The

Reference Shelf®

Racial Tension in a "Postracial" Age

The Reference Shelf
Volume 88 • Number 1
H.W. Wilson
A Division of EBSCO Information Services

Published by
GREY HOUSE PUBLISHING
Amenia, New York
2016

The Reference Shelf

The books in this series contain reprints of articles, excerpts from books, addresses on current issues, and studies of social trends in the United States and other countries. There are six separately bound numbers in each volume, all of which are usually published in the same calendar year. Numbers one through five are each devoted to a single subject, providing background information and discussion from various points of view and concluding with an index and comprehensive bibliography that lists books, pamphlets, and articles on the subject. The final number of each volume is a collection of recent speeches. Books in the series may be purchased individually or on subscription.

Publisher's Cataloging-In-Publication Data
(Prepared by The Donohue Group, Inc.)

Names: H.W. Wilson Company.
Title: Racial tension in a "postracial" age / [compiled by] H. W. Wilson, a division of EBSCO Information Services.
Other Titles: Reference shelf ; v. 88, no. 1.
Description: Amenia, New York : Grey House Publishing, 2016. | The reference shelf ; volume 88, number 1 | Includes bibliographical references and index.
Identifiers: ISBN 978-1-68217-063-2 (v.88, no.1) | ISBN 978-1-68217-062-5 (volume set)
Subjects: LCSH: United States--Race relations--History--21st century--Sources. | Racism--United States--History--21st century--Sources. | Post-racialism--United States--History--21st century--Sources. | Equality--United States--History--21st century--Sources.
Classification: LCC E184.A1 R33 2016 | DDC 305.800973--dc23

Contents

2

3

4

In School and on Campus

5

A New Civil Rights Movement and Current Perspectives on Race

Preface

The Formation of Race

Race is a complex phenomenon, both biological and sociological, involving the development and maintenance of human subgroups. From an evolutionary perspective, all humans belong to a single species, *Homo sapiens*. Over thousands of years of isolation and independent development, different groups of humans evolved to have different physical characteristics, forming the basis of what humans later called "race." Because all humans are the same species, the physical differences between individuals in different "racial" groups are largely superficial physical variations rather than substantial genetic variations. However, amplified through cultural divergence, these minor physical differences in the human body have fueled some of the most influential, destructive, and creative events in human history.[1]

One Species, Many People

Humanity originated in Africa, on the plains and in the scrub forest of the Rift Valley where constant equatorial sun threatened our early ancestors with radiation burns and skin diseases. The earliest humans had darker skin and other physical traits to help protect against this constant radiative bombardment. Between 80,000 and 60,000 years ago, humans began the "Great Migration" that took the species from Africa through Asia and Oceana and then to the rest of the world. Around 40,000 years ago, the first humans colonized Europe. Over thousands of years, populations of humans arriving in new areas began developing different physical characteristics. Lighter skin color, for instance, is believed to have evolved in colder climates as light skin allows the body to absorb more vitamin D from limited solar rays. It is believed that the "light skin" variant of the human species did not develop until as recently as 8500 years ago.[2]

It took tens of thousands of years for humanity to settle the globe, and human communities in different regions developed unique cultural traditions reflecting the particularities of their environments. Over thousands of years, the migration was lost from human memory and cultures in various continents began believing that they had originated from different parts of the world. When the great societies that formed in isolation came face to face with each other again after thousands of years apart, they failed to recognize each other as members of the same species. During the colonial era, as European explorers visited and colonized the New World, Africa, India, and anywhere else local populations lacked the military capability to repel them, colonizers often described the people they encountered as "primitive" or "inferior." These perceptions, the beginnings of a still existent pattern of racial hierarchical categorization, resulted in hundreds of years of persecution and exploitation. Massive populations of indigenous inhabitants on many islands and in the Americas were wiped out by European colonists as they traveled the globe capturing territory for their native monarchies and empires.

The Atlantic Slave Trade from the 1500s to the 1800s was perhaps the ultimate expression of racial conflict. Viewing the native African tribes they encountered as "primitive" or "inferior," European profiteers captured between 9 and 13 million African men, women, and children and shipped them around the world for use as slave laborers. Millions died at sea or through mistreatment by slave traders or slave owners, but the Atlantic African Diaspora resulted in populations of African descendants around the world. As the slave trade came to a close, through the gradual development of ethical and moral opposition to the practice, populations of African descendants continued to face racial discrimination and injustice in a long, arduous struggle toward racial integration and equality.[3]

Race as a Construct

In the twentieth century, sociologists proposed that race was better viewed as a "social construct" rather than a "biological reality."[4] According to this view, concepts of race are created within societies through shared prejudices, fears, and theories about the *meaning* of physical and cultural differences. Most of the races commonly recognized in the twenty-first century differ in skin color. Those with lighter skin have come to be called *white*, while the terms *black, colored, red, brown,* and a variety of other descriptors have been used to describe populations having higher concentrations of melanin and thus having skin that is, on average, darker than the pink-skinned people who initially created existing systems of racial categorization.

In 1950, a now famous research program from the United Nations Educational, Scientific, and Cultural Organization (UNESCO) argued that race was not a biological reality, but a myth created through social and cultural conflict. The UNESCO findings were based on the realization that there appears to be no significant genetic or even genetically linked behavioral differences between humans, despite outward differences in skin color and other superficial physical characteristics.[5] As of 2015, science has not discovered any significant differences between humans of different races or ethnicities that could legitimately be used to prove that any one race, however defined, is superior to any other.

At the level of the society, race and racial concepts are constantly in flux and are refined and altered in each generation. For instance, different "tribes" of white Europeans once saw each other as different races, but these subtle differences have been largely abandoned in the formation of a more generalized European "white race." Racial concepts are deepened through cultural divergence and intentional isolation from other races, even those living in the same area, and also reflect the historical treatment and relative level of economic/social dominance achieved by individuals identified with a specific race. At the level of physical observation, race is about recognizing similarity and difference, and racial divisions are most obvious, lasting, and persistent between populations that look distinctly different.

Defining Racism

Racism, like race, can be defined in a variety of ways. On the most basic level, racism involves a set of beliefs about the significance of racial differences. Racism emerges when these differences are used to assign value and construct racial hierarchies based on prejudice, bias, xenophobia, and dubious observational evidence to create in turn the belief that some types of humans are superior to other types.

For some, race is solely about color, and so some opponents of racism argue that humanity should strive to become "colorblind," ignoring skin tone and other superficial physical differences. Critics of this approach argue that race cannot be reduced to "color" or addressed by promoting "colorblindness." Such a reductive approach may lead to the belief that racism can be seen as isolated incidents in which an individual is subjected to "differential treatment" because of his or her racial identification. However, some sociologists argue that racism is better understood as a system of cultural traditions, norms, stereotypes, and behaviors that serve to maintain a social hierarchy connected to the physical traits and social behaviors lumped together as "racial characteristics." Any behavior, activity, or general philosophy that maintains, deepens, or furthers this hierarchical view of race can therefore be seen as a manifestation of racism. In this view, racism is a long-standing system that encourages people to identify themselves, their families, their cultures, and their place in society in terms of the racial hierarchy. The struggle to defeat racism in society then becomes the struggle to end this *system* rather than the far more superficial effort to treat people "equally" in everyday interactions.[6]

Harmony and Tension

As of 2014, more than 50 percent of the 20 million young children in the United States were members of the nation's racial minorities, meaning that the "white race" of America is rapidly becoming a minority. There are few aspects of American culture that have not benefitted from the melting pot of race and ethnicity in the United States. In the United States, the mixing of "racial" cultures and artistic styles has resulted in unparalleled cultural creativity and innovation. The African slave population in the United States, creating new art forms in, for instance, music and dance, with influences from European traditions as well, developed the seeds of musical and artistic innovations—like jazz and blues music—that have since spread around the world. Though the meeting of different races and cultures has been the source of tremendous innovation, much strife has resulted from the socially constructed hierarchy of race, which continues to justify prejudice, bias, and inequality that to this day keeps societies stratified along racial lines.[7]

In August of 2015, a Pew Research study found that 59 percent of Americans agreed that the United States needs to continue making changes to achieve racial equality.[8] Among the racial groups currently recognized by the United States Census Bureau, "white" Americans are less likely to see racism, race relations, and racial prejudice as among the nation's top issues. In a 2015 Gallup Poll, 4 percent of white Americans identified race relations as the nation's "most important issue," compared to 13 percent of black/African American respondents.[9] It is perhaps not surprising that individuals in the racial group at the top of America's racial hierarchy are less concerned with race relations or racial conflict than America's marginalized minorities, though most white Americans also rank race as an important issue.

The white/black divide is America's most widely explored and widely debated racial division, but America also hosts large populations of Asians, Indians, Native Americans, and Hispanic/Latinos, and these individuals too have been repeatedly marginalized, stereotyped, and subjected to racial prejudice. In the twenty-first century, the complex ideological wars fought around the world between radical Islamist groups and governments aligned with the western powers have intensified racism and prejudice against Muslims and people of Middle Eastern descent. Most recently, fear over the Syrian terrorist group ISIS has resulted in attacks and racial violence against Syrian immigrants living in Europe and North America. This phenomenon shows that race and racial prejudice are fluid concepts, changing as broader cultural transformations alter the way that individuals see themselves and each other with regard to race.

Since the 2008 election of America's first nonwhite president, the term *postracial* entered the American lexicon. *Postracial* refers to the concept of an emerging culture, or an imagined future, in which race no longer matters in society. Numerous sociologists, cultural theorists, and social activists have passionately argued against the perception that America is now (or will become in the near future) a postracial society.[10] For some, the very idea of a postracial society may seem offensive as this vision seeks to eliminate or disregard the unique characteristics that have developed among racial groups. Opponents of the postracial view therefore argue that racial equality is not about erasing the differences between people, but about encouraging people to adopt an illuminated view that embraces the value of individuals, regardless of their unique physical and cultural characteristics.

Micah L. Issitt

Notes

1. Hadjiargyrou, Michael, "Race is a Social Concept, Not a Scientific One."
2. Gibbons, "How Europeans Evolved White Skin."
3. Falola, Toyin, *The African Diaspora*
4. Riese, Matt, "The Biological Meaning of Race."
5. Sussman, Robert, "The Myth of Race."
6. Bouie, Jamelle, "Why Do Millennials Not Understand Racism?"
7. Wazwaz, Noor, "It's Official: The U.S. Is Becoming a Minority-Majority Nation."
8. "Across Racial Lines, More Say Nation Needs to Make Changes to Achieve Racial Equality," *Pew Research*.
9. Brown, Alyssa, "Views of Race Relations as Top Problem Still Differ by Race."
10. Coates, Ta-Nehisi, "There Is No Post-Racial America."

1
Race in the Media

Viola Davis accepts the award for Outstanding Lead Actress in a Drama Series at the 67th Primetime Emmy Awards in Los Angeles, California on September 20, 2015. The first African American to win this award, Davis spoke about the lack of opportunity faced by women of color in Hollywood while applauding those writers and producers who have worked to reverse this trend in recent years—"people who have redefined what it means to be beautiful, to be sexy, to be a leading woman, to be black."

Racial Representation and Fictionalization in American Media

The American media—a vast mega-industry made up of thousands of participating companies with annual revenues in the tens of billions—plays an influential role in creating *and* reflecting American culture. News media provides information and opinions on domestic and foreign politics while entertainment media creates films, television shows, and musical products reflecting different aspects of the American experience. However, the media not only reflect, but also shape the ways in which people see themselves, their cultures, and each other. In the complex history of media and race, the media has, in some ways, been an important tool in the development of a more egalitarian and informed view of human culture. However, in other ways, the media reinforces prejudices and biases against certain racial groups, and in this way perpetuates racial discrimination and injustice.

Race in the History of Media

Long before men and women of African descent achieved citizenship in Europe, William Shakespeare wrote *Othello*, a play about a dark-skinned soldier who became a military leader in a society dominated by "white" men. Believed to have been written around 1600, *Othello* contains racial epithets like "thicklips" as other characters express the belief, common at the time and still often espoused, that individuals with darker skin are somehow inferior to individuals with pink or white skin. In *Othello,* Shakespeare portrays racism as a complex social evil that creates assumptions about the value of individuals based on their physical traits.[1] Unfortunately, the complexity of Shakespeare's *Othello* was unique at the time and, over subsequent centuries, thoughtful portrayals of race remained rare in "white" media.

The media helped to create the racial hierarchies that still exist in the Western world, reflecting, deepening, and legitimizing the belief that white, light-skinned individuals represent the pinnacle of human development, while portraying darker-skinned populations as inferior, savage, or intellectually/culturally deficient. In some cases, minorities are depicted as "savage" or "animalistic," either directly or through associations with other symbols of nature and prehistoric culture. In other cases, popular literature has reinforced a hierarchical racial order through the mythical archetype of the cultured white "savior" who brings religion, education, or culture to poor minority populations.[2]

Whatever the method used, such reductive portrayals condense an enormous diversity of cultural characteristics into a set of repeated stereotypes that reinforce prejudicial beliefs about race relationships. Not always obvious or intentional, these patterns of misrepresentation and cultural reduction often occur due to unconscious biases and prejudices on the part of writers, producers, directors, and other architects of media content.

Misrepresentation to Underrepresentation

The representation of race in American media demonstrates long-standing racial concepts to new generations and influences the way that individuals identify themselves as belonging to certain groups. A *Sports Illustrated* report from 2013 revealed that there are 15 times more African American physicians and 12 times more lawyers than there are African American athletes, and yet African Americans are far more likely to be portrayed on television as athletes than professionals. The overrepresentation of African American athletes sends a message to young African American viewers that achieving sports stardom is one of the primary ways to earn social acceptance in white-dominated culture. Given a lack of African American involvement in politics, science, and engineering, the choice of how to portray African Americans on television can influence generations through the demonstration of potential life goals, careers, and possibilities for advancement.[3]

Similarly, studies in the 2000s indicated that African American and Latino/Hispanic Americans are far more likely to be portrayed as "poor" in news broadcasts, despite the fact that two-thirds of the population living in poverty are white. A 2015 study by researcher Travis Dixon found that depictions of race in television news have improved since the 1990s, with realistic and varied depictions of minority individuals becoming noticeably more common. However, significant areas of racial bias were also found. For instance, reporters interviewing or showing police on camera in Los Angeles chose a white officer to profile/interview in 73 percent of instances, while only 53 percent of police in the region are white. About 16 percent of police officers shown on California television news were Hispanic/Latino, despite the fact that Hispanics/Latinos constitute over 30 percent of the police force. Essentially, white males are more likely to be depicted in "power" positions, as executives or police officers, while minority individuals are more likely to be portrayed as poor laborers or criminals.[4]

Even when the architects of American media actively attempt to avoid racism or racial insensitivity, subtle misrepresentations present a distorted version of reality that supports the preferences of white audiences and the overarching racial hierarchy. The rarity of realistic minority depictions may be linked to the dearth of minorities in the news and media industries. In the film industry, for instance, more than 94 percent of studio executives were white and 100 percent were male in 2014. A full 92 percent of film studio managers are white, as well as 93 percent of television senior managers.[5] A Pew Research study from 2012 found that only 12 percent of the newspaper workforce were minorities, with little increase in diversity since the early 1990s.[6]

The situation is little better on the other side of the camera. An analysis of the 100 top-grossing films in 2012 by the University of Southern California, found that only 10.8 percent of speaking characters in films were black, while 5 percent were Asian, 4.2 percent were Hispanic/Latino, and 3.6 percent were of mixed race.

Studies like these, of which there are many, demonstrate how minorities are underrepresented in media, again reflecting a subtle and sometimes unconscious bias favoring the portrayal of white protagonists. In many modern television programs and films, minority characters are still portrayed in highly stereotyped ways. White protagonists may have "sassy" or "street smart" African American friends, or may have "Hispanic/Latino" maids or servants. In some cases, even attempts to depict minority individuals in positive ways still reflect racial reduction and bias. Asian Americans may be portrayed as scientists or "technical experts," which, while not entirely unflattering, represents a white stereotype holding that Asians are "good at math and science." Asian and Indian actors also are often cast as shop owners or immigrant cab drivers, reflecting certain roles that might be especially visible in American cities and therefore easy to stereotype but that fail to capture the diverse lives of minority Americans.

Misrepresentation and underrepresentation collectively contribute to a mythological version of American society in which white characters, particularly white males, are portrayed with relative depth and complexity, while minority characters and women often represent archetypes whose presence in the narrative serves only to reflect the white male protagonist's experiences. Commercialized attempts to introduce "diversity" are sometimes criticized as ineffective and superficial, with studios and executives meeting external "diversity requirements" through the addition of "token" minority characters. Critics of the modern media's handling of race argue that these superficial attempts to be more racially diverse result in stereotyped characters that continue to reflect underlying assumptions about minority cultures.

Cooptation to Collaboration

Different minority groups in the United States have created unique cultural expressions through art. In early America, there was a type of theater, called the "minstrel show," in which white actors and artists dressed in "blackface" and imitated the dances and songs that had developed among African slave populations. Minstrel shows have long been derided as an example of white exploitation of African American culture, but the popularity of minstrel shows demonstrates that, even as most white Americans may have believed African Americans were inferior at the time, those same white Americans begrudgingly admired the unique and beautiful artistic creations emerging from the slave population.

Various kinds of music and art created within minority communities, like hip hop, jazz, breakdancing, break beat, dub step, ska, R&B, soul, and reggae, have long fascinated individuals outside the cultures that created them. However, minority art and language represent particular shared experiences often created in direct response to the oppression of white European or American economic and cultural hegemony. As such, white artists attempting to use minority music and language are often accused of cooptation, which is a form of exploitation in which an artist from outside a particular culture imitates, mocks, or appropriates forms of expression formed within another culture. Cooptation does not involve only music and art and occurs whenever members of a dominant racial group appropriate forms of cultural expression unique to marginalized societies.[7]

There is a fine line, however, between cooptation and legitimate innovation, and popular culture around the world has been greatly enriched through the blending of different art forms and other cultural expressions. The musical genre of jazz, for instance, though originating within the unique mélange of influences in black American culture in the early 1900s, spread to Europe during World War II, where it was transformed into new genres through the involvement of white Europeans and the also marginalized "gypsy" or "roma" minorities in places such as France and Belgium. Back in the United States, jazz and blues gave rise to R&B music, which was the first step in the creation of American "rock 'n' roll" music. This transition, from minority to majority music, involved cooptation by artists like Elvis Presley, who imitated African American innovators like Chuck Berry and T-Bone Walker and thus brought this innovative new art form to the white American public. In the fluid formation of culture and art, appropriation can be an unfortunate first step towards collaboration and innovation.[8]

Ultimately, media both reflects and helps to form ideas about race and racial values. The democratization of art through digital media has only begun to transform the American cultural landscape, opening the door for numerous alternative forms of art that might once have been rejected by the predominantly white male executives who decide what news and entertainment will be most profitable or productive for their purposes. Whereas racial portrayals were once overtly designed to reinforce racial stereotypes, in the twenty-first century, cooptation, misrepresentation, and underrepresentation, even when unintentional, still have pervasive effects on popular conceptions about various racial groups. But unintentional, racial bias is perhaps even more important to address because it speaks to the insidious underlying level of racial prejudice that colors all media and continues to reinforce racial hierarchies both locally and around the world.

Micah L. Issitt

Notes

1. "Othello," *PBS*.
2. Child, Ben, "Hollywood Fails to Represent US Ethnic Diversity, Study Says."
3, Fulwood, Sam III. "Race and Beyond: The Media's Stereotypical Portrayals of Race."
4. Dixon, Travis, "Good Guys Are Still Always in White?"
5. "2015 Hollywood Diversity Report: Flipping the Script," *Bunchcenter*.
6. Guskin, "5 Facts About Ethnic and Gender Diversity in U.S. Newsrooms." *Pew Research*.
7. Nilsen and Turner, *The Colorblind Screen*.
8. Gioia, *The History of Jazz*.

Race and Beyond: The Media's Stereotypical Portrayals of Race

By Sam Fulwood III
Center for American Progress, March 5, 2013

I'm no longer sure that seeing is believing.

As a former newspaper journalist, I'm disheartened to say that what you now see in the media isn't always an objective reality. Even when an article or broadcast reports the truth, the accompanying pictures and images can sometimes impress upon readers or viewers another set of facts that may be at odds with the story.

Harvard University professor Henry Louis "Skip" Gates, for example, delights in detailing how he used the gross distortion of media imagery of black men in sports to win a bar bet with the folks at the Veterans of Foreign Wars, or VFW, post in his hometown of Piedmont, West Virginia.

In an essay written for *Sports Illustrated*, Gates, an authority on African American literature and culture, told his drinking buddies that there were approximately 35 million black people living in the United States. He then wagered $5 to anyone who could tell him how many African Americans make a living playing professional sports in the United States.

The group of sports-loving men smiled, knowing they had a sucker in their midst. Everyone at the VFW post knew that blacks dominate some of the most popular sports in America. All they had to do was turn on their televisions, right?

Gates, a great raconteur, tells the story:

"Ten million!" yelled one intrepid soul, too far into his cups.

"No way ... more like 500,000," said another.

"You mean all professional sports," someone interjected, "including golf and tennis, but not counting the brothers from Puerto Rico?" Everyone laughed.

"Fifty thousand, minimum," was another guess.

At the end of the day, nobody won the money—all of the men grossly exaggerated their numbers. As Gates reported in *Sports Illustrated*, the facts about black athletes in America at the time his article was published were stunningly low:

This article was created by the Center for American Progress (www.americanprogress.org).

- There were 1,200 black professional athletes in all U.S. sports.
- There were 12 times more black lawyers than black athletes.
- There were 20 times more black dentists than black athletes.
- There were 15 times more black doctors than black athletes.

Arkansas Gazette sportswriter Jon Entine surveyed all professional sports teams in 2008 and figured that while 13 percent of the nation's population is black, 80 percent of the players in the National Basketball Association and 67 percent of the players in the National Football Association are black. Or, to put it another way, Entine calculated that the odds of a black teenager in America becoming a professional athlete are 4,000-to-1.

Such hard-to-believe facts contradict what so many Americans imagine they know based on what they see on TV. After all, this is a sports-crazed nation, and what sports fan doesn't watch ESPN—and especially its popular "SportsCenter" program—where black people are overrepresented as athletes and announcers? The sports media industry doesn't have to say explicitly that black athletes dominate sports. They just show an endless highlight reel of slam dunks and touchdown runs, and the pictures speak for themselves.

But a picture can—and often does—lie.

Which brings me to the cover art of last week's *Bloomberg Businessweek* magazine. Illustrating a story about the rebounding U.S. housing market, the *Bloomberg* editors chose inexplicably to run a cartoonish drawing of people with overt racial and ethnic features apparently swimming in a cash-filled house.

The cover drew almost immediate—and all negative—reactions. My colleague at ThinkProgress, Alyssa Rosenberg, described the cover as "awful as art" and quoted media critic Ryan Chittum's description of the cover in the *Columbia Journalism Review* as "awful as journalism."

Of course, a *Bloomberg Businessweek* editor soon apologized. "Our cover illustration last week got strong reactions, which we regret," Josh Tyrangiel, the magazine's editor, wrote in a statement sent to several news outlets. "Our intention was not to incite or offend. If we had to do it over again, we'd do it differently."

But that's not good enough. As Rosenberg argues, the magazine's editors and publishers need to come clean, not issue a mealy mouthed apology. "If you want to walk a line and publish edgy covers, you have a particular obligation to think about where the line is," she writes. "And if you want forgiveness, you need to actually look at yourself and your practices in a systemic way."

The NAACP, the National Council of La Raza, the National Fair Housing Alliance, and the Center for Responsible Lending have taken up the charge as well, demanding a full explanation and apology for the offensive cover. In an email sent to NAACP supporters, Dedrick Muhammad, senior director of the NAACP Economic Department, condemned the magazine:

> The insulting part of this cover isn't just the derogatory and cartoonish depiction of racial and ethnic minorities, but rather the insinuation that homeowners—coincidentally all people of color—are somehow greatly profiting today as the housing sector slowly recovers. . . We know where the fault really lies: unscrupulous banks and predatory

lenders who exploited our most vulnerable citizens with reckless abandon. It is these institutions who have had a "Great American Rebound" as the article itself notes.

But that's not what the image shows. Whether in professional sports or big business, stereotypical images steep into the collective consciences of those who view them and mistakenly believe they've seen the entire truthful picture.

Crime Coverage in Media Perpetuates Racial Stereotypes

By Christopher Benson
Chicago Reporter, April 15, 2014

It was a provocative question. Simple and complex all at once. "What are the consequences of media failure to cover social difference effectively?"

The students attending the two-day regional summit of National Association of Black Journalists campus chapters wanted an answer. But they wanted something more from the panel of journalism professionals and professors brought together by NABJ student organizers at the University of Illinois, Urbana-Champaign, last weekend.

They wanted a vocabulary to deal with the issues of media responsibility they undoubtedly will confront as professionals. Because today the news organizations they will one day be working for seem to be falling short when it comes to meaningful coverage of race and ethnicity.

The consequences of this failing can be far-reaching and enduring. Nowhere is this seen as clearly as with media coverage of crime. And the vocabulary in this conversation starts with "A" for agenda setting.

After all, the public agenda in effect is set by the media. They tell us what is important through the time and space devoted to a story and where that story is placed in a newscast or in the newspaper.

These are important considerations. Particularly for TV, which is more immediate, more visual, more visceral and has more of an impact than print. But the biggest reason this is so important is—stop the presses—most people get their news from television. Local television. And what the public is getting deserves a closer look.

Not only does crime coverage dominate the lead segment, but it also makes up a significant percentage of a 30-minute local newscast. More on the weekends. The message: This issue is the most important matter on the media agenda, so it is the most important item on the public agenda.

George Washington University professor Robert Entman and University of Illinois, Chicago, associate professor Andrew Rojecki studied television coverage in Chicago as part of the work leading to their book, *The Black Image in the White Mind*. They found that the excessive coverage of crime on television news tends to create a misperception among the public that crime is a bigger problem than it really is. Even in periods when reported crime actually is down.

Even worse, the media do more than merely tell us what is important to think through agenda setting. They also tell us how to think about it. Sadly, they tell us how to think about crime by showing it to us in blackface.

Too often, according to Entman and Rojecki, that "B" roll in TV news—the images that are used to show the story while the reporter in voiceover tells the story—tends to include images of African Americans or Latinos in prison settings. More specifically, according to a study by professor Travis Dixon of the University of California at Los Angeles, mug shots and orange jumpsuits are more likely to be shown in TV reports when the accused is a person of color.

The effect of this is powerfully enduring, Dixon wrote when he was on faculty at Illinois. Even when the image of an accused is not included in a crime story, people still tend to think the accused is a person of color. Worse still, some people will view a plainclothes African-American police officer being interviewed in a TV report about a particular crime and think that officer is the accused. Such is the mediated reality of TV. It is tough to see a different reality—the actual one—when it is presented.

Consider the actual reality presented by the FBI's 2012 Uniform Crime Reports, which show whites are twice as likely as African Americans to be arrested and charged with committing most listed crimes, although the rate for murder charges is pretty evenly split between the two racial groups at slightly less than 50 percent each. Why, then, are African Americans overrepresented in crime stories? Clearly, the people putting these stories together are so caught up in building a broadcast they ironically distort the very reality they are trying to present.

Language has a potent effect, too, in framing stories and the people in them. Words create and reinforce certain associations—positive or negative. In the classic example, a person might choose to use the word "aroma" or "stench" to describe the same smell. If we have never experienced that smell ourselves, that description

Mug shots and orange jumpsuits are more likely to be shown in TV reports when the accused is a person of color.

becomes our reality. This "semantic differential," the measurement of connotative meaning, was developed by the late psychology professor Charles Osgood, director of the Institute of Communications Research at Illinois, and helps us understand how the terms "inner city" or "South Side" in a news story have suggestive significance. Typically, African American. Frequently, crime related.

Students who have never visited Chicago's South Side tend to react negatively to the term in my classes. They think it is an area dominated by crime. We can only imagine how they perceive the people who live on the South Side. I am one of those people, by the way.

For the students attending the NABJ summit, the consequences were now clarified. The consequences and the challenges. It is vital for this next generation of media leadership to engage in media-literate conversations in their newsroom. About words and images and meaning.

This is especially appropriate at this moment, some 46 years after the National Advisory Commission on Civil Disorders, known as the Kerner Commission, reported that we were headed for "two societies, one black, one white—separate and unequal." The commission stated that media should be responsible for presenting a fair and balanced picture of America—one that includes context and deeper understanding. That challenge is one we still must meet.

Race Science Rears Its Ugly Head

By Gavin Evans
New Internationalist, March 2015

Things I've read recently: Europeans evolved to be smarter than Africans because of the ice age; there's a gene variant making sub-Saharans less intelligent; the reason poor people are poor is because they are inherently stupid, which is why there are more poor black people; the prime cause of poor health is low IQ, which is why Africa suffers; infectious diseases affected the genomes of Africans, making them innately stupider; the brightest people on earth are Ashkenazi Jews and the dumbest, "Bushmen."

After a post-Holocaust lull, the ancient habit of race science has returned in brazen form in the 21st century, with proselytizers from British and US universities taking the lead.

The most recent blast comes from science writer Nicholas Wade whose book, *A Troublesome Inheritance*, tells us that African tribalism (along with English enterprise, Japanese authoritarianism and Finnish drinking) has a "genetic basis" and that the "adaptation of Jews to capitalism is another such evolutionary process." Wade, by the way, insists he is not a racist.

In recent years, racial science has arrived in four related forms. At the top of the feeding chain are the big promotion books like Wade's, and Richard Herrnstein and Charles Murray's *The Bell Curve*, the 1990s book regarded as the bible of this calling.

Second come the respected academic journals, where race science papers are occasionally published, only to be discredited once the experts review them (with the critiques always enjoying far less media attention than the original articles).

Third, a branch of evolutionary psychology, with its fundamentalist faith in genetic determinism, periodically spills into racial territory. Their papers, often published in their own house journals, are peer reviewed by others of their persuasion.

Fourth, at the bottom of the feeding chain is the perpetual stream of articles and books published by the race-obsessed Right, which seem immune to counter-argument.[1] Articles by the pitch-forkers of race science, like University of Ulster evolutionary psychologist Richard Lynn, play a major supply role for the higher levels.

What all these have in common is the part played by universities. Most of the main players in race science are tenured academics, and the rest retain close links with their alma maters, which, inadvertently, give them protective cover.

The universities' approach to academic freedom—of leaving tenured academics to their own devices and not interfering with papers published in refereed journals—can lead to curious results.

When the London School of Economics–based evolutionary psychologist Satoshi Kanazawa wrote in the *British Journal of Health Psychology* that intrinsically low intelligence was why sub-Saharan Africans were unhealthy, LSE turned a blind eye.

However, when he wrote in *Psychology Today* that black woman evolved to be unattractive, they slapped him on the wrist. Saying Africans were stupid in an academic journal was OK; saying black women were ugly in a magazine was a bit too much.

Rants and Flaws

Yet articles in refereed journals can be no less troublesome than magazine rants. Take the much-trumpeted academic paper by a team of Utah anthropologists who claimed that Ashkenazi Jews were inherently more intelligent than anyone else.

Oddly, this is often assumed to be a relatively benign contention, somehow different from saying a particular group is innately less intelligent, even though one follows from the other.

It is based on the view that the Ashkenazim were genetically isolated, but contemporary research shows otherwise: a recent gene-search by 19 scientists found that European women were the main female founders of the Ashkenazi population, suggesting inter-marriage between Jewish men and non-Jewish women was commonplace.

> If opinion-makers come to accept that poor Africans (or poor anybody) are poor because they are inherently stupid, then they might also conclude that there's little point trying to undo the damage—a prejudice that in one form or another takes us back to slavery and beyond.

The paper's other genetic and historical contentions have also been lambasted by academic critics but it continues to be cited.

As with almost all of the recent examples of race science, its key flaw comes from its misplaced faith in IQ tests. There's certainly legitimate debate about the heritability of IQ within a given population, but scant room for dispute when it comes to variation between populations.

The reason relates to the "Flynn Effect," named after intelligence theorist Jim Flynn. This shows that IQs have risen steadily over the past century, making IQ tests ever more difficult. This has nothing to do with genetics and everything to do with environment—particularly increased exposure to abstract logic.

The IQs of some groups have therefore risen faster than others—the Ashkenazi average early in the 20th century was well below the 100 mean, whereas now it is well above, and recently it has been Kenyans who have shown the fastest IQ growth. This illustrates how facile it is to compare scores of different "races"—the silliest being Richard Lynn's claim that the average "Bushman" IQ is 54, based on apartheid data.

In their own words . . .

"We remain the same species, just as a poodle and a beagle are of the same species. But poodles, in general, are smarter than beagles, and beagles have a much better sense of smell."
Andrew Sullivan, *Race and IQ. Again*, 2013.

"[I am] inherently gloomy about the prospect of Africa [since] all our social policies are based on the fact that their intelligence is the same as ours - whereas testing says not really."
James Watson, quoted in *The Sunday Times*, 2007.

"[I]ndividuals in wealthier and more egalitarian societies live longer and stay healthier, not because they are wealthier and more egalitarian but because they are more intelligent."
Satoshi Kanawawa, "Mind the gap... in Intelligence: Reexamining the Relationship between Inequality and Health," *British Journal of Health Psychology*, 2006.

Lynn insists cold European weather prompted selection for intelligence 40,000 years ago. This is a view discredited by recent archaeological studies showing that cave art, and other signs of modern cognition, was flourishing in Africa 100,000 years back—a clear indicator that our intelligence evolved far earlier than previously realized.

Human populations have certainly evolved in other ways (skin color, ethnic diseases, lactose tolerance, etc.), but these usually involve single genetic mutations. Intelligence involves networks of thousands of genes.

Despite this weight of evidence, it looks likely that the flow of papers and books punting race-based science will continue, as will their exposure in a media climate that latches on to claims of difference based on misplaced faith that genetics can explain behavior.

What has changed is that in the past race science was fervently opposed, particularly in academic circles. When Arthur Jensen published a now-infamous paper on black American intelligence in the *Harvard Educational Review* in 1969, it was met by 29 academic rebuttals and a wave of student protest, prompting the publication to refuse reprints or even to allow him to respond to letters of criticism.

When a chapter in *The Bell Curve* was published by *The New Republic* in 1994, the staff threatened editor Andrew Sullivan with mass resignation and were only appeased when he agreed to published rebuttals by 19 writers, while scores of leading academics ripped to shreds the book's contentions.

In contrast, in 2014 *A Troublesome Inheritance* arrived with a Wade-penned cover story in *The Spectator* and an amused *Newsnight Review* interview with Jeremy Paxman. Six months later 139 of the world's leading evolutionary theorists signed a *New York Times* letter refuting Wade's premises and conclusions, but by then it was too late.

The implication of not challenging these views immediately and robustly is worrying in all sorts of ways, quite aside from the flawed science.

To take just one: if opinion-makers come to accept that poor Africans (or poor anybody) are poor because they are inherently stupid, then they might also conclude that there's little point trying to undo the damage—a prejudice that in one form or another takes us back to slavery and beyond.

Note

1. In particular, Mankind Quarterly, Personality and Individual Differences and Washington Summit Publishers.

Why We Need to Talk about Doc McStuffins and Race

By Jennifer Harvey
Huffington Post, September 30, 2014

She's African-American. Kids know it—and not just kids of color. White kids know it too.

And boys know she's a girl.

And that is all awesome.

Doc McStuffins is a crossover hit ($500 million in sales last year). Her "blockbuster sales" suggest she's adored not only by African-American girls, but by girls and boys from many racial demographics.

But for some reason, we adults seem to have a problem with the fact that our kids know Doc McStuffins is Black and female.

Adult explanations of Doc McStuffins' success reveal volumes about the way we adults—white adults in particular—think about race. At the moment, these revelations are pretty disappointing and have huge implications for how we talk about race and model racial behavior to and for our children.

I'll tell you why.

It starts with "colorblindness," an ideology that's a total dead end if we are serious about the development of white children along a pathway of healthy racial identity. By healthy racial identity, I mean what Janet Helms means: an identity that manifests a genuine and interested embrace of diversity while being comfortable in one's own skin, a strong antiracist sensibility as part of one's own white racial identity, and an ability to navigate a multiracial world without presuming oneself to be the dominant, "generic," or race-less norm.

If any of these attributes fail to become a deep and formative part of how our white children (becoming teens, young adults, etc.) understand themselves and their relationships with others, they will not be the able participants in a truly plural, diverse democracy that those of us who claim to value equality and justice want them to be.

On top of this, colorblindness also erases the interesting and beautiful value of difference (e.g., ask most Latino or Black folks if they want their race to be seen and usually the answer is "yes"). It's also based on the degrading assumption that there must be something "wrong" with "color." If there wasn't, why wouldn't we want to notice it?

"Why We Need to Talk About Doc McStuffins and Race" by Jennifer Harvey. Originally published by *The Huffington Post*, September 30, 2015.

So, colorblindness is a big "no, no" in my book. And, I think many of us, white parents included, increasingly recognize it as a big "no, no."

Yet we continue to talk about white kids as if they are colorblind. We do this 1) as if this were true and 2) as if (if it were true) this were a good thing. Meanwhile, neither of these things is the case.

This all came up for me again while reading a recent *New York Times* article on Doc McStuffins' success. Much of the article was great. It explored the importance of Doc McStuffins' visibility for young African-American children, girls especially, in a media market where positive images of blackness and Black femaleness are shamefully few and far between.

I agree.

The article lauded the evidence that both boys and white kids (girls and boys) are embracing her in remarkable numbers. I love it.

Go Doc McStuffins!

But the article also repeatedly suggested that Doc McStuffins' crossover success is due to white kids not seeing her as Black (and boys not recognizing her as a girl).

Consider the statement by Doc McStuffins' creator Chris Nee: "The kids who are of color see her as an African-American girl, and that's really big for them . . . And I think a lot of other kids don't see her color and that's wonderful as well."

The "other kids" (a.k.a., white kids) don't see her color?

Again 1) I doubt this is true and 2) if it was, this would not be cause for celebration (and the fact that we think it is reveals a lot).

To the first point: The depth and savvy with which young kids do see color, relentlessly in a society as racialized as ours, has been documented over and over.

Colorblindness does not exist in the United States. Not even for 2-year-olds. That reality alone has huge implications for how we should be engaging white kids on race.

To the second point: What's going on that so many adults continue to celebrate the fallacious belief that white kids don't see color? More frightening, if that's where we adults are at, how are we possibly going to enable our kids' healthy racial identity development? (I'm pretty convinced here that lots of adult talk about kids and race says a whole lot more about adults' racial identities than about kids'.)

> **It starts with "colorblindness," an ideology that's a total dead end if we are serious about the development of white children along a pathway of healthy racial identity.**

The article goes on to engage Dr. Margaret Beale Spencer, professor of comparative human development, who explains: "Children's play is serious business . . . They are getting ideas about who they are from these objects."

As a parent, I didn't need to read the studies to tell you that she's absolutely right. I watch what characters, books and shows do to the psyche and self-image of my daughters every day; how they shape the worlds they imagine to be possible.

And that is precisely why a character like Doc McStuffins, as a Black female, is so important for all of our children.

Yes, I agree with Spencer's emphasis on how important it is for African-American girls to see a powerful and confident character who looks like them. In a society that denigrates blackness and femaleness, the chance for these girls to identify power and confidence with both is indeed a kid toy success.

The stakes are higher for children of color. But Doc McStuffins is important to my young, white daughters too, and would be doubly so if they were sons. And not because "they don't notice." We who teach and parent white kids should never encourage them to see Doc McStuffins as a raceless, genderless person.

White kids need to associate power and confidence with blackness and femaleness too!

And the thing is, I think (at least in the moment of their adoration of Doc McStuffin's) they already do. Or they will. Or they could.

If only we adults would stop relentlessly overlaying our "colorblind" ideologies (anxieties?) over what our white kids are actually racially experiencing in the world. If we don't, eventually they'll absorb our myth, separate themselves from their actual experiences and then live all of this out in ways that will do more to help keep our current oh-so-inadequate racial order just as it is. All while smiling proudly about how "colorblind" they are.

Our kids are not colorblind and we should help them to remain that way.

That's the least we can do for the sake of all of our children. After all, my white kids are going to be the schoolmates, colleagues, coworkers and, I hope, allies of children, teenagers and adults of color now and in the years to come.

So when they think they see Black and female manifested as powerful and confident? And, even better, when they accept and love what they see? Our jobs are simply to say this: "Why yes, yes, in fact, you do."

Rachel Dolezal's Story, a Study of Race and Identity, Gets "Crazier and Crazier"

By Maria L. La Ganga and Matt Pearce
Los Angeles Times, June 15, 2015

Rachel Dolezal has sparked a national conversation about some of the most sensitive issues in American life—race, gender, identity and cultural inheritance. Chances are, however, it is not the teachable moment the self-made civil rights activist once dreamed about.

Dolezal, 37, resigned Monday as president of the Spokane, Washington, NAACP chapter amid revelations that she is a white woman posing as black. Her charade was exposed last week by her white parents, who live in Montana and have not seen their estranged daughter in years.

Dolezal's story raises questions about the power of race in a nation that has been publicly debating the issue since Eric Garner and Michael Brown died last summer in altercations with police, giving rise to protests, arrests and the rallying cry "Black Lives Matter."

Dolezal's case highlights Americans' conflicting sentiments about the country's increasingly multicultural population and about who gets to decide what race people identify with. The swift, loud response to her startling situation swirls around the issue of white privilege and the co-opting of a cultural identity.

This much is known for sure: An ambitious activist in a mid-sized city in a far-flung corner of the Lower 48 last Thursday unleashed a storm of anger and sympathy that spread coast to coast and shows no sign of abating. She was scheduled to speak publicly about the controversy Monday night, but canceled her appearance. Instead, she sent a letter of resignation to the NAACP's national headquarters and posted a lengthy explanation on the Spokane chapter's Facebook page.

She spoke about the fight that lies ahead to move "the cause of human rights and the Black Liberation Movement along the continuum . . . and into a future of self-determination and empowerment." She did not address the allegations that she lied about her race. She did not apologize for the controversy.

"Despite the fact that many people have liberal and malleable ideas about race, they're really stuck in a very black-is-black and white-is-white ideology," said Baz Dreisinger, author of *Near Black: White-to-Black Passing in American Culture*. "When a scenario like this comes around to upend those categories, it's a shocker. . . .

"This is very bold," she said, "and it keeps getting crazier and crazier."

Dolezal has been lauded for revitalizing Spokane's chapter of the 106-year-old civil rights organization. But according to court documents obtained Monday by *The Times*, when she was a graduate student in art at Howard University, she sued the historically black school in Washington, D.C., charging that she was a victim of racial discrimination.

Dolezal—who was married to a man named Kevin Moore and known as Rachel Moore at the time—claimed that university officials removed some of her artwork from a student exhibit in 2001 "for a discriminatory purpose to favor African American students" over her, according to an appeals court's summary of her arguments.

She also claimed university officials took her scholarship away and denied her a teaching assistantship because she was pregnant. Her claims were dismissed by upper and lower courts alike. A spokeswoman for Howard University declined to comment Monday, calling the matter resolved.

The couple divorced in March 2005, according to court documents. That year, she told the court that she taught science and art part-time at a school called River City Christian Academy and was an adjunct professor at North Idaho College in Coeur d'Alene, which is across the Washington-Idaho border from Spokane.

Dolezal recently walked away from a TV reporter who confronted her about her race. The reporter from KXLY in Spokane showed Dolezal a photograph of an elderly black man whose picture was on the Spokane NAACP's Facebook page and asked whether it was her father. "Yes, that's my dad," she replied. Then, when asked whether she is African American, Dolezal replied, "I don't understand the question," and walked away.

Dolezal's mother and father, who adopted three African American children and one Haitian child, say she has passed as black despite not having any African American heritage.

"She may have felt that she had some advantage in her activism by being portrayed as a black woman," her mother, Ruthanne Dolezal, said on NBC's "Today" show Monday. "We hope that Rachel will get the help she needs to deal with her identity issues. Of course we love her, and we hope that she will come to a place where she knows and believes and speaks the truth."

Rachel Dolezal's father said they had not spoken about their daughter's race before because they had never been asked.

"We had never been asked to be involved, we had never been questioned before, but just short of a week ago, we were contacted by the Coeur d'Alene Press," Lawrence Dolezal said on the "Today" show.

"I guess it was part of some investigative reporting that was being done and somehow they got wind of us as her parents as a possibility, so they contacted us to see if we were, in fact, her parents," Lawrence Dolezal said. "We taught our children, as we raised all six of them, to tell the truth, always be honest. So we weren't going to lie; we told the truth: Rachel is our birth daughter."

Rachel Dolezal has not spoken publicly about the uproar; on Tuesday she is expected to appear on the "Today" show.

In an interview Monday with *The Times* after Dolezal resigned, the NAACP's national president, Cornell William Brooks, said that the disgraced former chapter leader was widely liked and respected in Spokane, where there is "a great deal of disappointment and pain now."

Brooks also insisted that "racial identity is not a qualifying or disqualifying characteristic for leadership or membership within the NAACP. It's just not something that's a criterion . . . . It would be surprising to me that it even comes up."

What is important is the organization's "institutional integrity," Brooks told *The Times*. "Having credibility in terms of truth-telling is critically important."

When pressed about the fact that Dolezal had lied about her identity, Brooks said: "No. Lying is not consistent with our values."

Ed Prince, executive director of the Washington State Commission on African American Affairs, said the outrage over the Dolezal case "goes to the heart of white privilege.

> **"Despite the fact that many people have liberal and malleable ideas about race, they're really stuck in a very black-is-black and white-is-white ideology."**

An African American can never wake up and say, 'I'm gonna make my hair blond, put on white makeup and go through my day as a white person.' Not that [Dolezal] consciously thought, 'If I don't like it I can go back and be a white lady,' but she appropriated."

Jody Armour, a professor of law at USC and author of *Negrophobia and Reasonable Racism: The Hidden Costs of Being Black in America*, said it was ironic that just a week or so ago there was public celebration about Bruce Jenner's transition to become Caitlyn, but Dolezal is being castigated for changing her racial identity. Still, that argument can be taken only so far.

"I can't get up in the morning and tell a police officer, 'I'm transracial today. Treat me as a white man,'" Armour said. "Michael Brown couldn't be transracial . . . . When you walk into prisons and jail cells, you see cellblocks brimming with bodies that are conspicuously black. Those black bodies had no choice in how they were perceived."

But Camille Gear Rich, a professor of law and sociology at USC, argues that the uproar over Dolezal's situation is discriminatory in itself and devalues black women—particularly the back and forth on social media about the activist's mental health.

"Being a black woman is such a stigmatized identity that someone who would opt out of whiteness into blackness is 'showing a sign of mental illness,'" Rich said. "There are lots of reasons why her decision to become aesthetically black is not a sign of mental illness."

Among them, Rich said, is that she was raised with adopted siblings who are black, there are reports that she has a son who is black, and she might have acted "to be part of her family."

"I think her decision is regrettable," Rich said. "But she is sympathetic."

Iggy Azalea's Post-racial Mess: America's Oldest Race Tale, Remixed

By Brittany Cooper
Salon.com, July 14, 2015

As a white female rapper mistakes appropriation for artistry, black women remain pushed to the sidelines

Recently, my nine year-old nephew came running into the room, eager to find a seat to watch a performance by Iggy Azalea on an awards show. He sat, enraptured by her performance, yelling, "Iggy!" utterly oblivious to the look of chagrin and dismay on my face, as I, too, tuned in to watch this white girl from Australia, turned ATL-style rapper, caricature everything I love about Southern Hip Hop.

The look and feeling of chagrin has stayed with me each time I turn on my radio and hear Iggy's hit song, "Fancy" coming through my speakers. And some of the dismay I feel is at myself, because almost without fail, I immediately start bobbing my head to the beat.

Iggy is a protégé of T.I., one of my all-time favorite rappers. Though T.I. is known for Atlanta-style, crunk Southern bravado that is a hallmark of Black culture in that city, according to journalist/blogger Bené Viera, T.I. recently expressed disappointment that "we're at a place in America where we still see color." Apparently, color is only relevant when he's talking about racist acts against Black men, but not when he has to think through his complicity in white appropriation of Hip Hop music.

As a born-and-raised Southern girl, who believes that lazy summer evenings are best spent with your top back or your sun roof open, bass-heavy music booming through nice speakers, while you slowly make a few blocks through the neighborhood, to see who's out and what's poppin,' I resent Iggy Azalea for her co-optation and appropriation of sonic Southern Blackness, particularly the sonic Blackness of Southern Black women. Everytime she raps the line "tell me how you luv dat," in her song "Fancy," I want to scream "I don't love dat!" I hate it. The line is offensive because this Australian-born-and-raised white girl almost convincingly mimics the sonic register of a downhome Atlanta girl.

The question is why? Why is her mimicry of sonic Blackness okay? Though rap music is a Black and Brown art form, one does not need to mimic Blackness to be good at it. Ask the Beastie Boys, or Eminem, or Macklemore. These are just a smattering of the white men who've been successful in rap in the last 30 years and generally they don't have to appropriate Blackness to do it. In the case of Southern rappers like Bubba Sparxx or Paul Wall, who do "sound Black" as it were, at least it is clear that they also have the accents of the places and communities in which they grew up.

Not so with Iggy Azalea, who left Australia at age 16. To be clear, I know *all* of the problems with the phrases "sound Black" and "sonic Blackness." As a kid, I was mercilessly teased for and accused of "talking white," "acting white" and basically attempting to "be white." I learned during those difficult days to dissent from social norms that suggested that the only English for Black people is a vernacular English that stands adjacent to "corporate," "standard," or white English. I balked at such suggestions and reveled in my ability to master "standard" English.

Still I knew that at home, around my family and especially around my Grand-mother, my tongue got lazier, as I spoke of things I was "fin (fixing) to do," as I yelled at my cousins about how "nary a one of them" (which sounded more like "nair one") treated me right, as "th" sounds at the beginning of words easily became "d" sounds, and as the "g" sounds fell off the end of -ing words. At home, in the safety, comfort and cocoon of my Southern Black family, I talked how my people talked.

In the predominantly white classrooms of my school days though, proficient use of "standard" English showed those white folks that I had every right to be there, that I was just as good if not better. What I'm describing is what communications scholars have called for decades "code switching." The kind of literacies necessary to master communicating with different communities of people is a hallmark of what it means to grow up as a minority subject in the U.S. and any other country with a history of colonization and slavery.

Iggy Azalea interlopes on this finely honed soundscape of Southern Blackness to tell us "how fancy" she is, and ask "how we love dat." Her recklessness makes clear that she does not understand the difference between code-switching and appro-priation. She may get the science of it, but not the artistry. Appropriation is taking something that doesn't belong to you and wasn't made for you, that is not endemic to your experience, that is not necessary for your survival and using it to sound cool and make money. Code-switching is a tool for navigating a world hostile to Black-ness and all things non-white. It allows one to move at will through all kinds of com-munities with as minimal damage as possible.

Hollywood "Race Casting": What the Industry Is Getting Wrong about Diversity

By Britt Julious
The Guardian, March 25, 2015

There's no such thing as too much of a good thing, at least when it comes to diversifying media. Hollywood remains light years behind the ethnographic makeup of the US and industry leaders have, for years, used a variety of different excuses to hide their money-hungry, "safe" and downright racist decisions in casting actors of color for film and television roles.

The number of television roles for actors of color dropped dramatically over the last 15 years and it was not because of the various reasons given by Hollywood executives. Change is swift, but it's also most likely not as prominent as we imagine. The numbers from the 2015 diversity report on Hollywood, entitled Flipping the Script—a product of UCLA's Ralph Bunche Center for African American Studies—are only marginally better than previous years.

Consistent with previous reports, there is a major discrepancy between the actual population within the US and the representation of that population on TV. Minorities account for more than 40% of the US population and yet they are significantly underrepresented in the television industries. According to the report, minorities remain underrepresented nearly six to one in broadcast scripted leads and nearly two to one among cable scripted leads.

The numbers for series creators [are] even worse. Minorities are underrepresented at greater than six to one among the creators of broadcast shows, greater than three to one among the creators of cable scripted shows, and greater than seven to one for creators of digital platform and syndicated shows.

The demographics show that a greater percentage of black people in particular watch and engage with television than white audiences. According to a 2013 report from Nielsen, African Americans are more "aggressive consumers" of media. For example: "Blacks watch more television (37%), make more shopping trips (eight), purchase more ethnic beauty and grooming products (nine times more)," which translates to the two largest forces in television creation: numbers and advertisers. Despite those strong numbers and clear evidence, Hollywood insisted on practicing the same forms of structural racism as they have in the past.

However, Hollywood is a business at its core, and business, at least in terms of successes with minority leads and shows, is good. Longer running shows, like

Shonda Rhimes's *Scandal* and *Grey's Anatomy,* as well as cable hits like *The Walking Dead,* demonstrate a willingness from audiences to continue watching diverse shows. And after the success of Fox's *Empire,* as well as smaller successes with ABC's *Fresh Off the Boat, How to Get Away With Murder,* and *Black-ish,* it makes commercial sense to continue the "trend" of featuring more people of color on television screens.

But Nellie Andreeva's article in *Deadline* suggests a rapid, almost misguided sense of action on Hollywood's part and an underlying premise of "affirmative action"–type policies at work within Hollywood. Andreeva wrote: "Instead of opening the field for actors of any race to compete for any role in a color-blind manner, there has been a significant number of parts designated as ethnic this year, making them off-limits for Caucasian actors, some agents signal."

The tone of Andreeva's article suggests that this is a wrong practice. And yet it also negates mentioning this same practice had routinely been employed by Hollywood for years, but in exclusion of people of color. "From the earliest days of the industry, white males have dominated the plum positions in front of and behind the camera, thereby marginalizing women and minorities in the creative process by which a nation circulates popular stories about itself," wrote Darnell Hunt, head of UCLA's Ralph Bunche Center.

According to Andreeva, one year of targeted change and representation suggests those in charge have gone too far. Andreeva continues: "Many pilot characters this year were listed as open to all ethnicities, but when reps would call to inquire about an actor submission, they frequently have been told that only non-white actors would be considered." "Basically 50% of the roles in a pilot have to be ethnic, and the mandate goes all the way down to guest parts," one talent representative said.

According to the report, minorities remain underrepresented nearly six to one in broadcast scripted leads and nearly two to one among cable scripted leads.

Rather than state facts, Andreeva's scathing takeaway from the 2014–2015 television season, as well as the current pilot season casting process, gave greater weight to the opinions of disgruntled casting directors. Readers can't know for certain if their words are true or if they are upset that their legion of subpar actors who previously slipped into roles on broadcast, cable, and online television shows could no longer do so at the frequency of the past.

But if TV executives are actually, finally paying attention to audiences, this new system of change will soon become the norm, one in which casting directors defer to what people actually want and respond to and not discriminatory exclusions.

Andreeva's article suggests that rather than restrict minority actors to roles that regularly represented uniquely minority experiences (the underlying trend of the most recent television season with shows such as *Black-ish* and *Fresh Off the Boat*), networks instead aim to include minority actors in a broad array of shows and characters. Which, obviously. Why wouldn't they?

Compared to past discriminatory hiring practices, incorporating more minority representation on television just makes more business sense. As the Flipping the Script report notes: "Median 18–49 viewer ratings (as well as most median household ratings among whites, blacks and Latinos) peaked for broadcast and cable shows that at least match the minority share of the population in terms of overall cast diversity."

Past reports from the Bunche Center show similar statistics. In 2013, they reported that, "during the 2011–12 season median household ratings were highest among cable television shows with casts that were from 31% to 40% minority (0.88 ratings points)." And in contrast to those numbers, "ratings were lowest among shows with casts that were 10% minority or less (0.39 ratings points)."

To increase ratings in an increasingly diversified field of options for entertainment consumption (the internet, video games, reality television shows), it would be foolish to ignore facts and simply play by the same rules which don't work in the 21st century. This is not merely a case of the pendulum swinging, "a bit too far in the opposite direction," as Andreeva wrote. Important change is often radical, but it doesn't mean that it's wrong. In order to greater diversify television to satisfy both the storytelling process and the bottom line of ratings, studio heads are finally waking up.

Working on the Race Beat

By Jamil Smith
The New Republic, March 1, 2015

In November 2013, Tanzina Vega, a young reporter for *The New York Times*, pitched Jill Abramson, the paper's then-executive editor, the idea of devoting a reporting beat on the national desk to coverage of race and ethnicity. Abramson liked the idea, and Vega became the beat's sole reporter, publishing over the course of the next year an array of stories that directly engaged with the interests of people of color.

Vega's stories demonstrated her ability and interest as well as the broad opportunity that race reporting provides. She published a widely discussed article on "microaggressions," in which she assessed the "subtle ways that racial, ethnic, gender and other stereotypes can play out painfully in an increasingly diverse culture." She hosted the *Times*' "Off Color" video series on racial humor, investigated the inequities in school discipline outcomes for African American girls, and documented the crossover appeal of a black doll from Disney's "Doc McStuffins" cartoon. She looked into issues confronted by the growing population of Latino farmers in the United States and the problems the Census Bureau has had accurately counting an increasingly nonwhite population. Vega also investigated the subculture of black gun enthusiasts at the National Rifle Association's annual convention. Last August, she was in Ferguson, Missouri, to cover the aftermath of the shooting death of Michael Brown. Her stories, giving historical context to the protest movement and chronicling the shortcomings of local white leadership, set a new standard for nuance and complexity in American race reporting.

Then, on January 26, the *Times* abruptly discontinued Vega's beat and reassigned her to the metropolitan section. Her new beat has her covering a criminal courthouse in the Bronx.

An internal *Times* staff memo, acquired by several media organizations, offered a sunny justification for shuttering the paper's sole race-focused reporting operation. "Tanzina Vega showed how varied and powerful a national beat focusing on race could be. . . . But as we've told many a Foreign correspondent, you don't need to travel abroad to find adventure: The Metro desk can accommodate you right here in New York." Vega, who has not spoken publicly on the matter, declined comment for this article.

I learned about the *Times*' decision when I noticed several fellow journalists of color discussing it on Twitter. NPR blogger and former *Times* reporter Gene

Demby began the conversation: "So the @nytimes has scuttled its race beat, helmed by @tanzinavega. Okay, gang." Justin Ellis, a reporter with the Nieman Journalism Lab, replied, with more than a little sarcasm, "Listen, man, 2014 showed race is clearly not an important issue in America any more." Associated Press video producer Claritza Jimenez wrote directly to Vega: "I'm hoping you still find a way to incorporate race/ethnicity reporting." *Washington Post* reporter Wesley Lowery wondered how many national-level race and ethnicity reporters were left at traditional media outlets.

Through a spokesperson, Dean Baquet, the *Times'* executive editor (and the first African American to hold the post), issued a statement downplaying the significance of Vega's reassignment: "Suffice it to say we believe race is a big story and we will cover it aggressively." He declined to discuss the reasons for the decision. Margaret Sullivan, the *Times'* public editor, acknowledged in a column that the move

> **Collectively, we have not yet reached the point where we can "wait and see" how race coverage plays out without a race beat. And efforts to diversify newsrooms require time to yield inclusive journalism about race.**

was "not well received by some readers" and that it seemed "counterintuitive to increase and improve race coverage by discontinuing the race-and-ethnicity beat." When I spoke to Alison Mitchell, the *Times'* national editor, she echoed Baquet. "I think after Ferguson, it became pretty clear that everyone has to be writing about race," she said. I asked her how she would respond to skeptics who question the paper's commitment to keeping reporters conscious of writing about race without coverage dedicated to it. "I think people will have to wait and see and judge us on what we do," she replied.

Race beats began appearing in American newspapers in the 1950s as a necessity born of racial ignorance. White editors in white newsrooms felt they needed black reporters to tell black stories, particularly ones related to the civil rights movement. A July article in the *Columbia Journalism Review* (*CJR*) explained that race beats became more common in the late sixties and early seventies, although generally they weren't called that. Papers tended to refer to them euphemistically as "urban affairs" or "metropolitan" coverage.

In 1969, New York's *Newsday* assigned Les Payne, a black reporter who would later win a Pulitzer Prize, to be its "minority affairs specialist." Payne told *CJR* that along with reporting "black stories," his job was to "flag other stories for reporters on other beats—sports, for example. At the time there were so few reporters that we needed a dedicated beat, otherwise stories wouldn't be written about. We needed a stop-gap measure to ensure black news would flow into the normal flow of news." Charlayne Hunter-Gault, Chuck Stone, John Blake, Earl Caldwell, and other notable black journalists worked race beats during this period.

As the number of black journalists in newsrooms inched up in the 1990s, the number of formal race beats declined. Racial coverage began to migrate to media organizations and websites that covered it full time. *Colorlines*, a racial justice magazine, launched in 1998. Racialicious, a blog that examines the intersection of race and pop culture, started in 2006. The next year, PostBourgie began publishing, and served as a launching pad for celebrated black journalists, like Jamelle Bouie of *Slate* and Shani O. Hilton, executive editor of BuzzFeed News. In 2008, comedian Elon James White debuted This Week in Blackness, which features podcasts, video series, and a news blog. These sites don't bring in corporate dollars like Vox or FiveThirtyEight, but they have survived and even thrived by concentrating their coverage on issues affecting people of color, and by providing opportunities for writers to write on these subjects with a frankness rarely seen in mainstream publications.

A couple of years ago, Portland's *Oregonian* newspaper assigned a white reporter named Casey Parks to cover the race beat. I asked Parks how much criticism she receives for her skin color in this particular job. "I think I gave myself way more crap than anyone else has," she said. She also points out that Portland, which according to Census figures is just 6.3 percent black, is "a different kind of beat than *The New York Times*. My job is figuring out how you get a bunch of middle-class white people to read these stories when they may not know what white privilege is." Parks considers herself a "translator," someone trying to "figure out how to move white people a little bit."

"More black and brown voices are participating in important conversations in a very public way," said Akoto Ofori-Atta, a journalist doing a Knight Fellowship at Stanford University. "I think it's very slowly starting to influence editorial strategy at some publications."

For some, the best strategy is to end race beats altogether. Last summer, Cord Jefferson published "The Racism Beat," for Matter, which described his exhaustion as a black journalist writing stories of black politics and struggle in America. Publications, he said, shouldn't "assign [minorities] to specific stories that go along with their minority group. Give them jobs in your company."

As African Americans, and as a country, we can't wait for diversity to permeate media via hiring. Collectively, we have not yet reached the point where we can "wait and see" how race coverage plays out without a race beat. And efforts to diversify newsrooms require time to yield inclusive journalism about race.

The race beat does not ghettoize race coverage. It embeds it in the body of the publication and makes it an essential part of its mission. Those who report on race can also instruct their colleagues on how to integrate a nuanced and educated understanding of race into every narrative. Someday, perhaps, racial coverage in this country will reach a point where it is autonomously intersectional, and these kinds of checks and balances can fade away. But we aren't there yet.

2
Health and Wealth

Taken on April 30, 2015, this photo captures a row of abandoned homes in the streets of North West Baltimore. Lending of subprime mortgages throughout the 2000s preyed upon ethnic minorities and led to widespread defaulting and foreclosure of homes in largely African American communities.

The Modern American Dream

The phrase "American dream" is believed to have been coined by James Truslow Adams in his 1931 book *The American Epic*, in which Adams described the *dream* as the belief in a land where "life should be better and richer and fuller for everyone, with opportunity for each according to ability or achievement."[1] The millions of migrants who collectively founded the United States came to America to escape the aristocratic hegemony common in much of Europe that concentrated wealth and social mobility among a small social/religious/economic elite. Over more than two centuries, America came to embrace a new social hierarchy similar to the one that initially motivated the colonial exodus to the new world. In the United States, deep racial divides are one of the characteristic features of the nation's economic stratification.

For many Americans, there is a clear goal for America's future: to erase the remaining boundaries and barriers preventing people of any background, race, creed, or ideology from achieving the American dream, defined generally as the potential to lead an economically stable, healthy, and happy life and of passing these benefits on to one's children. While, in each generation, hundreds of families make strides toward this goal, millions of Americans face severe economic and social disadvantages that complicate their efforts to do so.

The Wealth Gap and the Race Gap

In 2011, thousands of Americans gathered in cities or connected through social media, joined in the "Occupy Wall Street" movement, protesting the growing "wealth gap" in America that some believe has created an economic elite that exploits and profits from the labor and effort of an underpaid, economically disadvantaged majority.[2] While movements like Occupy Wall Street call attention to deep economic inequities affecting millions of Americans across ethnic and racial lines, numerous sociological studies demonstrate that the wealth gap is far more pronounced for racial minorities. The median wealth holdings for white households across the nation was measured at $111,146 in 2011, as compared with $7,113 for African American households and $8,348 for Latino/Hispanic households. Census Bureau studies indicate that the average minority household has around 6 percent of the wealth of an average white household.[3] Evidence for a racial wealth gap is so pronounced that few economists or sociologists deny its existence. However, there is little current agreement about the best way to address this ongoing issue.

The mythology of the American dream holds that America, more than any other nation, makes it possible for a person to rise from humble beginnings to economic wealth. In academic terms, this is called "economic mobility," and the belief that the United States provides greater mobility than other nations has long been a cornerstone of American patriotism. In creating this mythology, American media agents and history textbooks give disproportionate attention to anecdotal stories of individuals who made this economic leap, including seminal American figures like Benjamin Franklin and Henry Ford. However, by some measures, the United States has far lower levels of economic mobility than many other Western nations. Pew Research studies indicate that more than 65 percent of Americans will stay in the social strata into which they are born and that family wealth is the most important determinant of eventual economic success in America.[4] Children born into wealthy families have greater freedom to engage in personal development and have access to the best training and tools to help them on the road to professional achievement. Social networks allow the children of the wealthy to find better jobs and to achieve acceptance to the best educational programs. In essence, wealthy individuals utilize a branching network of favoritism and nepotism to secure economic advantages irrespective of their personal intellectual skills, economic acumen, or effort. The more economic advantages a person has, the easier it becomes to maintain these advantages.

In addition to the general "wealth gap" in America, there is also a related, but distinct, "race gap," affecting the economic advancement of minority Americans specifically. Numerous independent studies indicate that the gap in wealth between white and minority Americans has grown wider since the 1960s.[5] The race gap occurs where economic disadvantages combine with racial prejudice, bias, and persistent institutional racism to create unique barriers preventing minority Americans from achieving the same level of mobility as white contemporaries, even within the same economic groups.[6] A 2015 study from the Federal Reserve Bank of St. Louis, for instance, indicated that African American and Hispanic/Latino Americans with college degrees are less likely to achieve the same level of economic success as similarly educated white Americans. This racial divide is linked to racial discrimination in hiring and college enrollment and to a lack of social networks and specific job training available to minority students and young professionals.[7]

To see how race continues to play an important role in economic stability, the phenomenon of home and property ownership provides an interesting example. Homes can be passed down within families, used to secure loans and credit, and enable families to store economic resources in the form of home equity. Home and property ownership have therefore long been seen as one of the primary ways for a family to achieve economic stability and mobility. However, homes in neighborhoods that are 10 percent or more African American appreciate far less than homes in white neighborhoods, even in white neighborhoods with similar income levels. A 2001 Brookings Institution study found that, across economic levels, black-owned homes were worth approximately 18 percent less than white-owned homes in any neighborhood. This disparity has far reaching consequences as it effectively penalizes white families who want to integrate or who might consider moving into neighborhoods that are 10 percent or more African American owned, and paradoxically, minorities purchasing homes in predominantly minority neighborhoods are economically punished for choosing to invest in their own neighborhoods.[8]

Health and Wellness

In America's free market healthcare system, those with economic advantages are able to afford better healthcare and alternative therapies unavailable to those at lower ends of the economic spectrum. This wealth gap in healthcare also involves nutritional health, where economic status again provides the ability to afford better, more nutritious food, and also provides the option for more leisure time that can be used for exercise or to engage in a variety of other "wellness" activities.

Studies published in 2014 issues of the *New England Journal of Medicine* found that American healthcare is more egalitarian than at any point in history, but that minority patients are still disadvantaged when compared to white patients with similar levels of income. On the broad scale, life expectancy is 5.4 years shorter for an African American man than a white man, a gap that can be clearly connected to the likelihood of receiving adequate preventative care to delay or prevent the onset of certain diseases and illnesses. A deeper examination of these trends found that "specialist doctors" charge the highest rates for their services, and that access to these medical specialists plays an important role in racial and economic differences in life expectancy.[9] Studies indicate that socioeconomic status is one of the most important determinants of health and wellness and that race and socioeconomic status remain intimately linked, thus producing a system in which the socioeconomic challenges more acutely facing minority Americans also affect minority health and wellness.

In a 2014 Gallup Poll, more than 77 percent of respondents listed "healthcare policy" as one of the top issues facing America, and yet there is no current consensus on how to address the healthcare disparities. While some support fully socialized medicine systems that use tax revenues to provide free healthcare for all citizens, critics argue that such systems pose an unfair tax burden on some members of the populace and reduce the quality of care through lower wages for physicians and researchers. As of December 2015, as Americans are adjusting to changes in the healthcare model under the most recent round of reforms, studies indicate a persistent lack of satisfaction in the state of the current medical system, but no universal agreement on how to address the many complex problems that affect healthcare outcomes for the majority of Americans.[10]

Achieving the Dream

The American dream can be viewed as a philosophy about social justice and equality. The dream says that in America a person has greater access to the means to build a happy, healthy, and prosperous life than anywhere else in the world. Throughout American history, the mythology built around the increasingly small number of Americans who have achieved the ultimate expression of this dream—rising from abject poverty to wealth—contrasts sharply with the reality for most Americans, and it continues to be more difficult for people of color to achieve the dream than their white counterparts. The resurgent race debate of the 2010s brings new hope as new voices and theories enter the conversation and continue to develop our collective ideas about race and social justice, but it remains to be seen whether the United States can rise to the challenge of addressing the race gap in years to come.

Micah L. Issitt

Notes

1. Clark, Jonas, "In Search of the American Dream."
2. Levitin, "The Triumph of Occupy Wall Street."
3. Shin, Laura, "The Racial Wealth Gap."
4. DeParle, "Harder for Americans to Rise from Lower Rungs."
5. "Nine Charts about Wealth Inequality in America," *Urban Institute*.
6. Kochar and Fry, "Wealth Inequality Has Widened along Racial, Ethnic Lines Since End of the Great Recession."
7. Cohen, Patricia, "Racial Wealth Gap Persists Despite Degree, Study Says."
8. Brown, Dorothy, "How Home Ownership Keeps Blacks Poorer Than Whites."
9. Hamblin, James, "Medicine's Unrelenting Race Gap."
10. Newport, Frank, and Joy Wilke, "Americans Rate Economy as Top Prority for Government."

Why So Many Minority Millennials Can't Get Ahead

By Mel Jones
The Atlantic, November 29, 2015

He died on a Saturday.

My mother and I had planned to pick my dad up from the hospital for a trip to the park. He loved to sit and watch families stroll by as we chatted about oak trees, Kona coffee, and the mysteries of God. This time, the park would miss him.

His skin, smooth and brown like the outside of an avocado seed, glistened with sweat as he struggled to take his last breaths.

In that next year, I graduated from grad school, got a new job, and looked forward to saving for a down payment on my first home, a dream I had always had, but found lofty. I pulled up a blank spreadsheet and made a line item called "House Fund."

That same week I got a call from my mom—she was struggling to pay off my dad's funeral expenses. I looked at my "House Fund" and sighed. Then I deleted it and typed the words "Funeral Fund" instead.

My father's passing was unexpected. And so was the financial burden that came with it.

For many Millennials of color, these sorts of trade-offs aren't an anomaly. During key times in their lives when they should be building assets, they're spending money on basic necessities and often helping out family. Their financial future is a rocky one, and much of it comes down to how much—or how little—assistance they receive.

A seminal study published in the *Journal of Economic Perspectives* on wealth accumulation estimates that as much as 20 percent of wealth can be attributed to formal and informal gifts from family members, especially parents. And it starts early. In college, black and Hispanic Millennials are more likely to have to work one or two jobs to get through, missing out on opportunities to connect with classmates who have time to tinker around in dorm rooms and go on to found multibillion-dollar companies together. Many of them take on higher levels of student debt than their white peers, often to pay for routine expenses, such as textbooks, that their parents are less likely to subsidize.

"Student debt is the biggest millstone around Millennials, period, and an even larger and heavier one around the necks of black Millennials," said Tom Shapiro, the director of the Institute on Assets and Social Policy. "It really hits those doing

"Why So Many Minority Millennials Can't Get Ahead" by Mel Jones, published in *The Atlantic*, November 29, 2015 courtesy of *Washington Monthly*.

the right thing. [They're] going through all the hoops." He explained that, unlike in previous decades when college tuition was drastically lower, the risks of educational costs are now passed down to the individual.

Recent polls indicate that a large portion of Millennials receive financial help from parents. At least 40 percent of the 1,000 Millennials (ages 18 to 34) polled in a March *USA Today*/Bank of America poll get help from parents on everyday expenses. A Clark University poll indicated an even higher number, with almost three-quarters of parents reporting that they provide their Millennial children with financial support. Another survey saw nearly a third of Baby Boomers paying for Millennials' medical expenses. A quarter of Boomers subsidized "other expenses" so their Millennial offspring could save money. Black and Hispanic Americans are less likely to be the recipients of this type of support.

Ironically, even though black and Hispanic Millennials are less likely to receive financial support from parents, their parents are more likely than white parents to expect their kids to help financially support them later on. According to the Clark poll, upward of 80 percent of black parents and 70 percent of Hispanic parents expect to be supported. And most studies show that a primary reason why people of color are unable to save as adults is because they give financial support to close family. This is important because when emergencies happen, many Millennials won't have the reserve money to cover them.

A Millennial who gets regular financial gifts and support from parents will either have the money to cover an emergency themselves, or (more likely) have a parent or grandparent cover it so there's no damage to their credit. They won't have to borrow from predatory-lending institutions, move into unsafe neighborhoods to save on rent, or start from financial scratch each time.

It doesn't even have to be a life emergency. In the decision between paying for a professional networking event or a cell-phone bill, the latter is likely to win out. It should come as no surprise that Millennials who are free to choose both are likely to benefit more in the long run. When this happens once or twice on a small scale, it's not a big deal. It's the collective impact of a series of decisions that matters, the result of which is displayed among ethnic and class lines and grounded in historical privilege.

And the help doesn't end when Millennials enter the next stage of adulthood. It's not just young, out-of-work Millennials who get help from parents or family members, according to the *USA Today* poll: Even Millennials making $75,000 or more said they had gotten money from their parents for basic necessities. Twenty percent of parents paid for their children's groceries, and more than 20 percent contributed money for clothing. Even 20 percent of cohabiting Millennials still had a parent paying for expenses like cell-phone bills, according to the poll.

Shapiro said the numbers of Millennials receiving support from family are "absolutely underestimated" because many survey questions are not as methodical and specific as those a sociologist might ask. "As much as 90 percent of what you'll hear isn't picked up in the survey," he said.

Shapiro's work pays special attention to the role of intergenerational family support in wealth building. He coined the term "transformative assets" to refer to any money acquired through family that facilitates social mobility beyond what one's current income level would allow for. And it's not that parents and other family members are exceptionally altruistic, either. "It's how we all operate," Shapiro said. "Resources tend to flow to people who are more needy."

Racial disparity in transformative assets became especially striking to Shapiro during interviews with middle-class black Americans. "They almost always talk about financial help they give family members. People come to them," Shapiro said. But when he asked white interviewees if they were lending financial support to family members, he said, "I almost always get laughter. They're still getting subsidized."

> **The gap in gifts, debts, and inheritances creates a vicious cycle with large ramifications for many black Millennials and their financial future**

These small savings add up over time. Commentary often centers on the dire circumstances Millennials inherited ("It's the recession, stupid!") or the defective attributes of recipients ("Millennials are too entitled!"). But these oversimplified viewpoints miss the point of how some Millennials and their parents are able to weather tumultuous financial terrain in the first place—and more, how intergenerational financial support contributes to these Millennials' long-term wealth-building capacity.

To many Millennials, the small influxes of cash from parents are a lifeline, a financial relief they're hard pressed to find elsewhere. To researchers, however, it's both a symptom and an exacerbating factor of wealth inequality. In a 2004 *CommonWealth* magazine interview, Shapiro explained that gifts like this are "often not a lot of money, but it's really important money. It's a kind of money that allows families to obtain something for themselves and for their children that they couldn't do on their own."

To be sure, gift-giving parents see it as a step in helping their Millennial children reach financial independence. But the bigger picture is that their support acts as a stabilizing factor now, and an inheriting factor later. The Institute on Assets and Social Policy's "The Roots of the Widening Racial Wealth Gap" found that every dollar in financial family support received by a white American yielded 35 cents in wealth growth. For a black individual, family support is much more essential to their financial trajectory: Every dollar received yielded 51 cents in wealth growth. Millennials of all backgrounds would certainly benefit from increased financial family support, but where one winds up depends a lot on where one started.

Wealth inequality can't be discussed without talking about race; within the American context, they are inseparable. So the fact that Millennials of color feel the impact of a precarious financial foundation more acutely is not a surprise. For black Millennials in particular, studies point to a legacy of discrimination over several centuries that contributed to less inherited wealth passed down from previous generations. This financial disparity stems from continuous shortfalls in their parents' net worth and low homeownership rates among blacks, which works to create an unlevel playing field.

As a result, the median wealth of white households is 13 times the median wealth of black households. In addition, the most recent housing bust is estimated to have wiped out half of the collective wealth of black families—a setback of two generations.

"It was just incredible," Shapiro said. "It hit hardest those groups latest to becoming home buyers." Homeownership makes up a large amount of black families' wealth composition, accounting for over 50 percent of wealth for blacks, compared with just 39 percent for whites. Shapiro also pointed out that the people impacted by the housing crisis were likely to be the parents of Millennials.

Even with equal advances in income, education, and other factors, wealth grows at far lower rates for black households because they usually need to use financial gains for everyday needs rather than long-term savings and asset building. Each dollar in income increase yields $5.19 in wealth for white American households, but only 69 cents for black American households. In addition, while many Americans don't have adequate savings, the rate is far higher for families of color: 95 percent of African American and 87 percent of Latino middle-class families do not have enough net assets to meet most of their essential living expenses for even three months if their source of income were to disappear. If Millennials of color aren't getting as much financial help, it's because there's just not as much help for their families to give.

It's more than just lack of "pocket money" from parents that impacts Millennials of color. The last significant stop on life's journey is often an economically definitive one too, when parents and grandparents pass away and leave an inheritance.

According to the Institute on Assets and Social Policy, white Americans are five times more likely to inherit than black Americans (36 percent to 7 percent, respectively). And even when both groups received an inheritance, white Americans received about 10 times more. "It's really a double whammy," Shapiro said. On the flip side, black Millennials and other low-asset groups are much more likely to go into debt when a family member passes away. It's not uncommon for some families to throw bake sales and engage in other fund-raising activities to bury their relatives.

A 2013 *Washington Post* article also noted that "black families rarely benefited from inheritances and gifts to help them make down payments on homes. The result was that black families typically bought homes eight years later than whites, giving them less time to build equity."

"That's an eight-year window of not paying rent and building equity," Shapiro said.

And the life cycle of homeownership-related matters is an onerous one for black Americans to begin with. The researchers Kerwin Charles and Erik Hurst found that black mortgage applicants were almost twice as likely to be rejected for a loan in the first place, even when credit profile and household wealth were controlled for.

The same study found that almost half of white Americans got money from a family source for a home down payment, while nine in 10 black Americans had to come up with their entire down payment on their own—which had the effect of disincentivizing younger black renters from buying. "Even when they were able to buy a home," the *Post* article said, "the typical black family did not see that property appreciate as much as did the typical white family."

It all adds up to a slice of the racial wealth gap that's hard to grasp because it's made up of many smaller inequalities instead of one massive one. It's not the difference between a silver spoon and a dirt floor—it's the one between textbook money and a campus job. It's not the difference between the 1 percent and the destitute—it's the one between a birthday card from Grandma and paying her hospital bill. The gap in gifts, debts, and inheritances creates a vicious cycle with large ramifications for many black Millennials and their financial future—and when combined with redlining and unequal returns on income and education, the odds are stacked in a terrible way.

My father left me with many things of value: a love of creation, an affinity for literature, a deep sense of integrity, and a penchant for easily making friends out of strangers. He loved America, despite the times it relegated him to the back doors of its restaurants as a "colored man." He placed glossy graduation photos of me from high school and college in nooks around the house like prized medallions. They symbolized his version of the American dream, in which his children—his Millennials—would accomplish more than he ever could.

For his sake and mine, I hope he's right.

Tech Jobs: Minorities Have Degrees but Don't Get Hired

By Elizabeth Weise and Jessica Guynn
USA Today, October 13, 2014

Top universities turn out black and Hispanic computer science and computer engineering graduates at twice the rate that leading technology companies hire them, a USA TODAY analysis shows.

Technology companies blame the pool of job applicants for the severe shortage of blacks and Hispanics in Silicon Valley.

But these findings show that claim "does not hold water," said Darrick Hamilton, professor of economics and urban policy at The New School in New York.

"What do dominant groups say? 'We tried, we searched but there was nobody qualified.' If you look at the empirical evidence, that is just not the case," he said.

As technology becomes a major engine of economic growth in the U.S. economy, tech companies are under growing pressure to diversify their workforces, which are predominantly white, Asian and male. Leaving African Americans and Hispanics out of that growth increases the divide between haves and have-nots. And the technology industry risks losing touch with the diverse nation—and world—that forms its customer base.

On average, just 2% of technology workers at seven Silicon Valley companies that have released staffing numbers are black; 3% are Hispanic.

But last year, 4.5% of all new recipients of bachelor's degrees in computer science or computer engineering from prestigious research universities were African American, and 6.5% were Hispanic, according to data from the Computing Research Association.

The USA TODAY analysis was based on the association's annual Taulbee Survey, which includes 179 U.S. and Canadian universities that offer doctorates in computer science and computer engineering.

"They're reporting 2% and 3%, and we're looking at graduation numbers (for African Americans and Hispanics) that are maybe twice that," said Stuart Zweben, professor of computer science and engineering at The Ohio State University in Columbus.

"Why are they not getting more of a share of at least the doctoral-granting institutions?" said Zweben, who co-authored the 2013 Taulbee Survey report.

An even larger gulf emerges between Silicon Valley and graduates of all U.S. colleges and universities. A survey by the National Center for Education Statistics showed that blacks and Hispanics each made up about 9% of all 2012 computer science graduates.

> **"There are these subtle biases that make you think that some person is not what you're looking for, even when they are."**

Nationally, blacks make up 12% of the U.S. workforce and Hispanics 16%.

Facebook, Twitter, Google, Apple and Yahoo declined to comment on the disparity between graduation rates and their hiring rates.

LinkedIn issued a statement that it was working with organizations to "address the need for greater diversity to help LinkedIn and the tech industry as a whole."

Google said on its diversity blog in May that it has "been working with historically black colleges and universities to elevate coursework and attendance in computer science."

In his blog post on diversity, Apple's CEO Tim Cook cited improving education as "one of the best ways in which Apple can have a meaningful impact on society. We recently pledged $100 million to President Obama's ConnectED initiative to bring cutting-edge technologies to economically disadvantaged schools."

All of the companies have insisted they are hiring all of the qualified black and Hispanic tech workers they can find.

In an interview earlier this year, Facebook Chief Operating Officer Sheryl Sandberg said the key to getting more women and minorities into the technology field had to start with improvements to education.

"We are not going to fix the numbers for under-representation in technology or any industry until we fix our education system," she said.

Others say tech giants simply don't see the programmers right in front of them.

Janice Cuny directs the Computer Education program at the National Science Foundation. She says black and Hispanic computer science graduates are invisible to these companies.

"People used to say that there were no women in major orchestras because women didn't like classical music. Then in the 1970s they changed the way people auditioned so it was blind, the listeners couldn't see the players auditioning. Now the numbers are much more representative," she said.

The same thing happens in the tech world, said Cuny. "There are these subtle biases that make you think that some person is not what you're looking for, even when they are."

One of the key problems: There are elite computer science departments that graduate larger numbers of African-American and Hispanic students, but they are not the ones where leading companies recruit employees. Stanford, UC-Berkeley, Carnegie Mellon, UCLA and MIT are among the most popular for recruiting by tech companies, according to research by *Wired* magazine.

"That is the major disconnect," said Juan Gilbert, a professor of computer and information science at the University of Florida in Gainesville.

"The premise that if you want diversity, you have to sacrifice quality, is false," he said. His department currently has 25 African-American Ph.D. candidates. Rice University in Houston has a large number of Hispanic students.

"These are very strong programs, top-ranked places that have excellent reputations," he said. "Intel has been hiring from my lab, and they say our students hit it out of the ballpark."

Justin Edmund says he was fortunate to attend Carnegie Mellon. Today he's the seventh employee at Pinterest and one of the top designers at the San Francisco start-up valued at $5 billion.

He's also one of the few African Americans in his company.

"There's a lot of things that can be done to fix the problem, but a lot of them are things that Silicon Valley and technology companies don't do," Edmund said. "If you go to the same prestigious universities every single time and every single year to recruit people . . . then you are going to get the same people over and over again."

African-Americans Are Still Being Victimized by the Mortgage Market

By David Dayen
The New Republic, May 27, 2014

Ta-Nehisi Coates' brilliant essay, "The Case for Reparations," recounts centuries of ongoing and persistent racism in America. The sprawling article incorporates slavery, Jim Crow laws, sharecropper abuse, lynching, and many other forms of oppression. But Coates in large part illustrates formal racism by looking at housing policy, specifically in the Chicago neighborhood of Lawndale in the 1960s.

Housing is an appropriate lens. The most direct way for the American middle class to acquire wealth in the postwar era has been through their homes. And as Coates points out, African-Americans were simply cut off from that opportunity, broadening a racial wealth gap that exists to this day. From the 1930s to the 1960s, a period when homeownership rates doubled, the Federal Housing Administration refused to insure houses in African-American neighborhoods, specifically shaded on maps in red. Restrictive covenants in mortgage documents prevented homeowners in white neighborhoods from reselling to black Americans, lest they lower property values. As a result, a generation of African-Americans were "red-lined" into segregated spaces.

As banks wouldn't lend to the black community, this service was left to contract sellers—speculators who bought up homes on the cheap (often by scaring whites out of the neighborhood by telling them black families were moving in, a practice known as "block-busting") and resold them to African-Americans at a markup. They would not issue a mortgage to allow the home occupiers to build equity. "The seller kept the deed until the contract was paid in full," Coates writes. One missed payment would cause not only eviction, but also a forfeiture of the original down payment. Contract sellers used all sorts of tricks to recapture the home and sell it back to another unsuspecting family. These speculators preyed on vulnerable people, and stripped them of their wealth and opportunity.

That last sentence should sound familiar, because the nation just went through virtually the same experience with the housing bubble and eventual foreclosure crisis. That doesn't normally get labeled as a racist policy, but it certainly could. As Coates points out in a five-paragraph coda at the end of his article, modern-day predatory lenders also targeted black communities, deliberately concentrated in neighborhoods by decades of government-sanctioned segregation, and steered them toward subprime loans. "Plunder in the past made plunder in the present efficient," Coates writes.

It's worse than he describes. The Fair Housing Act of 1968 ended government redlining and segregation, allowing black families to accumulate wealth through homeownership. For sub-prime lenders, this was quickly seen as a prime opportunity: a largely low-income community strug-gling with stagnant wages and a rising cost of living, whom they could per-suade to use their homes like an ATM.. As far back

> **Contract sellers used all sorts of tricks to recapture the home and sell it back to an-other unsuspecting family. These speculators preyed on vulnerable people, and stripped them of their wealth and opportunity.**

as 1993, African-Americans were five to eight times more likely to hold subprime loans than whites. Even homeowners in *high-income* black communities were twice as likely to have subprime loans as homeowners in *low-income* white communities. And these loans were typically cash-out refinances (loans taken out for more than the home is worth, so the borrower can pocket the remainder cash) and lines of credit for homeowners with substantial equity—attempts by the lenders to get at the meager wealth created by black families and expropriate it.

But there is a key difference between the housing policies of the past and the present: the lenders themselves. In 1960s Chicago, contract sellers were the only people African-Americans could turn to if they wanted to purchase a home. But these days, banks pride themselves on lending to African-Americans; in fact, just last week their trade group, the Mortgage Bankers Association, charged *govern-ment* mortgage policies as racist.

Indeed, the key subprime loans in the 2000s were either originated by or funded by our biggest banks. Coates recognizes this, pointing out that the Justice Depart-ment successfully sued not fly-by-night originators, but Wells Fargo and Bank of America, over housing discrimination. Loan officers at Wells Fargo, the leading originator of home loans to ethnic minorities, referred to black customers as "mud people" and their offerings as "ghetto loans." The problem in the 1960s was that black people couldn't get loans from the banks; the problem in the present is that they can too easily.

In other words, the plausible deniability of the financial industry's role in racist housing policies has now withered. Coates writes that there used to be two housing markets—one legitimate and one lawless. Now there's just one, but it's largely law-less, backed by the government and controlled by our largest financial institutions. Government's laissez-faire attitude toward regulating the subprime sector allowed this transformation from exploitation by individual contract sellers to a formal Wall Street moneymaking scheme. The housing discrimination lawsuits, like most of the attempts at accountability for the predatory practices of the foreclosure crisis, re-sulted in a pittance compared to the actual impact. Restitution for banks deceiving borrowers with loans they couldn't afford and taking away their homes illegally was as low as $300.

Virtually all of the 1960s-era contract seller tactics that Coates describes have analogies today. Contract sellers loading up borrowers with payments they cannot meet? That's a good description of an adjustable-rate mortgage, which resets to unsustainable levels. The story of one woman who had an insurance bill added to her payment without her knowledge? There's a modern-day scam called force-placed insurance, where banks install high-cost junk insurance policies on borrowers whose homeowner's insurance has lapsed. Contract sellers lying about building code compliance? There's a long record of appraisal fraud that put buyers into homes at inflated prices.

I correspond with homeowners abused by the system on an almost daily basis. The majority of them are black or Hispanic. Many have tried to fight back exactly in the manner that the Contract Buyers League, the collection of black homeowners in Chicago, did in the 1960s. They have gone to the homes of bank executives and embarrassed them in front of their neighbors. They have filed class-action lawsuits alleging deliberate abuse. Like the Contract Buyers League, these actions unfortunately amounted to little.

Subprime abuse devastated African-American communities, eroding generations of wealth creation and progress. Research by Atif Mian and Amir Sufi shows higher unemployment rates in communities with the biggest decline in housing prices and the most foreclosures, and persistent, long-term unemployment affects lifetime earning potential. Additional research shows that foreclosures increase suicide rates, create health problems for the affected families and lead to public health crises. The pain heaped on foreclosure-ridden black communities goes well beyond the surface.

But Coates does not identify one important contributor to the stripping of black wealth: the cultural factor of mythologizing homeownership. Coates, in fact, falls into this trap. He calls homeownership "the emblem of American citizenship" and describes the home as Americans' "most sacred possession." This concept, fed by persistent propagandizing from both the government and Wall Street, leads vulnerable people to sink their savings into inherently unstable assets. In fact, the government grants huge benefits, in the form of the mortgage interest deduction, on families who reach to buy a home. Renters *are* implicitly seen as less than full citizens.

We don't have to live with this reality. Homeownership makes sense for some people, but not those on the poorest rungs of the ladder, who already spend 40 percent of their income on housing. We can redesign our housing and savings policies so people don't have to fall prey to unscrupulous lenders and play dangerous games with debt just to acquire wealth in America. We can create housing personal savings accounts to benefit first-time renters as well as homeowners who make larger down payments, and we can give many other inducements to savings, including higher wages, to reduce reliance on housing as a wealth-creation tool. We can redesign the 30-year mortgage so payments rise and fall with home prices, lowering the chance for a disastrous foreclosure crisis and subsequent recession. We can use government to stabilize communities disproportionately affected by downturns. And we can eliminate the stigma against renting that leads people to make bad choices with the biggest purchase of their lives.

Sadly, we're moving in the opposite direction. Mel Watt, an African-American from North Carolina, is arguably the most important person in housing policy today. As head of the Federal Housing Finance Agency, Watt oversees mortgage giants Fannie Mae and Freddie Mac, which currently own or guarantee 90 percent of all new home loans. And his first action at the FHFA was to loosen mortgage standards, making credit more available, but also making families more vulnerable to the same predatory lenders that abused them before. Re-inflating the housing bubble, not reimagining the housing market in general, seems to be the priority.

Black communities have clearly been decimated by the lending industry, in a variety of forms, for centuries. They deserve restitution for this theft, or at least a Truth and Reconciliation Commission to make plain, in Coates' words, "our collective biography and its consequences." But part of that restitution must include an alteration of the cultural biases that set up African-Americans, and actually many other would-be homeowners, for failure.

Supreme Court's Latest Race Case: Housing Discrimination

By Nikole Hannah-Jones
ProPublica, January 21, 2015

This week, the U.S. Supreme Court will take up one of the most important civil rights cases of the last decade. If you've never heard of *Texas Department of Housing and Community Affairs v. The Inclusive Communities Project*, you have company. The issue of housing segregation has never captivated the nation's attention like affirmative action or voting rights.

But today, two days after the Martin Luther King Jr. holiday, the court will hear arguments in the Texas case that many fear could gut the Fair Housing Act, the landmark 1968 law that was passed just days after King's assassination.

"This case has as broad of a reach as anything the court has decided in the last 10 years," said Myron Orfield, director of the Institute on Metropolitan Opportunity at the University of Minnesota Law School, because housing segregation is the foundation of racial inequality in the United States.

The case concerns whether the Fair Housing Act, which sought to end the long-standing segregation of America's neighborhoods, should be read to only bar intentional discrimination. For four decades, federal courts have held that the law should be interpreted more broadly, ruling again and again that if the policies of governmental agencies, banks or private real estate companies unjustifiably perpetuate segregation, regardless of their intent, they could be found in violation of the Fair Housing Act.

All 11 of the federal circuit courts that have considered the question have seen it that way. As well, the U.S. Department of Housing and Urban Development, the agency charged with administering the act, issued a regulation enshrining the principle in 2013.

The nation's highest court does not typically intervene in cases unless there's been disagreement in the lower courts. But this court has been determined to have its say on the housing issue and the legal theory that has come to be known as "disparate impact." The Texas case marks the third effort in as many years by the current justices to consider the intent and reach of the housing act. The other two cases were withdrawn or settled in deals reached before oral arguments, as fair housing advocates feared they would lose before the Roberts Court.

"It is unusual for the Court to agree to hear a case when the law is clearly settled. It's even more unusual to agree to hear the issue three years in a row," said Ian Haney López, a University of California, Berkeley, law professor.

The Texas case involves a nonprofit organization that works to promote integrated communities and the Texas state housing authority. The nonprofit, Inclusive Communities, showed that nearly all the affordable housing tax credits approved by the Texas housing agency had been assigned to Dallas' black neighborhoods and almost none of it to white neighborhoods. A federal judge did not find intentional discrimination on the part of Texas officials, but held that the outcome unacceptably increased housing segregation and that the housing agency could have taken steps to ensure that affordable housing units were allotted more equally.

Texas appealed the ruling, raising the stakes when it decided to challenge whether the Fair Housing Act allowed such "disparate impact" rulings at all.

For many, the Supreme Court's persistence signals a determination to install intentional discrimination alone as the standard for such cases. The Roberts Court is considered by a host of scholars and others to be the most conservative since the 1930s, and so such an outcome would be consistent with its more narrow interpretations of laws governing voting rights and school segregation.

"Those who care about eradicating housing discrimination have to be very concerned about the Supreme Court taking this case," said Erwin Chemerinsky, dean of the University of California School of Law, where he is a constitutional scholar.

Elizabeth Julian, president of the Inclusive Communities Project and the former Assistant Secretary of Fair Housing and Equal Opportunity at HUD [U.S. Department of Housing and Urban Development], is among those who are worried.

"Reversing essentially four decades of case law would send a message that is very concerning," Julian said.

A few generations ago, most housing discrimination was overt. Banks openly refused to lend to black homebuyers. Public housing officials used to announce that certain developments were for white residents, others for Latinos. But the nature of housing segregation has evolved over the years, and the fight against it has had to change as well. Today, banks may well charge higher loan rates in certain communities, but they can also insist it has nothing to do with those neighborhoods being black or Latino. Local planning boards can concede that most affordable housing efforts have been placed in black neighborhoods, but maintain that it was not by malicious design.

The theory of disparate impact, then, has often been the only tool to address ongoing housing discrimination. Landlords or lenders who implement policies or practices that disproportionately impact racial minorities can be found in violation of civil rights law if they cannot justify those practices—even if no one can show they acted out of racial animus.

The U.S. Department of Justice has used disparate impact to win record settlements from banks that charged higher rates to black and Latino borrowers with similar credit histories as white borrowers, but could not justify the practice.

A fair housing group used disparate impact to topple a "blood relative" ordinance passed by nearly all-white St. Bernard's Parish in the wake of Hurricane Katrina. The ordinance barred homeowners from renting to anyone who was not kin. Civil rights lawyers were convinced officials passed this law to keep out black renters, but could not prove racist motivations. But when St. Bernard's Parish could not come up with a plausible justification for the ordinance, a court struck it down.

This tool, for the first time, is in real jeopardy.

The Supreme Court has been weakening many civil rights protections for decades. The Rehnquist Court, for instance, was known for getting the courts out of the business of addressing racial inequities. But the Roberts Court has gone a critical step further, severely curbing efforts undertaken by Congress and the executive branch to address our nation's long history of discrimination.

In 2007, the Roberts Court came down against two school districts that were trying to maintain gains in integration. In 2009, the court ended the attempts of New Haven, Connecticut, officials to ensure that the city's promotion practices were fair after no black firemen passed a promotion exam, saying the efforts discriminated against white firefighters. In 2013, it held that a key provision of the Voting Rights Act intended to address the disenfranchisement of

> **"Those who care about eradicating housing discrimination have to be very concerned about the Supreme Court taking this case,"** said Erwin Chemerinsky, dean of the University of California School of Law, where he is a constitutional scholar.

black voters had expired. And last year, it upheld Michigan voter–approved ban on affirmative action.

"The Supreme Court is newly aggressive in the area of race," said Haney López. It is targeting efforts by other branches of society to remedy segregation and is striking them down."

Strikingly, if it ultimately rules against Inclusive Communities, in under a decade the Roberts Court will have limited pivotal protections in each of the three landmark civil rights laws passed in the 1960s: the 1964 Civil Rights Act, the 1965 Voting Rights Act and the 1968 Fair Housing Act.

The Court's aggressive tack has been welcomed by conservative groups, who believe the Fourteenth Amendment of the Constitution, intended to ensure former slaves equality under the law, requires strict legal colorblindness.

The Pacific Legal Foundation, an advocacy organization that promotes individual rights, has long looked forward to a showdown over the Fair Housing Act. It filed an amicus brief in support of the Texas housing agency..

Ralph Kasarda, a lawyer at the Pacific Legal Foundation, said that disparate impact puts an unfair burden on landlords, lenders and local governments.

He gives this example. A landlord requires a certain credit score for renters in order to ensure that they will pay their rent. For a host of societal reasons, African

Americans and Latinos tend to have lower credit scores. The landlord could find himself defending against a fair housing suit for a race-neutral policy.

"The problem that I have is imposing liability on someone for doing something without any intent to harm someone," Kasarda said.

Of course, even under the legal theory of disparate impact, legitimate business practices that can be justified do not violate the law even if they lead to different results among different racial groups.

But the Pacific Legal Foundation's chief gripe is race consciousness itself.

In order for Texas housing officials to ensure they were allotting subsidized housing in a racially balanced way, they would have had to take into account the racial makeup of the communities where the housing was to go. Kasarda and others argue that race-conscious policies designed to help racial minorities are no better than those designed to harm them.

"You have the case where a government or organization might resort to race-based decisions to avoid disparate impact," he said. "The Pacific Legal Foundation believes that is unconstitutional."

Julian, of Inclusive Communities, doesn't buy the conservative argument. The Fair Housing Act was designed to address the effects of racial segregation, she said.

"It doesn't require getting into the hearts and minds of people and motives of individuals because at the end of the day the motives don't matter. It's the perpetuation of segregation that is the harm," Julian said.

She offered an analogy: Say a driver is texting and hits someone with her car and puts them in the hospital.

"The fact that you did not mean to is beside the point," Julian said. "No, you didn't mean to hit them, but you are going to be held accountable because you engaged in behavior that you knew could cause harm, and you did it anyway."

The end of disparate impact policies and cases, she argued, would severely hamper advocates' ability to go after systemic housing discrimination in a nation where the segregation of black Americans has barely budged in many cities and where it is growing for Latinos. "It would be taken as a greenlight to say you can do anything you want, as long as you do not have the offending email."

Volume Editor's Postscript

On June 25, 2015, the Supreme Court, by a five-to-four margin, upheld the application of disparate impact under the Fair Housing Act ("FHA"), but the Court imposed significant limitations on its application in practice by placing a higher burden of proof on plaintiffs than previously existed and insisting that any "remedial orders . . . concentrate on the elimination of the offending practice" through "race-neutral means."

More Black Women Are Dying from Breast Cancer Than White Women—and the Disparity Is Growing Every Year

By Casey Gueren
Women's Health, March 20, 2014

While there have been amazing advances in breast cancer research over the last few decades, a new study suggests that not everyone is benefitting from [them]. There is a significant racial disparity between black and white women in breast cancer–related deaths in the U.S., according to a new study published in the journal *Cancer Epidemiology*. And even more shocking is the fact that this gap became even wider in many cities from 1990 to 2009. These startling findings pose the question: Why are more black women dying from breast cancer than white women each year?

The Frightening Findings

This latest research conducted by Sinai Urban Health Institute and the Avon Foundation for Women was prompted by their two earlier studies, which found these racial disparities in several cities across the country. After those findings came out, hospitals all over the U.S. asked them to take a look at the stats in their cities, too. So the researchers looked at breast cancer-related deaths in the 50 largest U.S. cities at four time points (1990–1994, 1995–1999, 2000–2004, and 2005–2009). Of those 50 places, they were only able to get data from 41 of the cities. The goal was to see the black/white disparity in breast cancer mortality (the difference between how many black women died from breast cancer and how many white women died from breast cancer), and how this disparity changed over time. Ideally, we would hope to see that the rates of black women and white women dying from breast cancer have both decreased at the same rate over time. Unfortunately, that wasn't the case.

Here's what they found: Between 1990 [and] 1994, the overall racial disparity for the U.S. was 17 percent. That means that at that time, black women were 17 percent more likely to die from breast cancer than white women were. That disparity varied for different cities, but only a few cities had a large disparity at that time. Fast forward to 2005–2009 and the U.S. disparity grew to 40 percent. Again, some cities were faring better than others; for instance, New York only had a 19 percent racial disparity, while Memphis had a 111 percent disparity. During 2005–2009, they saw a racial disparity in 39 of the 41 cities, and this gap grew over time in

35 of those cities. Essentially, the rate of white women dying from breast cancer was declining, while the rate of black women dying from breast cancer was not changing substantially.

The Reason for the Race Gap

The scope of these findings show that this difference cannot be blamed solely on genetics, says study coauthor Marc Hurlbert, executive director of the Avon Breast Cancer Crusade. "Other studies have shown that black women are more likely to get triple-negative breast cancer and more aggressive forms like inflammatory breast cancer," says Hurlbert. "But to go from almost no disparity in 1990 to a significant one in 2009—that change over time and that geographic variability shows that it has to be an issue of accessing care."

While the researchers can't be sure exactly why this disparity exists or why it's continued to grow, they have a few theories: "Certain technological advances related to screening and treatment that became available in the 1990s—such as digital mammography, advances in surgery, and new drugs for treatment—have been less accessible to black women, who are disproportionately poor and un- or under-insured and less able to obtain access to these advances," says lead study author Steve Whitman, Ph.D., director of Sinai Urban Health Institute in a press release.

In their earlier 2012 study, they found that cities with a larger poverty gap and cities that were more segregated had a larger disparity of breast cancer mortality between black women and white women. In areas like this, it wouldn't be uncommon for black women to have a harder time accessing the best, most comprehensive care—including the best hospitals, digital mammography, breast cancer specialists reading mammograms, and patient navigators helping women along the way. These are all things that have been proven to improve your chance of survival, says Hurlbert, but they aren't accessible to all women.

Closing the Gap

Since this data collection ended in 2009, the researchers aren't sure if the disparity continues to grow. "We're optimistic that the addition of Avon funded programs and the Affordable Care Act rolling out will mean more women will have access to insurance," says Hurlbert. "But that might take up to a decade [to affect the data]."

> "...to go from almost no disparity in 1990 to a significant one in 2009—that change over time and that geographic variability shows that it has to be an issue of accessing care."

In the meantime, Hurlbert suggests that all women get informed about their breast cancer risk and demand access to high-quality screening and treatment. "Find a center with a dedicated breast imager, ask who is reading your mammogram, demand timeliness," says Hurlbert, as research shows that getting your mammogram read by a breast cancer specialist (rather than a general radiologist) and starting treatment early are crucial steps that can make a huge difference in your outcome.

Hurlbert also suggests doing what you can do to lower your personal risk of breast cancer. For instance, we know that exercise can lower your risk, as well as maintaining a healthy weight and lowering your alcohol intake.

While these new findings are shocking, Hurlbert hopes they'll help point us in the right direction for future research: "Here's where we are now. Now how can we improve upon that going forward?"

The Racial Divide within Our Heart . . . Attacks

By Tom Jacobs
Pacific Standard, September 14, 2015

Besides "driving while black," and the more recently coined "laughing while black," new research has revealed another activity people of color would be particularly wise to avoid: suffering a heart attack.

The American Heart Association journal *Circulation* published today the latest study revealing health disparities among Americans of different races. It finds that, in a large sample, white Americans lived an average of 6.4 years following a heart attack, while black patients lived an average of 5.6 years.

Unexpectedly, the gap was much higher at the upper end of the socioeconomic ladder than the lower one. Among Americans living in well-off neighborhoods, post-heart-attack life expectancy was seven years for whites, compared to 6.3 for blacks. Among those living in the poorest areas, racial differences in life expectancy were quite small: 5.6 years for white patients, and 5.4 for blacks.

"The implication here is that black patients and poor patients are disadvantaged—and higher socioeconomic status does not eliminate racial disparities," Harlan Krumholz of the Yale University School of Medicine said in a press statement accompanying the study, which he co-authored with his colleague Emily Bucholz. "[The results indicate] that blacks with greater resources remain vulnerable to poorer outcomes."

The researchers used data from the Cooperative Cardiovascular Project, which identified Medicare beneficiaries who were hospitalized after suffering acute myocardial infarction—a heart attack, in layman's terms—and tracked their progress for the following 17 years.

The researchers used a random sample of 141,095 such patients whose heart attacks occurred between January 1994 and February 1996, when they were between the ages of 65 and 90. Using zip code information, they categorized each as living in one of three types of neighborhood: high socioeconomic status (in the top 15th percentile of median household income), low socioeconomic status (one in the bottom 15th), or medium socioeconomic status (the rest).

Not surprisingly, they found black patients (who made up 6.7 percent of the total) were more likely to live in the poorer neighborhoods: 26 percent did so, compared to 5.7 percent of white patients. But the data suggests blacks who made it up

> **"Because wealthy neighborhoods tend to have a greater concentration of white households, blacks living in these areas may experience less social cohesion and receive less support than those living in low-income areas."**

the economic ladder did not get the same health boost as whites.

"After 17 years of follow-up, the survival rate was 7.4 percent for white patients and 5.7 percent for black patients," the researchers report. But this gap varied with the socioeconomic level of the patients' neighborhoods.

Among those in the wealthiest areas, 9.1 percent of whites survived after 17 years, compared to only 7.1 percent of blacks. In middle-income neighborhoods, the survival rates were 7 percent for whites and 5.7 percent for blacks. The greatest amount of parity was found in the poorest neighborhoods, with a 5.4 percent survival rate for whites and 5.2 percent for blacks.

The reasons for this remain somewhat murky, although the researchers note that black patients in the study "had a higher prevalence of most cardiovascular risk factors, including diabetes, hypertension, congestive heart failure, and smoking."

Beyond that finding, they speculate that "because wealthy neighborhoods tend to have a greater concentration of white households, blacks living in these areas may experience less social cohesion and receive less support than those living in low-income areas."

The research team adds that "racial discrimination, whether perceived or actual, has been shown to increase cardiovascular disease risk and negatively impact health outcomes."

Indeed, a Northwestern University study released just last week reported the belief you are being discriminated against produces elevated levels of cortisol, a hormone associated with stress. This reaction, which has long-term negative health consequences, appears to be stronger among blacks.

So perhaps discrimination experienced during one's teen years, a particularly sensitive period in which stress can greatly impact a growing body, takes a toll much later in life. That's speculative, but it's an avenue worth pursuing. As Krumholz commented, "We have work to do to understand why blacks are disadvantaged, and immediately address it."

Racial Injustice Still Rife in Health Care

By Vijay Das and Adam Gaffney
CNN.com, July 28, 2015

Racism mars the history of health care in America. For years, black patients were relegated to separate—and appallingly unequal—hospitals and wards. Many were simply denied medical attention, either "dumped" into the care of other facilities or turned away at the hospital door.

Fifty years ago this week, that started to change as Lyndon B. Johnson signed into law two programs—Medicaid and Medicare—that constituted real progress in the cause of health care justice. For one, these programs greatly expanded health care access for the elderly and the poor, of all races. Also, building on years of civil rights work and legal challenges, Medicare was wielded to finally end explicit hospital segregation; hospitals hoping to become certified for the program were required to comply with Title VI of the Civil Rights Act.

Yet despite this important achievement, racial justice in health remains an aspiration, not an achievement.

After the death of Freddie Gray in April, and as the nation debated race and the criminal justice system, Americans were reminded of some disturbing racial inequalities in health. Not least among these were the differences in life expectancy between some of Baltimore's segregated neighborhoods, which were as high as one to two decades. Meanwhile, across the nation, black males in 2010 had a life expectancy almost five years lower than white males; black women could expect to live three years fewer than white females.

In addition to inequalities in health outcomes (which have many roots), disparities persist in health care access. According to a 2013 report, blacks and Hispanics have substantially higher uninsured rates than whites. And while many are pinning their hopes on the Affordable Care Act to address such inequalities, the act won't remedy the many deeply rooted racial injustices in America's health care system.

The ACA's primary instrument for increasing health coverage for people of color is the expansion of Medicaid to all those earning less than 138% of the federal poverty level. However, although Medicaid eligibility was meant to expand nationwide, the U.S. Supreme Court ruled that states could opt out. Some 19 states are doing exactly that.

Hopefully, with some combination of public shaming and political mobilization, common sense will prevail and Medicaid will be expanded nationwide. But even if the ACA's Medicaid expansion reaches all 50 states, the program's intrinsic weaknesses render it insufficient for reaching the goal of health care equality.

Most concerning is the problem of health care access. An audit of California's Medicaid managed care system last month, for example, raised disturbing questions about the adequacy of doctor networks for program participants in that state. Nationally, limited access to particular treatments is another problem. Last month, a study revealed that state Medicaid programs are limiting coverage of sofosbuvir, a potentially life-saving medication for those with Hepatitis C, a chronic condition disproportionately affecting minorities. The investigators called these cost-saving restrictions—which do not appear to have been based on any official, professional clinical guidelines—a potential "human rights violation" because they prevented patients from obtaining needed care.

Unfortunately, the problem of health care inequality is not limited to Medicaid. As a recent study suggested, some Obamacare plans effectively discriminate on the basis of drug affordability for certain diseases, like HIV/AIDS. By categorizing medications for particular conditions in the highest co-payment "tier," these plans price out patients with those ailments. These additional co-payments can result in thousands of dollars a year in extra expenses.

The reality is that people of color bear the brunt of a system that treats health care as a commodity at the same time as high out-of-pocket costs in the form of soaring deductibles become the norm. This point was underscored by the findings of the Commonwealth Fund, which found in 2014 that 31 million insured Americans were underinsured on the basis of high out-of-pocket expenses, which deter many from seeking treatment. Of course, these challenges affect everyone, but minority families may face particular distress.

We do not need to accept this status quo.

Just as Medicare helped spur hospital integration, it can usher in true universal health care—a single-payer system of "Medicare-For-All"—that will help lessen racial and class inequalities in health care. Such an expansion is consistent with the original goals of many advocates who created the 50-year-old program. But even as we expand Medicare to all, we must also improve it, including ending burdensome cost sharing requirements.

True universal health care cannot wait. Consider the tragic case of the late African-American Monroe Bird. This 21-year-old was shot by a private security guard in February. Though he was left paralyzed and critically ill, his private insurance plan reportedly denied him coverage for care in a rehabilitation facility. Bird returned home to be cared for by his family, who faced considerable financial stress in his complex care, owing up to $1 million in medical bills, according to the *New York Times*. Monroe died on June 30.

As we continue to confront the reality of structural racism in this country—where the criminal justice system disproportionately targets men and women of color, where the school-to-prison pipeline is the fate for far too many—we should also be aware that our for-profit health care system continues to fail too many people.

Racial and economic inequalities are intimately interwoven. There is now a record number of billionaires, yet as Vox notes, infant mortality is higher in West Baltimore than in the West Bank. The United States remains the only advanced nation that routinely forces families to start GoFundMe campaigns to pay for the medical treatment of their loved ones—and people of color are often bearing the brunt of this struggle. If we want to simultaneously improve American health care while opposing racial injustice, then let's expand and improve Medicare, and guarantee just and equal health care for all.

3
Criminal Justice and Racial Violence

Demonstrators face off with police officers during a protest in reaction to the fatal shooting of Laquan McDonald in Chicago, Illinois, November 27, 2015. McDonald, 17, was fatally shot by Jason Van Dyke, a Chicago police officer, in October 2014.

The Fight for Equality

In 2016, the criminal justice system remains one of the most controversial aspects of American race relations and the continuation of long-standing racial tension. Well-established statistics stretching back for more than a century show that police and the courts have disproportionately targeted minority Americans throughout American history and yet the underlying causes of this phenomenon are a matter of intense debate. In looking towards the future of criminal justice, police treatment, the effect of race in US courts, and the phenomenon of "mass incarceration" are among the most pressing issues.

Mass Incarceration

The rapid growth of the US prison population is one of the most widely debated topics in modern American criminal justice. The US prison population increased by 408 percent between 1978 and 2014, and the United States, with 5 percent of the overall population, has more than 20 percent of the global prison population. The United States, China, and Russia together house more than half of the global prison population, and the United States currently incarcerates more people each year than any other nation.[1]

Prison overcrowding is connected to various waves of "get tough" crime legislation that impose mandatory sentences and steeper penalties for both minor and major offenses. Proponents argue that these policies provide an effective crime deterrent and point to overall reductions in violent crime in the twenty-first century as proof that current strategies are working. Critics of America's current approach to incarceration argue that mass incarceration wastes millions in taxpayer funds, disproportionately targets individuals in certain racial and socioeconomic groups, and has had little impact on crime rates despite minor decreases in crime overall in the twenty-first century.

The American Civil Liberties Union (ACLU) argues that "extreme" sentencing laws and mandatory sentences fill prisons with young adult offenders guilty of minor crimes, including a variety of "drug crimes" that the ACLU argues are better addressed by treating drug addiction as a "disease" rather than a criminal activity. The ACLU also argues that the rise of private prisons and the "prison for profit" system has resulted in a situation where companies running correctional systems lobby against efforts to promote alternatives to incarceration.[2]

Targeting and Profiling

One of the most controversial problems in American criminal justice is the perception that police and courts disproportionately target minority offenders. Through a complex set of interwoven factors, minority Americans are more likely to be stopped or questioned by police, more likely to be arrested, and more likely to be convicted and sentenced to prison, than white offenders guilty of the same crimes. In many instances, this discrepancy is connected to "racial profiling" in which police learn to see racial characteristics as a signifier of possible criminal activity.

In 2015, African Americans and Latinos represent 56 percent of the prison population, but they constitute only 30 percent of the population as a whole. The subcategory of drug crime illuminates the situation. On the whole, drug-related crimes account for 14 percent of all arrests. Statistics from the 2012 National Survey on Drug Use and Health indicate that young white individuals (ages 12 to 25) are 32 percent more likely to sell drugs than African Americans of the same age. However, young black men and women are more than twice as likely to be arrested for drug crimes and more often receive prison sentences for drug offenses.[3] In total, African Americans constitute 59 percent of the population imprisoned for drug crimes.

Numerous other studies indicate that African Americans are also more likely to be stopped, questioned, and arrested by police than white offenders. In a 2014 study researchers found that in 70 police departments profiled from Connecticut to California, African Americans are arrested at 10 times the rate of white individuals.[4] African American author and activist Jason Riley argues in his book *Please Stop Helping Us* that African American communities have adopted a "culture of criminality" and that African Americans therefore commit *more crime* than any other racial group in America. Numerous criminologists and sociologists oppose this position, arguing that the targeting of African Americans has created the illusion that African Americans commit more crime than white Americans, a misconception supported and ingrained in American public opinion through depictions of African Americans and other minorities in popular culture.

Differential Justice

Since the 1960s, police departments around the nation have used arrest rates as a metric when attempting to measure the relative success of individual police districts and departments. Critics argue that police, looking to maintain arrest rates, tend to focus on poor neighborhoods where crime is more likely to occur in the open and where individuals who are stopped, detained, or arrested are less likely to have the means to legally defend themselves against police targeting. In New York City, for instance, police records indicate that young black men and woman were more than twice as likely to be targeted for "stop and frisk" operations or pulled over for traffic violations, and critics believe that this behavior continues because minority individuals are less likely to "fight back" within the justice system.

Targeting of minority youth has been a popular subject after the 2014 and 2015 police brutality controversies surrounding the death of Michael Brown in Ferguson, Missouri, and Eric Garner in Long Island, New York. The US Justice Department investigation in Ferguson, Missouri, found evidence of persistent prejudice in the way police and St. Louis County courts approach minority offenders. Attorney General Eric Holder stated that these patterns had created a "highly toxic environment" in which African Americans learn to view police as enemies persecuting them whether or not they are involved in crime.[5] The Department of Justice (DOJ) report found that, while approximately 67.4 percent of Ferguson residents are African American, police targeted African Americans in 86 percent of traffic stops, 92 percent of vehicle searches, and 92.7 percent of overall arrests.[6]

A 2014 study of DOJ statistics indicates that African Americans are also six times more likely to be convicted than white individuals arrested for the same crimes. A lack of racial diversity in jury selection and instances in which certain judges disproportionately recommend prison for African American offenders have been found to be contributing factors in the creation of racially divergent conviction rates. A 2001 analysis of DOJ statistics indicated that on average, minority offenders received 13 percent longer prison sentences overall than white offenders who were sentenced for the same crime.[7]

American public opinion is divided with regard to the treatment of minorities in the justice system. Polls from 2014 indicate that a slim majority (51 percent) believe that police treat minority suspects differently than white suspects. Nearly 6 in 10 white Americans believed that the Ferguson, Missouri, shooting was an isolated incident, not related to broader trends in police treatment of African Americans despite numerous studies and statistics indicating that the situation in Ferguson was indicative of a national problem in policing.[8]

Violence, Direct and Indirect

The South Carolina church shootings of 2015 and numerous similar incidents provide examples of situations in which individuals or racially-motivated, groups directly target individuals of certain races for violence. In 2014, 5,462 "hate crimes" were recorded by the FBI, 47 percent of which were motivated by race. With recent events surrounding the Syrian/Iraqi terrorist organization ISIS, the FBI has found that hate crimes against Muslims and Middle-Eastern Americans (especially those of Syrian descent) has intensified, with 154 incidents recorded in 2014. The targeting of Muslim-Americans demonstrates how racial tension changes in accordance with changing views of race in global politics, but, in the United States, African Americans, Hispanic Americans, and other minority groups have been targets for intense racial violence for the entirety of American history.

In some cases, racial violence takes the form of civil disobedience and "rioting," such as the 1992 Los Angeles riots and the more recent 2015 riots in Ferguson, Missouri. After the Ferguson riots, 58 percent of people interviewed by the *Wall Street Journal* said they believed the riots were an "excuse to loot," while 32 percent believed the Ferguson riots were the result of long-existing police persecution.[9] Race riots have been occurring in the United States since the 1700s, some involving former African slaves and their descendants and others involving Native Americans that had been attacked, persecuted, and forced to live in the equivalent of internment camps as white Americans settled the American West. Throughout history such incidents often intensify public debate about the treatment of minority Americans and as such have played an important role in past and current civil rights debates. The treatment of race in criminal justice is a complex and controversial issue and public opinion is often divided along racial lines. Moving forward, as in other efforts to address racial tension, it has become important to examine the way that structural racism and unconscious racial bias influence the justice system at every level, from the establishment of police procedure to the dispensation of justice in the court room.

Micah L. Issitt

Notes

1. Ye Hee Lee, "Does the United States Really Have 5 Percent of the World's Population?"
2. ACLU, "Campaign for Smart Justice."
3. Ingraham, Christopher, "White People Are More Likely to Deal Drugs, but Black People Are More Likely to Get Arrested for It."
4. Heath, Brad, "Racial Gap in U.S. Arrest Rates."
5. Levine, "Eric Holder; Ferguson Police Created 'A Toxic' Environment."
6. Goyette, Wing, Caded, "21 Numbers That Will Help You Understand Why Ferguson Is about More than Michael Brown."
7. "Report of the Sentencing Project to the United Nations Human Rights Committee," *Sentencing Project*.
8. Clement, Scott, "On Racial Issues, America Is Divided Both Black and White and Red and Blue."
9. Hook, Janet, "U.S. Split along Racial Lines on Backlash against Police."

The Price of Transgression

By Gary Younge
The Nation, November 17, 2014

When former president George W. Bush was questioned repeatedly about his cocaine use and heavy drinking as a young man, he responded jokingly, "When I was young and irresponsible, I was young and irresponsible." There is a wry logic to such an answer, even if Bush hardly exemplifies its most important lesson: there's only so much maturity one can expect from those who are not fully mature. (His shenanigans continued well into adulthood. He was arrested for drunk driving when he was 30 and didn't stop drinking until he was 40. "He tried everything his father had tried," wrote his former speechwriter David Frum. "And, well into his forties, succeeded at almost nothing.")

There's a reason why car insurers have higher premiums for young drivers, and young offenders are—or, at least, should be—treated with more leniency in the criminal-justice system. Adolescence is a stage in life with its own dynamic. Young people have the capacity to perform as adults—they can produce children, drive cars and kill people—without the life experience to always put those abilities to good use. They are more likely to take risks and less likely to understand what those risks entail. They are experimenting not only with substances (alcohol and drugs) but with relationships (sexual, familial, fraternal) and lifestyles. They are working out what kind of person they want to be, and in that process they are about as likely to make sound judgments as the elderly are to make rash ones.

The trouble is that the penalty for being "young and irresponsible" is not the same for everyone. Research shows that a black job applicant with no criminal record is no more likely to get the job than a white applicant who has just been released from prison. When, like Bush, you're white, wealthy and well-connected, your parents can pay for rehab, therapy, a good lawyer, [and] a decent education, and find a friend to put you on the payroll in the hope that you will one day sort yourself out and, who knows, maybe become president.

But when you're black and poor—more likely to be stopped and frisked, and unable to afford a lawyer—the price for youthful transgression is not only high; it could last a lifetime. Black and white youth, for example, use marijuana at about the same rate, but black youths are nearly four times as likely to be arrested for it. That setback triggers a cascade of others. "Once you're labeled a felon," writes Michelle Alexander in *The New Jim Crow*, "the old forms of discrimination—employment discrimination, housing discrimination, denial of the right to vote, denial of educational opportunity, denial of food stamps and other public benefits, and exclusion from jury service—are suddenly legal. As a criminal, you have scarcely more rights, and arguably less respect, than a black man living in Alabama at the height of Jim Crow. We have not ended racial caste in America; we have merely redesigned it."

The law is the law, and those who smoke marijuana (in most states) know it is illegal. But when the stakes are that high and the odds that skewed, black youngsters don't have the luxury to learn from their mistakes. "The great privilege of the Americans is to be able to retrieve the mistakes they make," wrote Alexis de Tocqueville in his landmark book, *Democracy in America*. But for black youth, the great American myth of personal reinvention is more elusive.

A primary-care physician recently described to me the lengths people go to keep their children out of trouble on the South Side of Chicago. "They create cocoons for these young people. They transport them everywhere. They don't get on public transportation. They don't go out and hang out in the parks, because it's just too dangerous." Not content with hobbling their childhood with poverty, poor education and insufficiently safe places to play, racism is stealing their youth. Their transgressions are treated as evidence of a deeper, intolerable and intractable pathology. The Obamas aren't poor, but it takes no great feat of imagination to understand how differently things would have gone if one of the Obama daughters had become a teenage unwed mother like one of the Palins.

As the reporting on recent police killings reveals, such warped reasoning follows them to their early graves. Take Michael Brown, the 18-year-old who was shot dead by a white policeman in Ferguson. Having taken his life, the authorities have since set out to disparage him in death. In the very week of his killing, police released video that allegedly showed Brown robbing a store; from the toxicology report from his autopsy, we have heard that he had marijuana in his bloodstream. The object of such selective leaks is clear: to suggest that, regardless of the circumstances surrounding his shooting, Brown had it coming.

The penalty for smoking weed or shoplifting (whether Brown did those things or not) is not summary execution. But if the punishment does not fit the crime, it nonetheless serves the mindset. To be young, black, poor and (usually) male is, in the eyes of the American state, to be guilty of something. The details will be worked out later. "You're working in Bed-Stuy, where everyone's probably got a warrant," Lt. Jean Delafuente told police officers at a roll call in 2008, explaining why they should easily be able to make their arrest quota in that neighborhood in Brooklyn. With crime and poverty thus racially codified, it is up to black youth to prove why they should not be gunned down or locked up. Those who cannot make the case that they are worthy victims are considered worthy of death or detention.

Last January, after 19-year-old Justin Bieber was arrested in Miami for drunk driving, the judge explained his lenient sentence thus: "Here is someone who is young. His whole life is ahead of him, and he just hopefully will get the message. He will grow up." That's the right call. But it's a disgrace that it isn't applied more fairly. Justin Bieber has his whole life ahead of him. Michael Brown does not.

Driving While Black

By Charles Epp and Steven Maynard-Moody
The Washington Monthly, January/February 2014

If there's one issue that won Bill de Blasio the New York Democratic mayoral primary in September, on his way to a crushing 74 percent to 24 percent victory in the November general election, it was his full-throated opposition to "stop and frisk." Under this policy, police officers stop, question, and frisk people they deem suspicious, usually with zero evidence that they've committed a crime. De Blasio's predecessor Michael Bloomberg and his GOP election opponent Joe Lhota strongly defended stop and frisk, arguing that it helps reduce the crime rate. But the voters of New York had clearly had enough of a policy that, in practice, overwhelmingly targets minorities, especially young blacks, only a tiny fraction of whom are ever found to be carrying drugs, or a gun, or indeed to have done anything wrong at all.

What few Americans (or at least white Americans) know is that stop and frisk is not limited to New York City. Versions of the policy are in place across the country. And just as in New York, whatever crime-fighting benefits derive from the policy come at the expense of contravening basic American principles of equal treatment under the law and of angering law-abiding minority citizens whose support and cooperation the police need to fight crime.

Until recently, there has been limited data on the degree to which stop-and-frisk policies, as opposed to other factors or police tactics, specifically cause alienation and resentment. But a first-of-its-kind survey we conducted in Kansas City makes that connection quite clear.

Although it is hard to document how widely police departments employ stop-and-frisk-like tactics, the data tells the same story nearly everywhere studies have been done on who is stopped by the police: racial minorities are stopped at considerably higher rates than whites. The underlying reason for this is not racism by individual officers. Rather, it is police department directives requiring officers to make large numbers of stops just to check people out. Police departments widely favor this practice because it allows officers to proactively seize guns and drugs, in officer-initiated stops, rather than waiting to respond to crimes.

Police officers have long checked out people who look suspicious, but in the 1970s several scholars, led by James Q. Wilson, proposed turning this happenstance occurrence into an organized, disciplined practice. In the 1980s, the Reagan administration's Operation Pipeline, a key war-on-drugs initiative that trained local

"Driving While Black" by Charles Epp and Steven Maynard-Moody, originally published in the Jan-Feb 2014 issue of *Washington Monthly.*

departments in how to make stops to find drugs, refined the technique and spread its gospel widely across the country. A study by the National Institute of Justice in the mid-1990s showed how to use investigatory traffic stops to seize illegally carried guns. The New York City Police Department then applied the practice to stop and frisks of pedestrians.

Police leaders know that it takes a lot of stops to find just a few illegal drugs or weapons. A widely used police training manual, *Tactics for Criminal Patrol*, declares that "[c]riminal patrol in large part is a numbers game; you have to stop a lot of vehicles to get the law of averages working in your favor." Or, as an officer put it to the late journalist Gary Webb, "you've got to kiss a lot of frogs before you find a prince." (The irony in this statement, of course, is that law-abiding citizens are the "frogs" and criminals are the "princes.") This numbers game helps to explain why 98.2 percent of the stops in New York City yielded no illegal weapon or drugs. This 1.8 percent "hit rate," as Columbia law professor Jeffrey Fagan has shown, is no better than chance.

To understand the phenomenon outside of New York City, where drivers rather than pedestrians tend to be the target of stop-and-frisk-type operations, we surveyed 2,329 drivers in and around Kansas City, a region typical of large, geographically segregated metropolitan areas in the country. The data from our survey allowed us to distinguish stops to enforce traffic safety laws—like speeding at fifteen miles per hour over the limit—from stops to investigate the driver. Our key finding is that these two types of stops differ from start to finish. In traffic safety stops, based on clear violations of the law, officers quickly issue a ticket or warning and let the driver go. In investigatory stops officers drag the stop out as they try to look at the vehicle's interior, ask probing questions, and ultimately seek consent for a search (drivers almost always agree, telling us that they feel they have no real choice in the matter).

The key influence on who is stopped in traffic safety stops is how you drive; in investigatory stops it is *who you are,* and being black is the leading influence. In traffic safety stops, being black has no influence: African Americans are not significantly more likely than whites to be stopped for clear traffic safety law violations. But in investigatory stops, a black man age twenty-five or younger has a 28 percent chance of being stopped for an investigatory reason over the course of a year; a similar young white man has a 12.5 percent chance, and a similar young white woman has only a 7 percent chance. And this is after taking into account other possible influences on being stopped, like how you drive. Police focus investigatory stops on younger people, and so as people grow older they are less likely to be stopped in this way. But a black man must reach fifty—well into the graying years—before his risk of an investigatory stop drops below that of a white man under age twenty-five. Overall, black drivers are nearly *three times* more likely than whites to be subjected to investigatory stops.

Being black is also the leading influence on how far police officers pursue their inquisition in investigatory stops. In these stops, full-blown vehicle searches are relatively common. After taking into account other possible influences, black drivers in our survey were *five times* more likely than whites to be subjected to searches in investigatory stops. Searches are remarkably rare in traffic safety stops, and the driver's race has no influence on whether the driver is searched in these stops.

These differences are not lost on African Americans. According to our survey, African Americans view normal traffic stops as legitimate exercises of law enforcement, and do so at about the same rate as whites do. Indeed, the main difference is that blacks, unlike whites, are even more likely to view a traffic stop as legitimate when the officer lectures them on driver safety, taking that lecture as a reassuring cue that they were in fact stopped for their behavior, not for the color of their skin.

> **After taking into account other possible influences, black drivers in our survey were *five times* more likely than whites to be subjected to searches in investigatory stops.**

By contrast, African Americans view investigative stops far more harshly, for reasons that are obvious when you hear their descriptions of the experiences, as we did conducting our survey. One gentleman, Billy, told a story about how, on the way to a job interview in Des Moines, he was pulled over by a Missouri highway patrolman for speeding even though he was going, at most, two miles over the speed limit. The trooper made Billy get out of his car and put his hands on the hood while he searched his car. Finding nothing, explained Billy, the trooper "came back and said, 'The reason why we checked your car is we've been having problems with people trafficking drugs up and down the highway.' So that was that." It was not the only time this happened to Billy. On another occasion, he, his wife, and his cousin were pulled over on their way to visit an ill relative and their rental van was searched for drugs by a Missouri sheriff's deputy.

Another man, Joe, told of being pulled over in Kansas City by an officer who drew his gun, handcuffed him, searched his car, checked his license, then let him go with "no ticket, no nothing." Asked why he thought the officer had stopped him, Joe said, "I don't know why, beside driving a nice vehicle, a nice car in the wrong neighborhood." Joe, too, experienced much the same thing a second time, when an officer pulled him over and checked his license for outstanding warrants (he had none). "I felt violated," Joe says of that episode. As well he should; warrant check stops are in fact illegal. But in some high-crime areas, an officer in a Kansas City–area department told us, "We stop everything that moves."

The numbers game that police play with investigatory stops is a recipe for giving offense to large numbers of innocent people. Pervasive, ongoing suspicious inquiry sends the unmistakable message that the targets of this inquiry look like criminals: they are second-class citizens. The vast majority of black respondents to our survey—64 percent, compared to only 23 percent of whites—said that you cannot always trust police to do the right thing. Twenty-two percent of black respondents agreed with the statement that "the police are out to get people like me." Only 4.5 percent of whites felt this way. The disproportionate personal experience of these stops among blacks is one source of this trust gap. Another is hearing stories of police disrespect from families, friends, and work and faith networks. Among respondents to our survey, 37 percent of black drivers, compared to 15 percent of whites, reported hearing these sorts of stories from members of their own household.

Investigatory police stops teach the lesson that the police are here to get racial minorities, not protect them. This is what Cornell law professor Sherry Colb calls the "targeting harm" of investigatory stops. It is the message that people like you are targets of surveillance, not the beneficiaries of protection. And while investigatory stops do enable police to find some lawbreakers and get them off the street, they also undermine the minority community's trust in law enforcement and thereby its willingness to share information vital to good police work. Sixteen percent of black respondents to our survey reported that they did not feel comfortable calling the police if they needed help, compared to only 5 percent of whites.

Police leaders say the solution is to train officers to be more polite and respectful. This is not enough. The people we surveyed certainly prefer to be treated politely in police stops. But investigatory police stops are fundamentally unjust—and, according to our survey, feared—no matter how polite the officer.

A more meaningful solution is one put forth by U.S. district judge Shira A. Scheindlin, who in August ruled that New York City's stop and frisks, as practiced, violate the Constitution. She ordered the New York City Police Department to better train officers in what kinds of justifications for these stops are constitutionally acceptable and to require officers to report the justification for stops in their own words (as opposed to simply checking a box to indicate the type of justification). Importantly, she also appointed a lawyer to monitor the police department's implementation of these directives. While her decision was suspended by an appellate court, it offers an excellent analysis of the constitutional problems in the practice of stop and frisk. We hope it serves to guide other judicial decisions.

Still, in our view, the judge's reform directives do not go far enough. The Constitution, at least as interpreted by the Supreme Court, sets the bar too low with regard to what is an acceptable justification for a stop. Police training *already* teaches officers to justify a stop with "specific, articulable facts and reasonable inferences there from," the language in the key Supreme Court decision *Terry v. Ohio*. It is too easy for officers to provide a right-sounding legal justification for what is, in fact, a stop based on inchoate suspicion.

The solution is to prohibit investigatory police stops. This will require a change in police norms. Police leaders celebrate investigatory stops and the few big busts they yield. Instead, these leaders—the heads of professional police associations, police chiefs, and police trainers—should acknowledge how much these stops cause palpable harm to the person stopped *and to trust in the police*. Departments should prohibit stops unless justified by evidence of a violation. Officers would still have the authority to make traffic safety stops to ticket or arrest drivers for speeding, blowing through red lights, or driving drunk. They would still have the authority to stop people who fit a clear description of a suspect. What they would not have the authority to do is to stop people out of curiosity or unspecified suspicion.

If law enforcement leaders won't act on their own, political leaders may force them into doing so. The New York mayor's race showed that stop and frisk has taxed the patience of a substantial number of voters. Our survey shows that New York City is not the only place where that's true.

The Milwaukee Experiment

By Jeffrey Toobin
The New Yorker, May 11, 2015

Like many people in the criminal-justice system, John Chisholm, the District Attorney in Milwaukee County, has been concerned for a long time about the racial imbalance in American prisons. The issue is especially salient in Wisconsin, where African-Americans constitute only 6 percent of the population but 37 percent of those in state prison. According to a study from the University of Wisconsin-Milwaukee, as of 2010 13 percent of the state's African-American men of working age were behind bars—nearly double the national average, of 6.7 percent. The figures were especially stark for Milwaukee County, where more than half of African-American men in their thirties had served time in state prison. How, Chisholm wondered, did the work of his own office contribute to these numbers? Could a D.A. do anything to change them?

The recent spate of deaths of unarmed African-Americans at the hands of police officers has brought renewed attention to racial inequality in criminal justice, but in the U.S. legal system prosecutors may wield even more power than cops. Prosecutors decide whether to bring a case or drop charges against a defendant; charge a misdemeanor or a felony; demand a prison sentence or accept probation. Most cases are resolved through plea bargains, where prosecutors, not judges, negotiate whether and for how long a defendant goes to prison. And prosecutors make these judgments almost entirely outside public scrutiny.

Chisholm decided to let independent researchers examine how he used his prosecutorial discretion. In 2007, when he took office, the Vera Institute of Justice, a research and policy group based in New York City, had just begun studying the racial implications of the work of the Milwaukee County District Attorney's office. Over several years, Chisholm allowed the researchers to question his staff members and look at their files. The conclusions were disturbing. According to the Vera study, prosecutors in Milwaukee declined to prosecute 41 percent of whites arrested for possession of drug paraphernalia, compared with 27 percent of blacks; in cases involving prostitution, black female defendants were likelier to be charged than white defendants; in cases that involved resisting or obstructing an officer, most of the defendants charged were black (77 percent), male (79 percent), and already in custody (80 percent of blacks versus 66 percent of whites).

Jeffrey Toobin/*The New Yorker*

Chisholm decided that his office would undertake initiatives to try to send fewer people to prison while maintaining public safety. "For a long time, prosecutors have defined themselves through conviction rates and winning the big cases with the big sentences," Nicholas Turner, the president of the Vera Institute, told me. "But the evidence is certainly tipping that the attainment of safety and justice requires more than just putting people in prison for a long time. Prosecutors have to redefine their proper role in a new era. Chisholm stuck his neck out there and started saying that prosecutors should also be judged by their success in reducing mass incarceration and achieving racial equality." Chisholm's efforts have drawn attention around the country. "John is a national leader in law enforcement, because he is genuinely interested in trying to achieve the right results, not only in individual cases but in larger policy issues as well," Cyrus R. Vance, Jr., the Manhattan District Attorney, told me.

Chisholm reflects a growing national sentiment that the criminal-justice system has failed African-Americans. The events in Baltimore last week drew, at least in part, on a sense there that black people have paid an undue price for the crackdown on crime. Since 1980, Maryland's prison population has tripled, to about 21,000, and, as in Wisconsin, there is a distressing racial disparity among inmates. The population of Maryland is about 30 percent black; the prisons and local jails are more than 70 percent black.

> "The racial disparity spoke for itself, starting with the disparities in the state prison system. . . .The one that stood out the most was low-level drug offenders— possession of marijuana or drug paraphernalia. There were clearly a disparate number of African-Americans being charged and processed for those offenses."

In 2013, former Attorney General Eric Holder announced an initiative, known as Smart on Crime, that directed federal prosecutors to take steps toward reducing the number of people sentenced to federal prisons and the lengths of the sentences. "Prison is very costly—to individuals, to the government, and to communities," Jonathan Wroblewski, a Justice Department official who was part of the Smart on Crime team, told me. "We want to explore alternatives." By 2014, federal prosecutors were seeking mandatory minimum sentences in only half of their drug-trafficking cases, down from two-thirds the previous year. The number of these prosecutions inched downward as well.

Last week, President Obama spoke to reporters about the criminal-justice system at the state and federal levels, saying, "If we are serious about solving this problem, then we're going to not only have to help the police, we're going to have to think about what can we do— the rest of us—to make sure that we're providing early education to these kids; to make sure that we're reforming our criminal-justice system, so it's not just a pipeline from schools to prisons; so that we're not rendering men in these communities unemployable because of a felony record for a nonviolent drug offense; that we're making investments so that they can get the training they need to find jobs. That's hard."

The next day, Hillary Clinton gave a speech at Columbia University, in which she called for a national rethinking of the criminal-justice system, and suggested, among other things, putting body cameras on police officers. "Today, smart policing in communities that builds relationships, partnerships, and trust makes more sense than ever," she said. "And it shouldn't be limited just to officers on the beat. It's an ethic that should extend throughout our criminal-justice system. To prosecutors and parole officers. To judges and lawmakers. We all share a responsibility to help re-stitch the fabric of our neighborhoods and communities." She added, "It's time to end the era of mass incarceration."

Chisholm's experiment is important on its own terms, but it is especially notable now. Scott Walker, the governor of Wisconsin and a presumptive Republican presidential candidate, is a fierce ideological adversary. Chisholm, a Democrat, who is fifty-two, and Walker, who is forty-seven, both grew up in the state and both attended Marquette University, in Milwaukee. Both have spent virtually their entire lives working for state and local government in Wisconsin. As a state legislator, Walker pursued a traditional law-and-order agenda, and he sponsored bills that sought to increase mandatory minimum sentences for a variety of crimes. He became a statewide figure by sponsoring Wisconsin's "Truth in Sentencing" legislation, which increased prison time and abolished parole for certain offenders. As governor, Walker has continued to oppose parole opportunities for prisoners. In 2010, the year before he took office, the state granted 13 percent of parole requests; in 2013, only 6 percent were granted. As the presidential campaign begins, the debate between these opposing visions of mass incarceration will play out across the nation.

Chisholm works in the Safety Building, an imposing structure built in 1930, in the days of municipal prosperity; it has terrazzo floors, and marble stalls in the bathrooms. At the time, the industrial might of Milwaukee rivalled that of Chicago, ninety miles away. But the declines of the 1980s hit Milwaukee hard, and the building looks as threadbare as the local economy. Wall clocks in the building haven't worked since a fire in 2013. Old records are stored in the cells of an abandoned jail. (The paperwork in the case of Milwaukee's most notorious criminal, Jeffrey Dahmer, is preserved there.)

After graduating from the University of Wisconsin law school, in Madison, Chisholm took a job as a junior prosecutor, worked through a variety of assignments in the trenches, and eventually held a senior position under E. Michael McCann, who served as Milwaukee's District Attorney for thirty-eight years. When McCann stepped down, in 2006, he endorsed Chisholm as his successor, and Chisholm has since won two races, virtually unopposed.

"I basically divide our world in two," Chisholm told me in his office. "There are people who scare us, and people who irritate the hell out of us. The first group includes the people charged with homicide and other gun crimes. It's about 10 or 15 percent of our cases, a relatively small group, and there's not much change with them from the old days. The most important thing we can do with those people is incapacitate them, so they can't do any more harm."

Chisholm decided to make changes in the larger pool—the "irritating" defendants. "The racial disparity spoke for itself, starting with the disparities in the state prison system," he told me. "But there were very significant disparities in specific categories. The one that stood out the most was low-level drug offenders—possession of marijuana or drug paraphernalia. There were clearly a disparate number of African-Americans being charged and processed for those offenses."

Even findings in the Vera report that seemed encouraging turned out to have a troubling subtext. In addition to the city, Milwaukee County includes more than a dozen suburbs, most of which are predominantly white. "When I first saw the data, I thought, here is some good news," Chisholm told me. "It said that we charge white offenders for property crimes at a higher rate than we do black offenders for those kinds of cases. So I thought, good, here is a disparity the other way. That must balance things out. But a deputy of mine pointed out that what the data really meant was that we devalue property crimes in the center city. We don't charge a car theft, because we think it's just some junker car that's broken down anyway. It meant that we were devaluing our African-American victims of property crimes—so that was another thing to address."

Chisholm decided to move to what he calls an evidence-driven public-health model. "What's the most effective way to keep a community healthy?" he asked. "You protect people in the first place. But then what do you do with the people who are arrested?" There are two basic models of prosecutorial philosophy. "In one, you are a case processor," he said. "You take what is brought to you by law-enforcement agencies, and you move those cases fairly and efficiently through the system. But if you want to make a difference you have to do more than process cases."

So Chisholm began stationing prosecutors in neighborhoods around Milwaukee. "If people view prosecutors as just the guys in the courthouse, who are concerned only with getting convictions, then you are creating a barrier," he said. He and his team started asking themselves in every instance why they were bringing that case. "In those that were seen as minor, it was the least experienced people who were deciding whether to bring them. And these people saw that we had generally brought those cases in the past, so they went ahead with them again. But we started to ask, 'Why are we charging these people with crimes at all?'"

In 2010, Michelle Alexander, a professor at the Ohio State University School of Law, published *The New Jim Crow*, a study of mass incarceration among African-Americans. Like many influential works, the book identified trends that had been apparent for some time. Alexander noted that the prison population in the United States had grown from roughly three hundred thousand, in the early nineteen-seventies, to two million, after 2000. "The United States now has the highest rate of incarceration in the world, dwarfing the rates of nearly every developed country, even surpassing those in highly repressive regimes like Russia, China and Iran," she wrote. Moreover, "the racial dimension of mass incarceration is its most striking feature."

This critique has grown in intensity in recent years. "Mass incarceration is ahistorical, criminogenic, inefficient, and racist," Paul Butler, a professor at Georgetown University Law Center, told me. "Throughout much of American history, we incarcerated about 100 people per 100,000 people in the population. After the 1980s, it moved to 600 or 700 per 100,000. Prisons are finishing schools for criminals, so they breed more crime. They cost a fortune to maintain. And the racism of the process just starts with drug crimes. Black people don't use drugs more than anyone else, but, with 13 percent of the population, black people make up close to 40 percent of inmates serving time for drug offenses."

Some prominent Republicans also have begun to criticize current policies. The Koch brothers have funded work by the National Association of Criminal Defense Lawyers which aims, among other things, at limiting mandatory minimum sentences in drug cases, and, in a broad effort to reduce prison sentences, they have joined forces with such unlikely allies as the American Civil Liberties Union and the Center for American Progress. Rand Paul, the Kentucky senator and Republican presidential candidate, has sponsored a bill with Cory Booker, the New Jersey Democrat, that would allow youthful offenders more opportunities to expunge criminal records.

Scott Walker has shown little interest in joining this movement. For the most part, he has focused his administration on tax cuts and budget cuts (especially for higher education) and on a successful battle against public-employee unions in his state. In terms of criminal justice, Walker's primary effort has been to expand gun rights. In 2011, he signed a law that allowed people to carry concealed firearms and one that endorsed the "castle doctrine," a presumption that homeowners act lawfully if they shoot an intruder on their premises. Chisholm opposed these measures.

One of the difficulties of criminal-justice reform is that power is spread so diffusely through the system. "Criminal justice is a system, and no one person or group is in charge of it," Alfred Blumstein, a professor at Carnegie Mellon University, told me. "You have legislators who decide what's a crime and establish the range of penalties. You have judges who impose the sentences. You have police who decide whom to arrest. And you have prosecutors who have wide discretion in what cases to bring, what charges to call for, and what sentences to agree to in plea bargains." Each of those participants has contributed to the rise in incarceration. "Are more people in prison because there is more crime?" Blumstein asked. "More arrests per crime? Better policing? Longer sentences imposed by judges? More mandatory minimum sentences established by legislatures? Tougher decisions by parole boards?"

Blumstein and others place some of the responsibility for mass incarceration on lawmakers who, in the 1980s and 1990s, dramatically increased sentences, especially for narcotics offenses. When Congress revised federal sentencing guidelines in the 1980s, it not only increased the length of most prison terms but established a sentencing disparity of a hundred to one between crack cocaine, often used by blacks, and powdered cocaine, favored by whites. (A 2010 revision of the law lowered the disparity to eighteen to one.)

But a recent quantitative analysis by John Pfaff, a professor at Fordham Law School, [and] who also has a Ph.D. in economics, argues that sentencing laws are not the main reason for the increase in the prison population. "For all the tougher sentencing laws, there is not much more time served in prison per prisoner," he told me. "Prisoners are serving about the same amount of time now as they did in the eighties." Rather, Pfaff points to prosecutors—more than cops, judges, or legislators—as the principal drivers of the increase in the prison population. "The real change is in the chances that a felony arrest by the police turns into a felony case brought by prosecutors," he said.

How this change came about defies easy explanations. The United States Department of Justice, through its U.S. Attorneys, plays a relatively small role in incarceration. Federal prisoners amount to just over 10 percent of the total prisoner count in the country. There are roughly 2,300 different local prosecutorial offices in the United States, most prosecutors are elected independently, and the lead lawyer in each office has considerable discretion in setting policies. In New York City, each borough elects its own district attorney, and the D.A.s' policies differ, sometimes significantly. (Kenneth P. Thompson, the Brooklyn District Attorney, has effectively decriminalized possession of small amounts of marijuana, while the city's four other D.A.s have not.) Still, as Pfaff said, "if you are going to reduce the prison population, prosecutors are going to be the ones who have to lead the way."

The most significant innovation in Chisholm's overhaul of the office involves an "early intervention" program, which begins after a defendant is arrested but before arraignment. Each defendant is given an eight-question assessment, which can be conducted in about fifteen minutes and is compared to the information on the rap sheet and in the police report. The questions include: "Two or more prior adult convictions?" "Arrested under age sixteen?" "Currently unemployed?" "Some criminal friends?" A low score can lead to an offer of "diversion"—a kind of unofficial probation that, if successfully completed, leaves the individual without a criminal record. A high score leads to a second, more detailed, fifty-four-question assessment. The questions include: "Ever walked away/escaped from a halfway house?" "Were you ever suspended or expelled from school?" "Does your financial situation contribute to your stress?" "Tell me the best thing about your supervisor/teacher." Results of the assessment may also lead to diversion or may lead to a more intensive kind of post-arrest supervision, known as deferred prosecution. People in this group will maintain a criminal record of an arrest but may have their charges reduced or dismissed. To participate in these incarceration alternatives, a defendant must commit to completing drug-treatment or other educational programs that are approved by Chisholm's office.

"The whole program is designed to reduce the number of people we are putting in jail or prison, but to do it in a smart, accountable way," Jeffrey Altenburg, a deputy district attorney, who oversees the early-intervention program, told me. "It's to get people back on track, based on their risk and their need." Every week, Altenburg, an eighteen-year veteran of the D.A.'s office, conducts a series of informal meetings with people in the diversion and deferred-prosecution programs who are in danger of being thrown out and returned to the traditional criminal-justice system.

A man I'll call John was the first offender at a recent hearing, which took place in a subdivided conference room in the Safety Building. Altenburg was joined by a lawyer from the public defender's office and a case manager from an outside agency. At nineteen, John had already spent a year in juvenile detention, for robbery, and his recent arrest was for possession

> To explain this year's crime rise, as well as the persistent racial disparities, Chisholm cites forces beyond his control—poverty, hopelessness, lack of education, drug addiction, and the easy availability of guns.

of marijuana. He had reported to the program supervisor that he had used Percocet without a prescription. "I don't have an addiction problem," he said. "It's more choices and decision-making." He was praised for reporting his violation, and told to attend a class on decision-making and return to the committee in two weeks. The case officer noted that John's girlfriend was pregnant. "Of course," the public defender muttered.

Jane, a fifty-two-year-old who was in diversion for shoplifting, had failed her fifth breathalyzer test for alcohol and tested positive for cocaine, but she had maintained her community-service obligation at the Salvation Army. "You've been in this program a long time," Altenburg said to her. "You have shown the ability to improve. You can get through this program. You need to work on your addiction." She promised to continue counseling.

Joe, who was in his mid-twenties, had received a deferred prosecution for a burglary, which involved stripping the contents of an unoccupied house. The police had recently charged him with disorderly conduct and had also found him passed out in a parking lot. His attorney said that he was sleeping off a drunk so he wouldn't drive while intoxicated. "He is not a bad guy, but he has trouble making smart decisions long-term," she said. Altenburg noted that Joe had committed other violations, and revoked his participation in the program. He would be convicted of felony burglary.

Bob had been arrested after he yanked the steering wheel from the passenger seat in a car, causing a crash. As part of his deferred-prosecution program, he was supposed to take a cognitive-behavioral-therapy class, but his attendance was poor, because he was caring for his girlfriend's two-year-old son, who has special needs. (Bob's girlfriend was pregnant again.) Altenburg pressed him for better attendance.

As a group, those in the early-intervention program seemed more like lost souls than like desperadoes, but they were all lawbreakers and, in many cases, repeat offenders.

Efforts by Chisholm and others to keep low-level offenders out of prison represent the core of the criminal-justice-reform movement—and these initiatives are passionately opposed by traditional law-and-order advocates. "The new mantra from the reformers is for 'evidence-based' solutions and assessments to determine who is low risk, and then we find that some of them go out and slaughter people,"

Michael Rushford, the president of the right-leaning Criminal Justice Legal Foundation, which publishes a widely read blog called Crime and Consequences, told me. "What the reformers never want to talk about is that, in the 1980s and 1990s, once we incarcerated a lot of people, the crime rate went down dramatically around the country." He went on, "Over the past ten years, we've been winning the war of attrition on crime, because the deterrent effect works. People don't commit crimes, because they don't want to go to prison. The reformers are teaching the opposite lesson. If a guy is stealing cars, and finds that he's never going to go to prison for stealing cars, what do you think he's going to do? He's going to steal a lot of cars and then move on to stealing something else." It is true that the overall level of crime has fallen in the United States over the past two decades, but the debate over whether mass incarceration is the reason for this decline has been inconclusive.

At the local level, Chisholm's aversion to incarceration has drawn the ire of probably the best-known law-enforcement figure in Milwaukee (and the only African-American in a senior position), David A. Clarke, Jr., who has been the sheriff of Milwaukee County since 2002. Clarke, whose responsibilities include supervising local jails, has a dashing public profile, thanks in part to a penchant for topping his black uniform with a cowboy hat. On Clarke's campaign Web site, he states, "My soft-on-crime opponents emerge from Candy Land to propose second chances, third chances, and fourth chances, in the process endangering our homes, neighborhoods, and schools." When I talked with him in his office, which is also in the Safety Building, he drank coffee from a cup bearing a portrait of John Wayne.

Clarke told me, "Their whole movement comes up with these cutesy phrases— 'those who scare us, those who irritate us'—but those who violate society's rules over time need to pay the price. They need to be punished for their misbehavior. That's how you change behavior." In particular, Clarke opposes Chisholm's predisposition for drug-treatment programs rather than jail or prison. "I'm not for government-funded drug-rehab programs," he said. "These individuals are making this choice. Those programs de-motivate people to address their own problems. So don't expect me to pay for your drug rehab. Find your own through the private sector."

Clarke believes that Chisholm's effort to reduce incarceration hurts those it's intended to help. "In the communities where most crime takes place, we do not have the support structures in place for social alternatives to incarceration. So you are putting them back into the community to claim more black victims. If you want to let people back on the street, you have to think about the people who are going to be dealing with them—my people, black people. What I've heard recently with criminal-justice reform is simply normalizing criminal behavior in a community that can least afford it—the ghettos."

Wisconsin has some of the most polarized politics in the country, and Clarke is a close ally of Scott Walker's. The split between Chisholm and Walker has been exacerbated by a long-running investigation by Chisholm of Walker's staff when Walker was the Milwaukee County Executive. The initial part of the investigation, which is known as the John Doe case, led to the conviction of six Walker aides, on charges ranging from theft to campaigning on government time. Since 2012, Walker's staff has been investigated for possible violations of campaign-finance laws by working too closely with outside groups, like the Club for Growth, which were advocating on his behalf. The investigation has been stalled since last year, and the Club for Growth sued Chisholm and his subordinates in both their professional and their individual capacities, on the ground that they had violated the free-speech rights of Walker's supporters. (The case is now on appeal.) Chisholm says that he can't comment on the investigation.

Advocacy for Walker in the Doe case has become a cause célèbre in conservative circles. "Some truly outrageous things have gone on in the state of Wisconsin that have happened as part of the effort to destroy Scott Walker," Rush Limbaugh said on his radio broadcast last month. "It was the kind of thing that Vladimir Putin does and we all laugh about because that's what we expect in a tyrannical dictatorship like the Soviet Union or Russia. We find out that it can happen here and has happened here, and there was no mechanism to stop it. The prosecutor's name is Chisholm, John Chisholm, and I hope his name is never forgotten."

The vast majority of the murders in Milwaukee take place on the north side, which is overwhelmingly African-American, with an unemployment rate above 40 percent. In 2014, there were eighty-seven homicides in Milwaukee, which has a population of just under 600,000. If New York City had Milwaukee's murder rate, there would have been more than 1,200 homicides in 2014; the actual number was 328. In Milwaukee, this year has got off to a dismal start. By the end of April, there were forty-eight homicides. As the Milwaukee *Journal Sentinel* noted in a recent headline, "HOW COULD THIS HAPPEN? NO EASY ANSWERS TO MILWAUKEE'S SPIRALING VIOLENCE." Chisholm told me, "This last patch has been a tough one."

Since 2008, the police chief in Milwaukee has been Edward Flynn, who is sixty-six years old and a longtime ally of New York's police commissioner, William Bratton. Like Bratton, he relies on crime data to direct officers to the most dangerous neighborhoods. "The reality for urban police practitioners is that we respond to the overwhelming victimization of black people," Flynn told me. "Every community meeting I go to in an African-American neighborhood is fueled by demands for more effective police services. The sad fact is that most violent offenders look like their victims. So that means everything we do is going to have a disparate impact on communities of color."

When I took a drive around north Milwaukee with Jacob Corr and Christopher Ladwig, community-based prosecutors in Chisholm's office, and Patrick Fuhrman, a sixteen-year veteran of the police force, in an unmarked car, they insisted that I wear a bulletproof vest. Corr was an early enlistee among Chisholm's lawyers in the field and, for a decade, has been assigned to the police station in north Milwaukee. "I'm a six-foot-four-inch bald white guy," he told me. "It was going to take me a while to generate trust here." In Ladwig's office were maps of the neighborhood marked with red dots for major crimes and blue dots for nonfatal shootings. He relies on data from "shot spotter" technology, which alerts the police every time a gun is fired in certain areas of the city; it goes off about eighteen times a day. Even in poor neighborhoods, Milwaukee still has a lot of sturdy housing, built in the early twentieth century, but the streets around Washington Park, a couple of blocks from Ladwig's office, bear signs of trouble. Most commerce takes place in "corner stores," as convenience stores are called here. They do a steady business in Jackpot cigars, which are emptied and filled with marijuana, and Chore Boy scrubbers, which can be used to make crack-pipe filters.

The prosecutors' duties go well beyond those of traditional prosecutors. In 2011, Ladwig helped persuade Habitat for Humanity to renovate some houses on a block in a particularly crime-ridden neighborhood, and the crime rate dropped precipitously. Ladwig has also worked closely with the Benedict Center, a nonprofit agency in the same neighborhood that is dedicated to helping both female victims of crime, usually domestic violence, and female offenders, usually prostitutes. Ladwig and his colleagues found that prostitutes who were treated at the Benedict Center had a better chance of staying off the street than those who were arrested. In a rare example of collaboration between Chisholm and Walker, in 2013 the governor provided more than $10,000,000 in funding for the Sojourner Family Peace Center, a nonprofit in Milwaukee that helps victims of domestic violence.

Back at the district police station, the magnitude of Milwaukee's problems comes into focus. One afternoon, Mallory O'Brien, an epidemiologist affiliated with the Medical College of Wisconsin, convened a meeting of the Milwaukee Homicide Review Commission, which she directs. Once a month, O'Brien brings together cops, prosecutors, parole agents, and judges to conduct brainstorming sessions about recent homicides in the area. Together, they suggest ideas about how the violence might be prevented. "For years, the federal government has had a review commission to look at every death on the highway and see what can be learned from it," O'Brien told me. "We're using the same idea for shootings in Milwaukee." After a series of crimes committed by people who had returned from prison, the review group helped create a team of officers and parole agents who visit parolees' families before and after they are released, to ease the transition.

Six homicides were reviewed at the meeting I attended, and they all seemed like variations on the same dismal theme. A drug transaction was planned or consummated. A dispute arose, usually near a bar. Suspect and/or victim were drunk or high. Shots were fired. All parties, including the witnesses, were African-American. More than 80 percent of both the perpetrators and the victims of Milwaukee homicides have criminal records.

This inventory from the homicide-review panel illustrates the limits of Chisholm's efforts. To some extent, he has succeeded in his goals. There are many fewer prosecutions of both blacks and whites for low-level drug offenses. Chisholm has stopped bringing cases for possession of drug paraphernalia, which were at the heart of the original Vera study. On his watch, the overall number of misdemeanor prosecutions in the county has dropped from 9,000 to 5,200. Likewise, once Chisholm instituted a policy that all burglary-case filings must be approved by a senior prosecutor, the disparity that led to more cases against white alleged thieves than black ones faded. The number of African-American residents of Milwaukee County sent to state prison on drug charges has been cut in half since 2006.

Still, Chisholm acknowledged that cases involving gun violence or homicide inevitably skew attempts to redress racial imbalances in incarceration. "Almost all of our shootings and almost all of our homicides are black-on-black crime, and that's an enormous problem," he told me. The prison population in Wisconsin has dropped from roughly 24,500 in 2007, to 22,000 today, and most of the reduction has come from Milwaukee County. Still, the change in the racial makeup of the prison population has been modest. Chisholm said, "We're no longer sending low-level drug offenders to state prison, but we are still sending violent criminals, and that's keeping the African-American numbers up. If we do this right, the people who are going to prison should be going to prison. The people who are going to prison are dangerous."

To explain this year's crime rise, as well as the persistent racial disparities, Chisholm cites forces beyond his control—poverty, hopelessness, lack of education, drug addiction, and the easy availability of guns. In this way, Chisholm's greatest lesson may have been in humility. "We redesigned our system, but we learned that no individual actor can change the dynamics of what goes on in a complex larger system like a city," he said.

Terrorism in Charleston

By Jelani Cobb
The New Yorker, June 29, 2015

During the second debate of the 2012 presidential campaign, Mitt Romney repeated the frequently levelled Republican charge that it had taken Barack Obama many days to refer to the attack upon the U.S. Embassy in Ben-ghazi as terrorism. Obama disputed that, and the two men argued back and forth until the moderator, Candy Crowley, intervened to say that the President had in fact referred to the incident as an "act of terror" the day after it happened. In the ensuing partisan scrum, conservatives and liberals debated the nuances between an "act of terror" and "terrorism," proper. Beneath this philological fracas lay a truth evident to political speechwriters, eulogists, and news anchors: in times of tragedy, language matters.

The Charleston police were quick to label what happened in the sanctuary of Emanuel African Methodist Episcopal Church last Wednesday night a "hate crime." Many crimes are motivated by hatred, yet we reserve the term "hate crime" for an act motivated by an animus that has been extrapolated beyond any single individual and applied to an entire segment of the populace. The murder of nine black churchgoers during Bible study is an act so heinous as to be immediately recognizable as a hate crime. But it was not simply this. We should, for all the worst reasons, be adept by now at recognizing terrorism when we see it, and what happened in Charleston was nothing less than an act of terror.

Yet the term was missing from early descriptions of the incident. Senator Lindsey Graham, of South Carolina, in his initial assessment, said, "I just think he was one of these whacked-out kids. I don't think it's anything broader than that." On Thursday, Governor Nikki Haley posted a statement on Facebook noting that "while we do not yet know all of the details, we do know that we'll never understand what motivates anyone to enter one of our places of worship and take the life of another." As a matter of morality, the actions of Dylann Roof, who confessed to the murders, may be a conundrum, but his motivations are far from inscrutable.

The Patriot Act defines "domestic terrorism" as activities that:

(A) involve acts dangerous to human life that are a violation of the criminal laws of the United States or of any State; (B) appear to be intended—(i) to intimidate or coerce a civilian population; (ii) to influence the policy of a government by intimidation or coercion; or (iii) to affect the conduct of a government by mass destruction, assassination, or kidnapping; and (C) occur primarily within the territorial jurisdiction of the United States.

At a minimum, the murders were intended to intimidate and coerce the black civilian population of Charleston, and beyond. A friend of Roof's said that he had talked about wanting to start a "race war"—something that Roof also reportedly confessed to investigators. And he apparently based his acts on vintage rationalizations for terrorist violence in American history.

When Tywanza Sanders, a twenty-six-year-old man who was in the church, urged Roof to spare the lives of the congregants, Roof stated that his actions were necessary. "You are raping our women and taking over the country," he reportedly told Sanders, before killing him. A century ago, the film *The Birth of a Nation* exalted the Ku Klux Klan's reign of terror during Reconstruction as the necessary deeds of men committed to defending white women from the sexual menace of newly emancipated black men. American antiterrorism law has its legislative roots in the Klu Klux Klan Act of 1871, which broadly empowered President Ulysses S. Grant to prosecute Klan members for abrogating federal law regarding black rights. Nine counties in South Carolina were so deeply suffused with Klan influence that they were placed under martial law. The Klan emerged not solely as an expression of concern for women but also in response to the growing political power of blacks in the postbellum South—people who, from the Klan's vantage point, were taking over the country. In "The Prostrate State: South Carolina Under Negro Government," published in 1873, the journalist James Shepherd Pike described a set of circumstances in which the white population was imperilled by the presence of black elected officials in the state legislature. The practice of lynching—there were more than 150 lynchings in South Carolina between 1877 and 1950—facilitated the disenfranchisement of blacks and the retention of political power in white hands.

Twenty years ago, when Timothy McVeigh bombed the Alfred P. Murrah Federal Building, in Oklahoma City, killing a 168 people, the act was quickly understood as terrorism. We tend not to recall, however, that McVeigh was trying to realize the plot of *The Turner Diaries*, an apocalyptic novel that details a white man's war against a federal government under the control of minorities and their white enablers. The FBI Web page on the Murrah bombing lists it as "the worst act of homegrown terrorism in the nation's history." That designation overlooks the Tulsa riots of 1921, in which a white mob, enraged by a spurious allegation that a black teenager had attempted to assault a young white woman, was deputized and given carte blanche to attack the city's prosperous black Greenwood section, resulting in as many as 300 black fatalities. From one perspective, the Murrah bombing was the worst act of domestic terrorism in our history, but, as the descendants of the Greenwood survivors know, it was likely not even the worst incident in *Oklahoma's* history.

Another word has remained absent from the discussion of the events in Charleston: Obama. The president is an unnamed but implicit factor in the paranoid assertion—attributed to Roof but certainly not limited to him—that blacks are taking over the country. In January 2008, Barack Obama won the South Carolina Democratic primary, largely on the strength of African-American votes; a state in the Deep

South gave a black candidate a crucial push in his campaign for the White House. The recalcitrant pledges to "take our country back" that began after the inauguration were simply more genteel expressions of the sentiments that Roof articulated.

The fact that Roof appears to have acted without accomplices will inevitably be taken as solace. He will be dismissed as a deranged loner, connected to nothing broader. This is untrue. Even if he acted by himself, he was not alone.

Unrest in Chicago after Police Officer Charged with Murder in Shooting of Black Teenager

By Mark Guarino, Wesley Lowery, Mark Berman,
and Justin Wm. Moyer
The Washington Post, November 25, 2015

A police officer who fatally shot a black teenager last year was charged with first-degree murder on Tuesday as graphic video of the killing, just released, sparked unrest.

Throngs of protesters filled the streets of downtown Chicago on Tuesday night, with a large crowd gathering outside a police building. Around 11:15 p.m. EST Tuesday, a crowd that had largely been peaceful turned confrontational.

Skirmishes broke out between protesters and police, who surrounded officers after they apparently made arrests. Protesters also tried to stop a police SUV from leaving with arrestees—an effort that failed. As the sound of sirens filled the air, police were met with shouts of "16 shots"—the number of times an officer fired at Laquan McDonald in October 2014—and demonstrators taking selfies. Some protesters showed up in gas masks, and some pushed against a police line, but no smoke or tear gas came.

Around 1 a.m. for about 15 minutes, hundreds of protesters moving west blocked one of downtown Chicago's main traffic arteries, Interstate 290. While most stopped at an I-290 on-ramp, others broke through a police line to block cars entering and exiting the interstate.

"You are obstructing the roadway," an officer said into a megaphone. "If you continue to be up here you will be subject to arrest."

Police ordered protesters to disperse, evidently arresting some. Eventually, marchers retraced their route back to State Street and traveled north. What had been a march turned into individual standoffs as temperatures fell. Dog owners walked their animals alongside protesters; a man on a treadmill on the second floor of a building looked down on the rally.

Asked early Wednesday for information about reported arrests, a police department spokesman said no information would be released until morning.

Chicago officials were worried about possible unrest in response to the video's release. The video depicts Jason Van Dyke, a white 14-year veteran of the police force, drawing his weapon on McDonald, an African American teen carrying a knife.

In the video, as McDonald veers away from officers, Van Dyke begins firing, felling McDonald immediately, and then shoots repeatedly into his prone body. A total of 16 shots were fired—all the ammunition in the officer's clip. It is rare for a police officer to be charged in a fatal shooting, and the first-degree murder count is the most severe Van Dyke could have faced.

Van Dyke's attorney, Daniel Herbert, said the officer feared for his life when he opened fire. Mayor Rahm Emanuel (D) took another view.

"We hold our police officers to a high standards and obviously in this case Jason Van Dyke violated . . . basic moral standard that bind our community together," Emanuel said at a news conference announcing the video's release.

"The officer in this case took a young man's life and he's going to have to account for his actions, and that's what today is all about," said Garry F. McCarthy, the Chicago police superintendent.

Van Dyke was the only officer to fire at McDonald, who police said used his knife to slash the tires of a squad car when he encountered the officers. He was on the scene near McDonald for less than 30 seconds before he began firing, said Anita Alvarez, the state's attorney for Cook County, Illinois. She said Van Dyke's actions "were not a proper use of deadly force."

"He abused his authority, and I don't believe the use of force was necessary," Alvarez said. She also said: "With these charges, we are bringing a full measure of justice that this demands."

Superintendent McCarthy called on city residents to demonstrate peacefully.

"People have a right to be angry," he said. "People have a right to protest, people have a right to free speech. But they do not have a right to commit criminal acts."

In a statement, the McDonald family asked "for calm in Chicago."

"No one understands the anger more than us but if you choose to speak out, we urge you to be peaceful," the statement said. "Don't resort to violence in Laquan's name."

In April, the Chicago City Council approved a $5 million settlement to McDonald's relatives. But some in the community say they are angry it took Alvarez's office so long to charge Van Dyke.

"There is no way this length of time should have gone on so long when the video showed all this evidence," Michael Pfleger, a Catholic priest in Chicago, said Tuesday. "Shame on them for being so late."

Chicago is not the only city in American roiled by officer-involved shootings and their aftermath—far from it. The video's release comes amid intensified scrutiny of police forces following fatal encounters between law enforcement and black men and boys. Police shootings, propelled into the public eye after the killing of Michael Brown in Ferguson, Missouri, last year, have led to demonstrations in city streets and debates on college campuses across the country.

Indeed, the rapid developments on Tuesday—an officer charged, a horrific video's release—recalled similar situations that unfolded this year. In North Charleston, South Carolina, and Cincinnati, similar videos showing officers fatally shooting black men were released; in both cases, officials announced murder charges the same day. In both cities, protests followed, but they were far less heated than those seen in cities such as Ferguson and New York after grand juries declined to indict officers.

Even as protesters filled Chicago streets, a similar drama unfolded in another large Midwestern city. Police in Minneapolis took three men into custody after gunshots were fired at a "Black Lives Matter" rally, wounding five demonstrators in an attack that inflamed tensions already high over the recent police killing of 24-year-old Jamar Clark, an unarmed black man.

The shooting Monday night, which occurred one block from a police station that protests had centered around, shook demonstrators who nonetheless said they would not be driven away.

"I'm out here to make sure those cowards know that they didn't scare anybody," Demetrius Pendleton, 46, who runs a local homeless shelter, said during a march on Tuesday afternoon. "We want to see justice, and we won't stop until we get it."

In a Facebook post, Black Lives Matter Minneapolis said that "white supremacists" attacked the group on Monday night "in an act of domestic terrorism," and the group vowed not to be intimidated.

Police said Tuesday they had three white men in custody: a 23-year-old arrested in Bloomington, a nearby city, as well as a 26-year-old and a 21-year-old who turned themselves in to investigators. A fourth person, a 32-year-old Hispanic man arrested in south Minneapolis, was released after it was determined he was not at the shooting scene, police said.

Minneapolis police said they received multiple 911 calls on Monday night about the gunfire, a block away from the Fourth Precinct. All five people, who had been protesting at the police building, suffered non-life-threatening injuries, officials said.

Protesters said the shooting occurred after a group of people—three men and a woman, all wearing ski masks—were seen filming the activity. The people in ski masks went down Morgan Avenue, and some demonstrators followed them.

A fight ensued and then gunshots rang out, said Henry Habu, who has been at the protests since Sunday. Habu said that protesters had been told to watch out for white supremacists wearing masks or camouflage clothing, and said the group filming the demonstrations matched those descriptions.

After the gunfire at 10:40 p.m. on Monday, police said dozens of officers rushed to the scene to investigate. Demonstrators rushed to tend to the injured, and others flocked to the area.

"It was very somber," said John Jacobson, who said he had arrived 30 minutes later after seeing a Black Lives Matter post on Facebook. "Like a wake, and you're looking for familiar faces."

One demonstrator was shot in the leg and was among "four boys on the ground," said Carrie Brown. "He just kept saying, 'Don't leave me, don't leave me,'" she said.

Federal authorities said Tuesday they were in close contact with local police.

"The Department of Justice is aware of the incident and is coordinating with the Minneapolis Police Department to assess the evidence and determine if federal action is appropriate," the department said in a statement.

Police have said that Clark, a suspect in an assault, was shot on November 15 when he interfered as paramedics tried to treat the assault victim.

"At some point during an altercation that ensued between the officers and the individual, an officer discharged his weapon, striking the individual," the Minnesota Department of Public Safety said in a statement.

The officers involved were Mark Ringgenberg and Dustin Schwarze. Both have served with the Minneapolis police for a little over a year, and each has been an officer for a total of seven years, according to the Bureau of Criminal Apprehension, the state agency investigating the shooting. Police have not said which officer fired the fatal shot.

The FBI announced it will conduct its own investigation into Clark's death. The U.S. attorney's office in Minnesota and Justice Department prosecutors said they will review evidence to see whether there were any federal civil rights violations.

Some witnesses said Clark was handcuffed when he was shot. Police said that did not appear to be the case. Drew Evans, superintendent of the Bureau of Criminal Apprehension, said authorities were still working to determine whether Clark was handcuffed when he died.

Demonstrators have called on police to release video footage of the shooting. Evans said there is no complete video, though investigators have multiple videos related to the encounter.

A march on Tuesday afternoon was much like those in dozens of American cities in the year since Brown was killed. The crowd danced to Kendrick Lamar's "Alright," shouted out the names of those killed by police in the last year—Brown, Tamir Rice in Cleveland, Walter Scott in North Charleston—and chanted, "No justice, no peace, prosecute the police."

"We want justice," said Jayme Ali, a local minister who marched near the front of the crowd.

Ali, 44, was born and raised here. She said it is time this city addressed issues of racial inequity, especially in policing. While she attended many of the first days of protests, she had not come out for three days because of an illness.

The shooting of the five activists on Monday night, however, got her back on the street. She wanted to show that she wasn't afraid. As she marched from the police station to City Hall, her hands gripped a homemade cardboard sign with a warning for the nation: "This could be your city next."

The Steep Cost of Incarceration on Women of Color

By Tanzina Vega
CNN.com, November 29, 2015

For Debra Henderson, love has come with a hefty price tag.

Her ex-husband was incarcerated multiple times, her boyfriend was recently released after serving seven months for a felony and her son has had a few brushes with the law. In all, Henderson, who is 40 and makes $60,000 a year working at an insurance company, has spent more than $32,000 on everything from bail bonds to lawyers to phone calls trying to maintain relationships with the men in her life.

Henderson is one of thousands of women who are shouldering the financial burden of incarceration of a loved one, particularly in black communities.

According to data from a CNN/Kaiser Family Foundation poll on race in America, 55% of black Americans said they either had been incarcerated themselves or had a close friend or family member who had been incarcerated compared to 36% of whites and 39% of Hispanics. Among these black Americans, nearly two-thirds said they earned less than $50,000 a year and only 21% said they had earned a college degree.

The financial costs of incarceration are steep. Inmates can be assessed fees for their daily stay in jail, probation and phone calls. In some cases, inmates accrued thousands of dollars in prison-related debt. Once released, many former inmates find that employers are reluctant to hire people with criminal records. As a result, it's often female relatives who are left footing a large percentage of the bills.

"Women of color are carrying the burden," said Gale Muhammad, the founder and president of the prison advocacy group Women Who Never Give Up. "It's all on us, the mothers, the wives, the sisters, the girlfriends."

Indeed, research on the financial costs of incarceration by the Ella Baker Center for Human Rights in 2014 showed that 83% of family members responsible for court-related costs were women. Families surveyed in the report also said they had trouble meeting basic needs like food, housing, utilities and transportation after a loved one was incarcerated.

The economic costs of loving someone in prison "has broken the black family," Muhammad said. "You've got women working two or three jobs to keep it together."

Henderson's troubles began with her ex-husband, who she met when she was 16. During their 15-year relationship they had three children and he was in and out

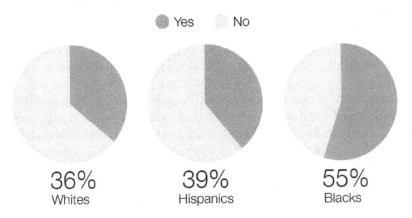

Have you or any of your family members or
close friends ever been incarcerated?

● Yes   ● No

36%
Whites

39%
Hispanics

55%
Blacks

Source: CNN/Kaiser Family Foundation Poll, Aug.-Oct. 2015

of prison. Once she gave him $5,000 to help pay for a lawyer. Then she helped pay for phone calls and sent him money for his commissary account and visited him in jail, spending money on gas, tolls and vending machine food. In 2007, she had just refinanced the house they lived in when her husband was arrested again. The $10,000 she received from the refinancing went to a bail bondsman instead. "That money was supposed to be used to fix my home," Henderson said.

It was the last straw and the couple separated shortly thereafter. She never received child support from her ex-husband, who is currently incarcerated, and now that two of her children are above the age of 18 and the youngest is 14, she doesn't expect she will.

In March 2012, Henderson declared bankruptcy.

But Henderson's financial woes didn't stop there. In August 2014, Henderson's current boyfriend landed in jail. Henderson said she spent $2,450 on phone calls with her boyfriend during his seven-month stint. In October, the Federal Communications Commission ruled to cap the cost of phone calls made between prisoners and their families, which had become prohibitively expensive. But for Henderson, the ruling came too late.

Henderson said she also paid fees ranging from $3.95 to $10.95 per transaction for putting money into his commissary account. After her boyfriend was released, he was placed on an intensive probation program that cost a total of $3,000. She helped him pay for half of it. Of the $4,000 in monthly expenses the family incurs, including a mortgage of $1,850, food, gas and utilities, Henderson pays $3,000 a month. Her boyfriend contributes about $1,000, earning money from odd jobs like landscaping and working at a gym.

"Where I'm standing at 40 years old, I should have better credit from helping everybody else that's taken from me," she said.

And now Henderson's son has had a few brushes with the law and the costs of bail and lawyers' fees are already hovering around $6,000.

Experiences like the one Henderson has had "reveal how profoundly gendered the whole incarceration story is," said Bruce Western, a sociology professor at Harvard University who focuses on criminal justice. Male relatives "come to rely on these small points of social and financial stability occupied by these women who have steady jobs" or Social Security and disability benefits or housing vouchers, Western said.

The incarceration of men also reduces the family income by about 20% to 30%, Western said.

Race is also a critical part of the equation, he said. Since the majority of the prison population are men of color, "the women in those families are doing most of the caring work for their loved ones who are incarcerated or recently released from prison or jail," Western said.

Just ask Belinda, whose two brothers were incarcerated 28 years ago. "We had to dig deep, get clothes for school, make sure Christmas was happy," Belinda, who asked that her last name not be used, said. "The whole family pulled together to make ends meet."

Her mother took on various minimum wage jobs, including working as a hotel maid and frying chicken at a fast food restaurant. The financial stress of having two sons in prison ultimately took a physical toll on Belinda's mother, who ended up struggling with cancer, hypertension and blindness in one of her eyes.

Often the emotional and financial challenges continue once the man is released from prison, said Muhammad.

"We're the ones with the credit, we're the ones with the job, we're the ones putting everything in our name," said Muhammad, whose husband died in prison halfway through a 24-year sentence. "They need a ride, they need a suit, they have to go job hunting? You're putting them up. You're their sponsor."

After her husband died, Muhammad met another inmate while doing advocacy work for prisoners. They fell for each other, but the relationship didn't last. Now, both widowed and in their fifties, the couple has reunited. But Muhammad said she still notices the financial strain. While her boyfriend has also become a prison advocate and has a job as a barber, Muhammad makes more money than he does. So occasionally she pays for dinner and makes other contributions to their relationship.

His contribution? "He cooks dinner for me, I get my feet rubbed and I get the companionship of a guy that I care about that I couldn't be with for nine years."

4

In School and on Campus

In this November 9, 2015 photo in Columbia, Missouri, student and activist Jonathan Butler, center, addresses a crowd following the announcement that University of Missouri President Tim Wolfe would resign after protests about pervasive racism at the university.

The Education Race

Colleges and universities are unique environments, partially sheltered from but still vitally connected to the states and cities they inhabit. Some of the world's most powerful and influential social movements have formed in these unique microenvironments, where students are introduced to numerous new ideas and encouraged to look for new ways of interpreting and understanding history and human culture. Colleges and universities played an essential role in the Civil Rights Movement at mid-century, and generations of minority individuals have used the knowledge and experiences gained in American higher education to become social and cultural leaders within their communities. However, there is a racial gap at every level of the American education system ongoing since the end of the Civil War and still playing a dramatic role in the power structure of America's racial environment. As America continues into the twenty-first century, activists and educators are trying to bring this issue to the forefront of the public debate on racism, eduation, and equal opportunity.

The Mobilization of Youth

During the Civil Rights era, colleges and universities became havens for activism. In the segregated south, historically black colleges and universities provided a safer environment for students and activist to gather and strategize, and helped to spread the message of equality among America's student population. Historians have noted that the success of the civil rights and antiwar movements of the 1950s and 1960s depended on the ability to mobilize America's youth. Thousands of white students joined minority students and activists to hold marches and demonstrations around the nation, and these became focal points in the national debate, eventually leading to the Civil Rights Act of 1964, and to the systems put in place since to promote the integration of America's school systems.[1]

After the 1960s, activism and political mobilization has remained a common theme in American educational environments but never again achieved the same level of national focus and/or influence as in the 1960s. However, a resurgence of college activism in the 2010s has led some in the media to speculate that the nation might be experiencing a renaissance of student activism. In 2014, for instance, protests at Bryn Mawr College in Pennsylvania and New York's Colgate University addressed institutionalized racism in college admissions and student relations. As the controversy of the Michael Brown shooting in Ferguson, Missouri, led to street-level marches and demonstrations in cities around the world, college campuses likewise held numerous protests and demonstrations against bigotry and the treatment of minorities by police and governments.[2]

The modern wave of student activism differs from the student movements of the 1960s in important ways. For one, the issues addressed by modern student movements are more varied and disparate, with demonstrations organized to protest everything from inadequate protection of student athletes and the preponderance of college rape and sexual crimes, to racial disparities in education and employment and the growing economic class divide in the workforce. Another difference is that the microenvironments of colleges and universities are not nearly as isolated as they were in the 1960s because students are linked to the larger world through social media, allowing the "hashtagged" calls to action from American universities to carry across the digital landscape with the potential to become the seeds of much larger youth movements. Essentially, student activism has been altered and made more powerful in some ways, by the potential for each group's message to "go viral" from the campus to the seats of political power. The resignation of the University of Missouri president and chancellor in November 2015, after a wave of student marches protesting the university's failure to address campus racism, demonstrates the impact that even an isolated student movement can have.[3]

Colleges and universities are fertile grounds for addressing forms of racism and racial prejudice often ignored in society as a whole. For instance, microaggressions, the everyday slights, comments, and other behaviors, often unconscious, reinforcing and representing underlying racial tension and stereotypes, have been the subject of intense debate and exploration at colleges and universities, where the environment that fosters social exploration and unabashed expression allows students to dig deeper into America's racial inequities.

Postracial Idealism Meets Racial Realities

While American colleges and universities have long provided a relatively safe stage for activism, studies of higher education indicate that minority students are underrepresented in the nation's elite institutions and that this disparity in student involvement plays a major role in perpetuating the patterns of racial disadvantage in both educational and professional environments. Georgetown University's Center on Education and the Workforce found that though minority student enrollment in American universities has grown far faster than white student enrollment, whites continue to dominate the world's 468 most selective, influential, and economically dominant learning institutions. The study also found that minority students are treated differently from white students within universities and that universities often fail to address the unique challenges faced by students from minority and low-income backgrounds.[4]

America's elite learning institutions have a disproportionate impact on American society. Alumni networks and college employment assistance programs help graduates from elite schools find employment at leadership levels in many of America's most powerful economic, social, and political institutions. The racial makeup of these institutions therefore plays a role in the formation of social power structures that affect all of society. While education analysts report that there remains a troubling "race gap" at every level of the American education system, solutions to this problem have become as controversial as the issue itself. In 2015, public opinion polls showed that a majority of Americans opposed preferential treatment of minorities in college/school admission, believing that such "differential treatment" constitutes a form of racial bias that discriminates against qualified white students.

In several widely publicized cases, white students and/or their parents have sued educational institutions for rejecting white students in favor of similarly qualified or less qualified minority students. Since 2000, a number of states have passed state laws prohibiting universities and other educational institutions from taking race directly into account when handling admissions. Critics argue that, while preferential admission of minority students may not be an ideal solution to the problem of racial bias in education, such measures are necessary to address the continued bias and disadvantages faced by minority students trying to compete in the educational environment. As white Americans increasingly turn against affirmative action, at least through preferential recruitment of minority students and educators, educational activists fear that the Supreme Court may abolish affirmative action before a suitable alternative has been found.[5]

Numerous writers and educational activists have noted that the young adults of the millennial generation view race far differently than members of the past generation. The growth of the multiracial population, the progress (however controversial) of affirmative action, and the remarkable success of African Americans and other minority individuals in achieving greater social and political power, have created a far more racially diverse environment for millennial adults. Many of these younger adults believe that racism and racial tension will become far less important once members of their generation achieve power. However, polls and studies of the millennial generation indicate that millennials espouse similar racial stereotypes as previous generations and that racism, as a whole, is equally pronounced among millennials as it is among members of Generation X.[6]

In some cases, members of the millennial generation have expressed a troubling apathy when it comes to discussing race and racism. In 2013, for instance, three white community college students in Minneapolis, Minnesota, complained about a teacher's lecture on "structural racism," objecting to the personification of white men as the "bad guys" in American history. After filing a complaint with the school's legal affairs department, the teacher was cited for creating a "hostile learning environment." Examples like this demonstrate how apathy among millennials wanting to leave the "race issue" behind as an artifact of the previous generation, coupled with a society that has become hypersensitive to potential litigation, can limit the debate on racism in the educational institutions that have long been a haven for honest exploration of these essential issues.[7]

The Gap in Education

From the 1940s to the 1960s, as racial integration occurred in American cities, white families moved away from the cities to peripheral suburbs and exurbs outside the cities and these communities, a phenomenon known as "white flight." Minority communities who remained in the cities after this exodus were left with few resources to support public institutions like schools and other services. Meanwhile, "county" and "suburban" school districts, fueled by tax revenues and financial support from middle- and upper-class white residents, constituted a new elite level of American public education. Though desegregation programs were put in place to promote racial diversity in both urban and suburban school districts, these controversial efforts do little to address the dire need for funding and modern technology available to the vast majority of America's minority students.

One area in which this disparity is most pronounced is in the science, technology, engineering, and mathematics (STEM) fields. Economists and educators say that STEM education is an essential facet of education that will become more important in the future, yet minority and female student involvement in the STEM fields is well below that of white males, which creates a generation of graduates unevenly prepared for employment in the modern professional environment. Federal and state programs to promote STEM education for minorities and women have attempted to address this gap, but progress toward this goal is slow and the STEM fields in general are still dominated by white males.[8]

The 2014 addition of the National Assessment of Educational Progress indicated that the gap in mathematics and reading between white and African American students of the same age has increased since the 1990s. The education gap at the K–12 level means that thousands of minority students are poorly prepared for higher education when graduating. Hispanic and African American graduation rates have increased since the 1990s, providing some hope for a reduction in the racial education gap, but studies indicate that even as more minority students graduate high school, the effort to prepare minority students for higher education environments has not been as successful. Proposals for how to address these problems often call for massive increases in spending at the state level, promoting improvements to the basic education system serving minority Americans. This goal, however, has been espoused for decades with only minimal improvements in state spending. The end of affirmative action incentives tied to federal funds could further delay attempts to make basic changes at the primary and secondary school levels and in the education system more broadly.

Micah L. Issitt

Notes

1. Anderson, Melinda D., "The Other Student Activists."
2. Wong, Alia, "The Renaissance of Student Activism."
3. Curwen, Song, and Gordon, "What's Different about the Latest Wave of College Activism."
4. Bidwell, Allie, "Report: Higher Education Creates 'White Racial Privilege.'"
5. Bouie, Jamelle "Easy AA."
6. Demby, Gene, "Is the Millennial Generation's Racial Tolerance Overstated?"
7. Cottom, Tressie McMillan, "The Discomfort Zone."
8. Bidwell, Allie, "STEM Workforce No More Diverse Than 14 Years Ago."

The School-to-Prison Pipeline

By Marilyn Elias
Teaching Tolerance, Spring 2013

In Meridian, Mississippi, police routinely arrest and transport youths to a juvenile detention center for minor classroom misbehaviors. In Jefferson Parish, Louisiana, according to a U.S. Department of Justice complaint, school officials have given armed police "unfettered authority to stop, frisk, detain, question, search and arrest schoolchildren on and off school grounds." In Birmingham, Alabama, police officers are permanently stationed in nearly every high school.

In fact, hundreds of school districts across the country employ discipline policies that push students out of the classroom and into the criminal justice system at alarming rates—a phenomenon known as the school-to-prison pipeline.

Last month, Sen. Richard Durbin, D-Ill., held the first federal hearing on the school-to-prison pipeline—an important step toward ending policies that favor incarceration over education and disproportionately push minority students and students with disabilities out of schools and into jails.

In opening the hearing, Durbin told the subcommittee of the Senate Judiciary Committee, "For many young people, our schools are increasingly a gateway to the criminal justice system. This phenomenon is a consequence of a culture of zero tolerance that is widespread in our schools and is depriving many children of their fundamental right to an education."

A wide array of organizations—including the Southern Poverty Law Center [SPLC], the NAACP and Dignity in Schools—offered testimony during the hearing. They joined representatives from the Departments of Education and Justice to shine a national spotlight on a situation viewed far too often as a local responsibility.

"We have a national problem that deserves federal action," Matthew Cregor, an attorney with the NAACP Legal Defense Fund, explained. "With suspension a top predictor of dropout, we must confront this practice if we are ever to end the 'dropout crisis' or the so-called achievement gap." In the words of Vermont's Sen. Patrick Leahy, "As a nation, we can do better."

What Is the School-to-Prison Pipeline?

Policies that encourage police presence at schools, harsh tactics including physical restraint, and automatic punishments that result in suspensions and out-of-class time are huge contributors to the pipeline, but the problem is more complex than that.

The school-to-prison pipeline starts (or is best avoided) in the classroom. When combined with zero-tolerance policies, a teacher's decision to refer students for punishment can mean they are pushed

> **In other studies, Losen found racial differences in suspension rates have widened since the early 1970s and that suspension is being used more frequently as a disciplinary tool. But he said his recent study and other research show that removing children from school does not improve their behavior.**

out of the classroom—and much more likely to be introduced into the criminal justice system.

Who's in the Pipeline?

Students from two groups—racial minorities and children with disabilities—are disproportionately represented in the school-to-prison pipeline. African-American students, for instance, are 3.5 times more likely than their white classmates to be suspended or expelled, according to a nationwide study by the U.S. Department of Education Office for Civil Rights. Black children constitute 18 percent of students, but they account for 46 percent of those suspended more than once.

For students with disabilities, the numbers are equally troubling. One report found that while 8.6 percent of public school children have been identified as having disabilities that affect their ability to learn, these students make up 32 percent of youth in juvenile detention centers.

The racial disparities are even starker for students with disabilities. About 1 in 4 black children with disabilities were suspended at least once, versus 1 in 11 white students, according to an analysis of the government report by Daniel J. Losen, director of the Center for Civil Rights Remedies of the Civil Rights Project at UCLA.

A landmark study published last year tracked nearly 1 million Texas students for at least six years. The study controlled for more than 80 variables, such as socioeconomic class, to see how they affected the likelihood of school discipline. The study found that African Americans were disproportionately punished compared with otherwise similar white and Latino students. Children with emotional disabilities also were disproportionately suspended and expelled.

In other studies, Losen found racial differences in suspension rates have widened since the early 1970s and that suspension is being used more frequently as a disciplinary tool. But he said his recent study and other research show that removing children from school does not improve their behavior. Instead, it greatly increases the likelihood that they'll drop out and wind up behind bars.

Punishing Policies

The SPLC advocates for changes to end the school-to-prison pipeline and has filed lawsuits or civil rights complaints against districts with punitive discipline practices that are discriminatory in impact.

According to the U.S. Department of Justice, the number of school resource officers rose 38 percent between 1997 and 2007. Jerri Katzerman, SPLC deputy legal director, said this surge in police on campus has helped to criminalize many students and fill the pipeline.

One 2005 study found that children are far more likely to be arrested at school than they were a generation ago. The vast majority of these arrests are for nonviolent offenses. In most cases, the students are simply being disruptive. And a recent U.S. Department of Education study found that more than 70 percent of students arrested in school-related incidents or referred to law enforcement are black or Hispanic. Zero-tolerance policies, which set one-size-fits-all punishments for a variety of behaviors, have fed these trends.

Best Practices

Instead of pushing children out, Katzerman said, "Teachers need a lot more support and training for effective discipline, and schools need to use best practices for behavior modification to keep these kids in school where they belong."

Keeping at-risk kids in class can be a tough order for educators under pressure to meet accountability measures, but classroom teachers are in a unique position to divert students from the school-to-prison pipeline.

Teachers know their students better than any resource officer or administrator—which puts them in a singularly empowered position to keep students in the classroom. It's not easy, but when teachers take a more responsive and less punitive approach in the classroom, students are more likely to complete their education.

Students See Many Slights as Racial "Microaggressions"

By Tanzina Vega
The New York Times, March 21, 2014

A tone-deaf inquiry into an Asian-American's ethnic origin. Cringe-inducing praise for how articulate a black student is. An unwanted conversation about a Latino's ability to speak English without an accent.

This is not exactly the language of traditional racism, but in an avalanche of blogs, student discourse, campus theater and academic papers, they all reflect the murky terrain of the social justice word du jour—microaggressions—used to describe the subtle ways that racial, ethnic, gender and other stereotypes can play out painfully in an increasingly diverse culture.

On a Facebook page called "Brown University Micro/Aggressions" a "dark-skinned black person" describes feeling alienated from conversations about racism on campus. A digital photo project run by a Fordham University student about "racial microaggressions" features minority students holding up signs with comments like "You're really pretty . . . for a dark-skin girl." The "St. Olaf Microaggressions" blog includes a letter asking David R. Anderson, the college's president, to address "all of the incidents and microaggressions that go unreported on a daily basis."

What is less clear is how much is truly aggressive and how much is pretty micro—whether the issues raised are a useful way of bringing to light often elusive slights in a world where overt prejudice is seldom tolerated, or a new form of divisive hypersensitivity, in which casual remarks are blown out of proportion.

The word itself is not new—it was first used by Dr. Chester M. Pierce, a professor of education and psychiatry at Harvard University, in the 1970s. Until recently it was considered academic talk for race theorists and sociologists.

The recent surge in popularity for the term can be attributed, in part, to an academic article Derald W. Sue, a psychology professor at Columbia University, published in 2007 in which he broke down microaggressions into microassaults, microinsults and microinvalidations. Dr. Sue, who has literally written the book on the subject, called *Microaggressions in Everyday Life: Race, Gender, and Sexual Orientation*, attributed the increased use of the term to the rapidly changing demographics in which minorities are expected to outnumber whites in the United States by 2042. "As more and more of us are around, we talk to each other and we know we're not crazy," Dr. Sue said. Once, he said, minorities kept silent about perceived slights. "I feel like people of color are less inclined to do that now," he said.

Some say challenges to affirmative action in recent years have worked to stir racial tensions and resentments on college campuses. At least in part as a result of a blog started by two Columbia University students four years ago called The Microaggressions Project, the word made the leap from the academic world to the free-for-all on the Web. Vivian Lu, the co-creator of the site, said she has received more than 15,000 submissions since she began the project.

To date, the site has had 2.5 million page views from 40 countries. Ms. Lu attributed the growing popularity of the term to its value in helping to give people a way to name something that may not be so obvious. "It gives people the vocabulary to talk about these everyday incidents that are quite difficult to put your finger on," she said.

To Serena Rabie, 22, a paralegal who graduated from the University of Michigan in 2013, "This is racism 2.0." She added: "It comes with undertones, it comes with preconceived notions. You hire the Asian computer programmer because you think he's going to be a good programmer because he's Asian." Drawing attention to microaggressions, whether they are intentional or not, is part of eliminating such stereotypes, Ms. Rabie said.

On the other hand, John McWhorter, a linguistics professor at Columbia University, said many of his students casually use the word when they talk about race, but he cautioned against lumping all types of off-key language together. Assuming a black student was accepted to an elite university purely because of affirmative action? "That's abuse," Dr. McWhorter said. "That's a slur." Being offended when a white person claims to be colorblind—a claim often derided by minorities who say it willfully ignores the reality of race? Not so fast.

> **Across college campuses and social media, younger generations have started to challenge those fleeting comments that seem innocent but leave uneasy feelings behind.**

"I think that's taking it too far," he said. Whites do not have the same freedom to talk about race that nonwhites do, Dr. McWhorter said. If it is socially unacceptable for whites to consider blacks as "different in any way" then it is unfair to force whites to acknowledge racial differences, he said.

Microaggressions: Comments That Sting

Across college campuses and social media, younger generations have started to challenge those fleeting comments that seem innocent but leave uneasy feelings behind.

Even when young people do not use the term overtly, examples of perceived microaggressions abound.

When students at Harvard performed a play this month based on a multimedia project, "I, Too, Am Harvard," that grew out of interviews with minority students, an entire segment highlighted microaggressions.

In one scene, students recite phrases they have been told, presumably by non-black students, including "You only got in because you're black" and "The government feels bad for you." In another scene, a black student dressed in a tuxedo and a red bow tie describes being at a formal university function and being confused for a waiter.

Tsega Tamene, 20, a history and science major, and a producer for the play, said microaggressions were an everyday part of student life. "It's almost scary the way that this disguised racism can affect you, hindering your success and the very psyche of going to class," she said.

Outside of college campuses, microaggressions have been picked apart in popular Web videos including a two-part video poking fun at things white girls say to black girls ("It's almost like you're not black") and another video called "What Kind of Asian Are You?" ("Where are you from? Your English is perfect").

But the trend has its critics. A skeptical article in the conservative *National Review* carried the arch headline "You Could Be a Racist and Not Even Know It."

Harry Stein, a contributing editor to *City Journal*, said in an email that while most people feel unjustly treated at times, "most such supposed insults are slight or inadvertent, and even most of those that aren't might be readily shrugged off." Mr. Stein took issue with the term "microaggressions," saying that its use "suggests a more serious problem: the impulse to exaggerate the meaning of such encounters in the interest of perpetually seeing oneself as a victim."

The comments on recent articles about microaggressions have been a mix of empathetic and critical. One commenter on a BuzzFeed article on the "I, Too, Am Harvard" project wrote: "Make up your mind, do you want to be seen the same as everyone because you're a human being, or do you want to be seen as a 'colored' girl, since not being seen as a 'colored' person is obviously offensive?" Another wrote, "I don't get bent out of shape if a white person asks me are you, like, Hindu or something? I just correct them."

Henry Louis Gates Jr., the Harvard professor and author, said the public airing of racial microaggressions should not be limited to minorities, but should be open to whites as well. "That's the only way that you can produce a multicultural, ethnically diverse environment," he said.

"We're talking about people in close contact who are experiencing the painful intersections of intimacy," he said. "The next part of that is communication, and this is a new form of communication."

U.S. Education: Still Separate and Unequal

By Lindsey Cook
U.S. News & World Report, January 28, 2015

The U.S. spends significantly more on education than other OECD [Organisation for Economic Co-operation and Development] countries. In 2010, the U.S. spent 39 percent more per full-time student for elementary and secondary education than the average for other countries in the [OECD], according to the National Center for Education Statistics.

Yet more money spent doesn't translate to better educational outcomes. In fact, American education is rife with problems, starting with the gaping differences between white students and students of color: More than 60 years after *Brown vs. Board of Education*, school systems in the United States are separate and unequal. By 2022, the number of Hispanic students in public elementary and secondary schools is projected to grow 33 percent from the 2011 numbers. The number of multi-racial students is expected to grow 44 percent.

As the percentage of white students in our education shrinks and the percentage of students of color grow, the U.S. will be left with an education system that doesn't serve the majority of its children properly; the gaps in education will prove especially problematic.

Since the killing of unarmed black teenager Michael Brown in Ferguson, Missouri, by a white police officer, *U.S. News* examined the persistent gaps between black and white Americans, finding both the health and the justice system full of disparities.

As with those areas, many factors contribute to disparities in education. Lower wealth, lower health, lower parental education levels, more dealings with the justice system and other circumstances create a perfect storm that leaves blacks without the same educational opportunities as whites.

A Different Starting Line

Educational expectations are lower for black children, according to Child Trends, a non-profit and non-partisan research center that tracks data about children. Black parents, most of whom are less educated than their white counterparts, don't expect their children to attain as much education as white parents expect. Lower expectations become self-fulfilling prophecies, contributing to lower expectations from the

Parents With Bachelor's or Higher, by Child's Race

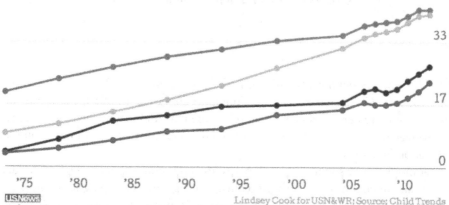

■White: Father ■White: Mother ■Black: Father ■Black: Mother   50%

33

17

0

'75   '80   '85   '90   '95   '00   '05   '10

USNews   Lindsey Cook for USN&WR; Source: Child Trends

student, less-positive attitudes toward school, fewer out-of-school learning opportunities and less parent-child communication about school.

By age 2, disparities already show between black and white children. Fewer black children demonstrate proficiency in development skills such as receptive vocabulary, expressive vocabulary, matching, early counting, math, color knowledge, numbers and shapes. While 91 percent of white children aged 3 to 5 who weren't enrolled in kindergarten were read to by family members three or more times per week, 78 percent of black children were read to with the same frequency.

Educational Attainment in U.S., by Race (2013)

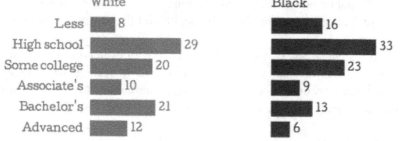

White   Black

	White		Black	
Less	8		16	
High school	29		33	
Some college	20		23	
Associate's	10		9	
Bachelor's	21		13	
Advanced	12		6	

USNews   Advanced is master's, professional or Ph.D. Lindsey Cook for USN&WR; Source: Census

Black parents may have less access to materials, have less time because of job and family obligations or be less comfortable reading. While the average number of words read correctly per minute for white adults with basic reading skills was 102, for blacks it was 85. Children's books also may not be as interesting to black children (or their parents) because of the lack of diversity in them: While about half of children under 5 are non-white, characters in children's books are overwhelmingly white.

Formal schooling starts at about the same time for black and white students. Black children who are about 4 years of age are just as likely to be involved in center-based care, thanks in large part to Head Start programs. But black children are much more likely than white children to be enrolled in low-quality day care. High-quality care environments have been shown to provide a lasting impact on the child's education, which prompted government attention in President Obama's recent State of the Union address when he mentioned plans to bring high quality childcare to more American families.

Formal Schooling, Same Inequalities

Once formal schooling begins, inequalities continue. More than 140,000 students were held back in kindergarten in the 2011–2012 school year. Black students are more likely to be held back, despite mounting research showing that holding back children doesn't benefit them socially or academically and makes them more likely to drop out later on. Retention rates for students hit a high in ninth grade, when 34 percent of students held back are black. While 12 percent of black students are held back in ninth grade, just 4 percent of white students are, according to the U.S. Department of Education's Civil Rights Data Collection. When all grade levels are combined, black students are nearly three times more likely to be held back as their white peers. They're also more likely to drop out before earning a high school diploma.

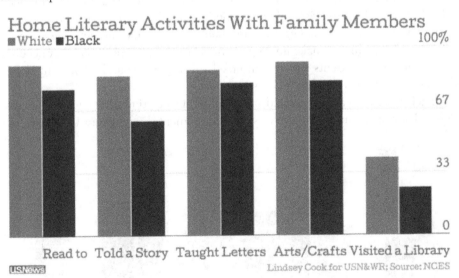

Home Literary Activities With Family Members
■White ■Black   100%

67

33

0

Read to Told a Story Taught Letters Arts/Crafts Visited a Library

USNews   Lindsey Cook for USN&WR; Source: NCES

As with retention, disparities in test scores start early, in kindergarten. Black students entering kindergarten for the first time score lower than their white counterparts in reading, mathematics, science, cognitive flexibility and approaches to learning—every category tested. The gaps persist throughout schooling, at fourth, eighth and 12th grades, according to a report from the Forum on Child and Family Statistics. On the SAT, black students had a mean score of 428 for critical reading

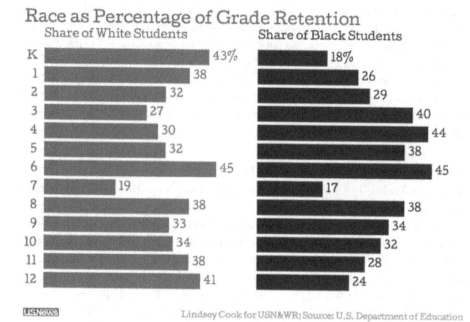

Race as Percentage of Grade Retention

Share of White Students | Share of Black Students

Lindsey Cook for USN&WR; Source: U.S. Department of Education

and 428 for math, compared with mean scores for white students of 527 for critical reading and 536 for math.

The elephant in the room when talking about racial disparities in American schools is the school-to-prison pipeline, another disparity that begins early.

Disparities in discipline begin in preschool and continue through every level of schooling. While blacks make up 18 percent of students in preschool, they account for 42 percent of students with an out-of-school suspension and 48 percent of students with multiple out-of-school suspensions.

Black Americans are suspended and expelled at three times the rate of white students. They make up 16 percent of school enrollment, but account for 32 percent

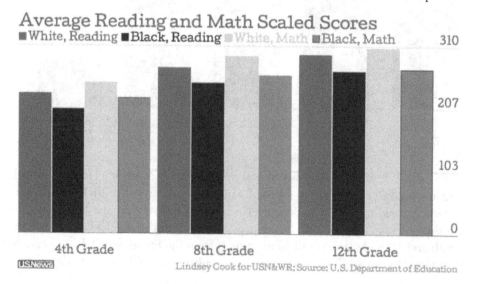

Average Reading and Math Scaled Scores
■ White, Reading ■ Black, Reading ■ White, Math ■ Black, Math

4th Grade   8th Grade   12th Grade

Lindsey Cook for USN&WR; Source: U.S. Department of Education

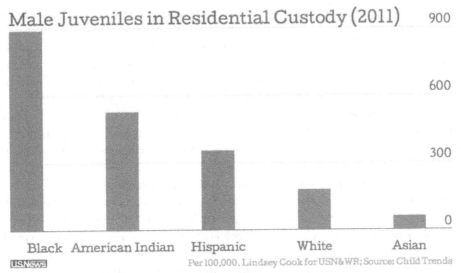

Male Juveniles in Residential Custody (2011)

Black   American Indian   Hispanic   White   Asian

Per 100,000. Lindsey Cook for USN&WR; Source: Child Trends

of students who receive in-school suspensions, 42 percent of students who receive multiple out-of-school suspensions and 34 percent of students who are expelled. Black students are arrested more and are referred to law enforcement more. The disparities in punishment even reach to black students with disabilities, who are more likely to receive out-of-school suspensions or to be subjected to mechanical restraint than their white peers.

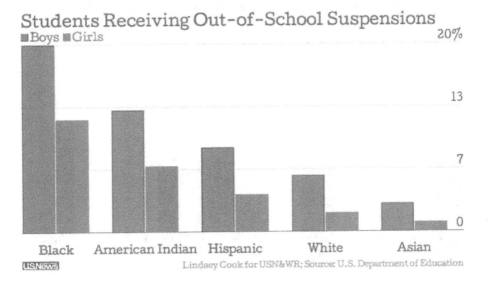

Students Receiving Out-of-School Suspensions
■ Boys ■ Girls

Black   American Indian   Hispanic   White   Asian

Lindsey Cook for USN&WR; Source: U.S. Department of Education

Separate and Unequal

More than 2 million black students attend schools where 90 percent of the student body is made up of minority students. Dozens of school districts have current de-segregation orders. Minority students represent 57 percent of the population in "dropout factories"—schools where the senior class has 60 percent or fewer students who entered as freshmen—but only 30 percent of the population in all schools.

On average, schools serving more minority populations have less-experienced, lower-paid teachers who are less likely to be certified. A report from the Center for American Progress found that a 10 percentage point increase in students of color at a school is associated with a decrease in per-pupil spending of $75.

Disparities in course offerings mean students of color have fewer opportunities to challenge themselves with more difficult courses—the type of courses needed to prepare for a four-year college degree or for a high-paying career in STEM [science, technology, engineering, and mathematics].

In seventh and eighth grades, blacks make up 16 percent of students, but account for 10 percent of students taking Algebra 1 and 9 percent of students passing the course. While nearly one in five white students took calculus in high school, one in 15 black students did. Fewer black students have access to a full range of high school math and science courses—algebra I, geometry, algebra II, calculus, biology, chemistry and physics. They are under-represented in gifted and talented programs. Black students take fewer Advanced Placement classes than white students and score lower on AP tests.

While black students disproportionately attend schools with higher minority populations, the teachers, principals and administrators who interact with the students are a different story. When the U.S. Department of Education collected data in the 2007–2008 school year, 80 percent of principals in public schools were white. Meanwhile, only 6.2 percent of high school public school teachers across all subject areas are black—the highest percentage is for health and physical education, where 9.2 percent of teachers are black.

Access to Full Range of Math/Science Courses 90%

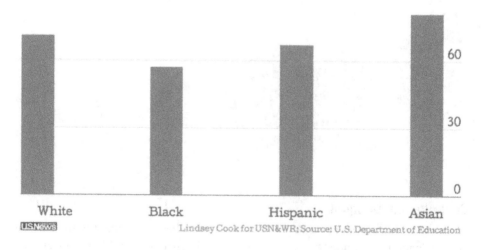

Lindsey Cook for USN&WR; Source: U.S. Department of Education

Percent of Students in Minority Schools, by Race

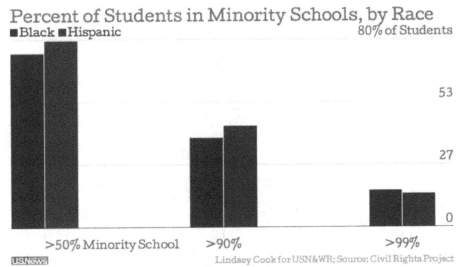

■Black ■Hispanic   80% of Students

53

27

0

>50% Minority School   >90%   >99%

USNews   Lindsey Cook for USN&WR; Source: Civil Rights Project

Different Schools, Different Neighborhoods

Part of the difference in educational outcomes likely stems from the different environments black and white children live in during their school years. Black children are far more likely to live in households that are low-income, extremely poor, food-insecure, or receiving long-term welfare support. Black children are less likely than white or Hispanic children to live in households where at least one parent has secure employment, and black children have the greatest rate of any race for families with children living in homeless shelters. Nearly 25 percent of black parents report their children live in unsafe neighborhoods, compared with 7 percent of white parents.

Black children are also more likely to have emotionally traumatic experiences impacting their childhood, such as abuse or neglect, the death of a parent or witnessing domestic violence. The child maltreatment rate (which signifies abuse or neglect of a child) was 14.2 per 1,000 black children and 8 per 1,000 for white children. More black high school students say they have been raped. Black youth at all age levels are more likely to be victims of violent crimes.

When a child doesn't know where her next meal is coming from, when she is dealing with the loss of a parent or living in a household rife with substance abuse or neglect, it seems obvious that these home circumstances would impact her ability to concentrate at school. When a child is living in poverty, it's easy to understand how lack of money for school supplies or lack of Internet or computer access would impede his ability to complete homework.

But it's more than that. These factors—a mix of race, poverty and family structures—are associated with a plethora of other problems: lower math and reading achievement, behavioral problems, grade retention, obesity, risky sexual behavior, greater risk of illness, greater risk of interpersonal or self-directed violence. The list is endless and the issues continue through adulthood, creating a cycle that proves difficult to escape for many. For those that do, however, disparities don't end with college enrollment.

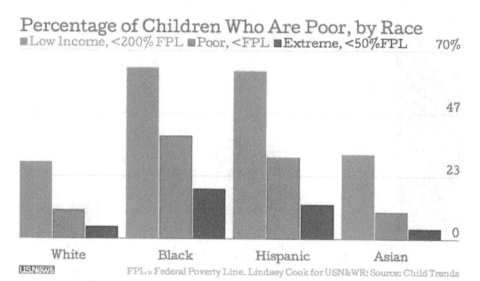

Percentage of Children Who Are Poor, by Race
■ Low Income, <200% FPL ■ Poor, <FPL ■ Extreme, <50%FPL   70%

White   Black   Hispanic   Asian

FPL = Federal Poverty Line. Lindsey Cook for USN&WR; Source: Child Trends

College and Beyond

Fewer black students graduate from high school (16 percent of blacks drop out compared with 8 percent of whites), meaning fewer are eligible for college enrollment from the beginning. Yet, disparities continue to snowball at every level.

Of individuals aged 16 to 24 completing high school or earning GED certificates in the last year, 56 percent of black students enrolled in a two or four-year college compared with 66 percent of whites. Fewer black students make it from enrollment to graduation and, for the ones that do, graduating takes longer. For the class starting at a four-year college in 2006, only 20 percent of black students graduated in four years versus more than 40 percent of white students. Within six years, 40 percent of blacks finished, but 60 percent of whites did.

Spending more time in college for the same amount of education means accruing more debt. While 90 percent of black students receive a federal, non-federal or

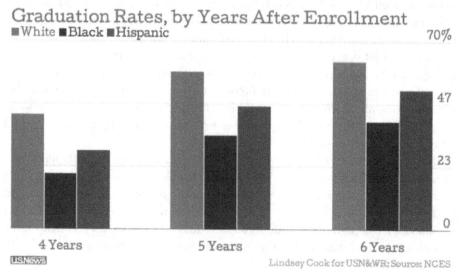

Graduation Rates, by Years After Enrollment
■ White ■ Black ■ Hispanic   70%

4 Years   5 Years   6 Years

Lindsey Cook for USN&WR; Source: NCES

PLUS loan by their fourth year in college, 65 percent of white students do. Even worse, for the majority of enrolled black students who don't finish college after six years, they may have to pay back federal aid and likely won't see the benefits of student loans. On average, black students have a slightly higher aid package than white students. Historically black colleges and universities are also more susceptible to economic dips because they have much smaller endowments than other, older schools. According to *Essence*, "If the endowments of all 105 HBCUs were added up, they'd still amount to less than 10 percent of Harvard University's endowment, which at upward of $30 billion is the wealthiest of any college in the world."

The disparities highlighted in this article, as well as many others, illustrate the severity of the unequal educational landscape. While more than one-third of whites held a bachelor's degree or higher in 2013, 19 percent of blacks did, according to the Census Bureau. But even if the educational landscape was equal, there would likely still be problems. A recent study found the unemployment rate for black college graduates was much higher than the rate for white graduates. Studies on labor market discrimination have shown that even when black and white candidates have the same qualifications, the black candidate is less likely to be called back for an interview.

Parents Tried to Desegregate Their Schools. The Roberts Court Said No.

By William Yeomans
The Nation, September 24, 2015

In June 2007, Chief Justice John Roberts mustered five votes to stymie public-school integration in the consolidated cases of *Parents Involved in Community Schools v. Seattle School District No. 1* and *Meredith v. Jefferson County Board of Education*. Supported by his colleagues on the right—Justices Antonin Scalia, Anthony Kennedy, Clarence Thomas, and Samuel Alito—Roberts declared that the voluntary efforts of Seattle and Louisville to desegregate their public schools violated the equal-protection clause of the Fourteenth Amendment. By doing so, Roberts converted the promise of the equal-protection clause—adopted to safeguard the rights of newly freed slaves—into a shield to protect white plaintiffs from the threat of attending racially inclusive schools. In the process, he rewrote decades of equal-protection law and announced a misguided denial of the nation's history in the name of a fictional color-blind Constitution.

The cases from Louisville and Seattle were litigated separately in the lower courts and consolidated for consideration in the Supreme Court. A federal court found in the 1970s that Louisville operated an unconstitutionally segregated school system and placed it under federal court supervision. Louisville submitted to a series of court-ordered desegregation plans, eventually convincing the lower court that local control should be restored. Because the city commendably wanted to maintain its progress, it kept the use of race as one factor in determining where children could attend school. The Supreme Court held that the city's warrant to take race into account in assigning pupils had expired when the lower court lifted its injunction. The race-conscious assignment plan was required by the Constitution one day but prohibited the next.

Seattle repeatedly adopted desegregation measures to avoid litigation that would have resulted in a finding that it operated an unconstitutional school system. The city implemented a race-conscious school busing program that Washington voters overrode by referendum, but that the Supreme Court implicitly embraced by invalidating the referendum in 1982. In *Parents Involved*, however, the Roberts majority reversed course, stating that the city could not voluntarily consider race as a tool to integrate its schools in the absence of a finding of discrimination by a federal court.

In other words, if Seattle had resisted desegregation, a court could have ordered it to consider race, but it could not voluntarily remedy segregation on its own.

Roberts's plurality opinion ripped the desegregation plans from their context, proclaiming that any consideration of race, no matter how benign or inclusive, was presumptively unconstitutional. He suggested that a desire to create inclusive schools—which he disparaged as "racial balancing"—was not a sufficiently compelling goal to justify consideration of race. He rejected arguments that diverse schools produce better educational outcomes and teach children the skills and attitudes that will help them live in a diverse society.

Most disturbingly, Roberts distorted the history of *Brown v. Board of Education* to support his opinion. *Brown*, decided in 1954, recognized that separate schools based on race were inherently unequal because they told African-American children they were inferior. Roberts disingenuously argued that the *Brown* plaintiffs had asked only to end the classification of children based on race. He found the inclusive Seattle and Louisville plans indistin-

> Meanwhile, despite passage of the Fair Housing Act in 1968, the country showed little stomach for a significant effort to attack residential segregation, the root of much school segregation.

guishable from the period before *Brown*, "when schoolchildren were told where they could and could not go to school based on the color of their skin." The *Brown* plaintiffs, however, argued for an end to racial classifications because they believed African-American children would then be integrated into schools with white students. The elimination of racial classifications was a means of achieving inclusion in integrated schools—the very result that the Seattle and Louisville plans sought.

Roberts also ignored the post-*Brown* rulings in which the Court responded to massive resistance by ordering school districts to desegregate. No earlier Court thought to question the authority of a well-intentioned school district voluntarily to assign students on the basis of race in order to create integrated schools. Indeed, in 1971, the Court explicitly stated that school districts had this power. Roberts dismissed that statement as mere verbiage.

Some downplayed the importance of the decision because the Court had long since weakened the push for school desegregation. After telling school districts to desegregate "with all deliberate speed" in *Brown II*, the Court largely stepped away until 1968, when it finally told school districts to eliminate their segregated systems "root and branch." The legal high-water mark for desegregation arrived in 1971, when the Court approved a comprehensive desegregation plan for Charlotte-Mecklenburg, North Carolina. Just three years later, the Court undermined desegregation in the North by making it virtually impossible for courts to craft remedies that would join urban and suburban school districts. It then loosened the requirements for escape from court supervision. Meanwhile, despite passage of the Fair Housing Act in 1968, the country showed little stomach for a significant effort to attack residential segregation, the root of much school segregation.

Yet *Parents Involved* was still enormously harmful. It told well-intentioned juris-dictions that efforts to create inclusive schools would meet legal resistance. More broadly, it announced the deep hostility of the Roberts Court to remedies for past and continuing racial discrimination. That hostility will be on display next year, when the Court once again considers the constitutionality of affirmative action in higher education.

The Roberts Court has set its sights on dismantling the nation's civil-rights laws just as many of the nation's too-comfortable assumptions about civil-rights prog-ress have unraveled. Police killings of unarmed African-Americans have highlighted long-standing tensions between the police and minorities, particularly those living in segregated pockets of entrenched poverty. Similarly, the slaughter of nine inno-cent people in a Charleston, South Carolina, church forced the country to reckon with its history of racially motivated violence. Despite the Court's misguided juris-prudence, vigorous enforcement of civil-rights laws governing police misconduct, housing and employment discrimination, voting rights, school integration, and ra-cially motivated violence remains crucial.

The harsh disconnect between the Court's assault on civil-rights protections and recent events that reinforce their necessity highlights the importance of the 2016

By the Numbers

The Impact of Resegregation

>Parents Involved was the final nail in the coffin of Seattle's integration efforts. In 2008, 34 of the city's 98 schools were considered "racially imbalanced," with a minority population 20 percentage points or more above the district average. This was in sharp contrast to the peak years of integration, when just one school was considered racially imbalanced.

>The racial achievement gap at Seattle schools has remained significant in the wake of Parents Involved. In 2012, fewer than 40 percent of black third-graders were meeting or exceeding math standards, compared with 85 percent of their white peers. Fourth-grade reading tests revealed similarly stark disparities (53 percent compared with 90 percent). Addressing the gap has emerged as a prior-ity in negotiations to resolve the city's teachers strike.

>Other districts across the country have seen even more dramatic declines. In August, for example, the *Tampa Bay Times* found that resegregation in Pinellas County (which includes the city of Tampa Bay) led to a precipitous drop in stu-dent performance at five elementary schools in predominantly black neighbor-hoods. The schools, which all had ratings of C or higher before resegregation in 2007, are now the "most concentrated site of academic failure in all of Florida." Ninety-five percent of black students in the resegregated schools received fail-ing scores on state math or reading exams.

presidential election. All of the conservatives on the Court owe their positions to Ronald Reagan, either because they came to prominence in his administration or because he appointed them to the Court. This Court is trapped in the conservative ideology of the Reagan administration, which is deeply rooted in the political and legal reaction against the gains of the civil-rights movement. Voters in 2016 will determine whether the Court will continue to obstruct the drive for racial equality or enable a new era of racial progress.

Race, Class, or Place?

By Sam Fulwood III
The Chronicle of Higher Education, March 20, 2015

By now, there's almost no debate that the nation's population is changing, becoming increasingly diverse both ethnically and racially. By a consensus of leading demographers, the United States population will soon become a smorgasbord of cultural identities—or, as some describe it, the nation will no longer have dominant white identity. Instead, the U.S. will be a "majority minority" nation.

Already, the changes are becoming apparent in our nation's schools. According to figures compiled by the National Center for Education Statistics (NCES), the number of white students enrolled in pre-kindergarten through 12th grade in U.S. public schools decreased from 28.7 million to 25.6 million, and their share of public school enrollment decreased from 60 percent to 52 percent.

The numbers show no sign of changing course, as white students dropped below 50 percent of all public school students in 2014 and, as NCES estimates, by fall 2023, white students are projected to make up 23.5 million, or about 45 percent of all students in public schools.

Such dramatic changes at the bottom of our national education ladder will have profound implications as the demographic shift works its way up, toward higher education. As the U.S. student population becomes increasingly diverse, ensuring access to selective colleges and universities will become more and more important—and the quest for admission will be more competitive.

For nearly two generations, the national effort to balance education opportunity for racial and ethnic minority students fell under the broad and sweeping rubric of affirmative action. But no more, as conservative activists have successfully beaten down federal and state efforts to permit highly selective schools to use race as a consideration in college admissions.

To be sure, the U.S. Supreme Court's recent decisions in *Fisher v. University of Texas* and *Schuette v. Coalition to Defend Affirmative Action* imposed new hurdles to considering race in university admissions, effectively muddling the fate of affirmative action. In the *Fisher* case, for example, the High Court agreed that diversity is a value worth preserving on college campuses and declined to strike down all race-based considerations in admission policies. For affirmative action proponents, that's the good news in the court's decision, but the court didn't stop there. It also demanded that public colleges and universities use race only as a final resort and only when all other approaches have failed to produce a diverse student body. Affirmative action antagonists cheered that part, believing such an order to be a repudiation of racial preferences.

In one specific case before the court, the justices' decision sidestepped the constitutionality of an admissions scheme at the University of Texas at Austin, and avoided ruling whether the plaintiff—Abigail Fisher, a white applicant to the university who was denied admission—was a victim of reverse racial discrimination herself. Instead, the court sent the case back to an appeals court, ordering it to reconsider the case under a stricter set of standards.

While the court kept the current regime in place for now, it set a very high bar for the University of Texas and other universities to meet: they basically have to prove that there is no better way to achieve diversity than one that takes race into account. If opponents can make any valid argument that another scheme would be better, the standard the court has imposed requires lower courts to side for the opponent.

That falls far short of an expected landmark decision. It neither gutted affirmative action programs nor enshrined them. So what does this all mean? In the short term, the nation's ongoing debate over race and opportunity continues unabated, with no clear end zone. In theory, diversity in education programs exists, but in practice, it might be much more difficult for race-based policies to be used and withstand legal challenges. Expect more lawsuits over affirmative action policies and, very likely, a return trip to the Supreme Court. After the most recent affirmative action ruling, the additional hoops that colleges and universities will now have to jump through will be tough but not impossible.

Indeed, a growing body of scholarly research suggests colleges can increase both racial and economic diversity through a variety of creative strategies that places family wealth ahead of race in the alchemy of college admissions.

One of the leading proponents of this reformulation of affirmative action is Sheryll Cashin, a Georgetown Law School professor. In her recently published book, *Place, Not Race: A New Vision of Opportunity in America* (Beacon Press, 2014), she poses a fresh challenge to status-quo arguments swirling around the decaying use of affirmative action to achieve diversity on U.S. college and university campuses.

Wedging her arguments between these two extremes, Cashin hasn't won many friends in the traditional civil rights camp that wants full restoration of affirmative action, nor with those who want to see it moldering in its grave. However, she does make a convincing case for the existence of a "perception gap" between people of color and whites about the extent of discrimination, which prevents political compromise on touchy racial issues.

A laundry list of studies and facts supports her thesis, she notes, including a 2009 CNN survey that "found 55 percent of blacks thought discrimination was a very serious problem, while only 17 percent of whites felt that way." Discussing yet another psychological study, she writes, "[W]hites and people of color have different perceptions about the extent of racial equality because they have different frames of reference."

Those "different frames of reference," Cashin accurately observes, are less a matter of race in the twenty-first century and increasingly an issue of where in the nation people live. Despite the melting pot theory, Americans are currently living separate lives in communities strictly outlined by race. As Cashin puts it, "[W]hites, blacks, Latinos, and Asians tend to experience diversity very differently in their daily lives."

So how can Americans achieve racial fairness if the bird's-eye view of the nation is a patchwork quilt and the on-the-ground experience is starkly segregated?

Richard D. Kahlenberg, a senior fellow at The Century Foundation in Washington, D.C., has studied the impact of alternative decision making in admissions policies, finding that schools that seek out economically disadvantaged students tend also to be more racially and ethnically diverse.

"It's not a one-for-one equation, substituting class for race," Kahlenberg said in an interview for "Convergence." He added, "But for the schools that are really serious about having diverse student bodies, they've not given up. They have invented new systems of affirmative action that in many respects are superior to the ones being replaced, as they are attentive to both economic and racial diversity."

> **In theory, diversity in education programs exists, but in practice, it might be much more difficult for race-based policies to be used and withstand legal challenges.**

Appearing at a June 2014 symposium co-sponsored by The Century Foundation and Lumina Foundation in New York City, Georgetown University's Anthony Carnevale and Jeff Strohl offered statistical support for Kalhlenberg's argument that highly selective colleges produce a disproportional level of influence in American society. As Carnevale explained to an audience of admissions officers, selective colleges and universities graduate equally qualified students at much higher levels than less selective ones.

This finding is reinforced in research by former Princeton President William Bowen. For example, Carnevale and Strohl's research notes that at the extreme end, only 10 percent of those who start community college end up with a bachelor's degree. Wages are estimated to be 5 percent to 20 percent higher for graduates of selective colleges. Moreover, extensive empirical data support Justice Sandra Day O'Connor's view that America's leadership class derives disproportionately from the ranks of top colleges and universities.

Cultural Cul de Sacs

As Florida State University political scientist Thomas Dye's research has found, 54 percent of America's corporate leaders and 42 percent of government leaders are graduates of just 12 institutions—Columbia, Cornell, Dartmouth, Harvard, Johns Hopkins, MIT, Northwestern, Princeton, Stanford, the University of Chicago, the University of Pennsylvania and Yale.

What all this points to is the need for having a diverse group of people entering and succeeding in the most selective colleges and universities. Whether affirmative action survives or exists by some other alternative formula, the increasing diversity of the nation demands that more people from disadvantaged communities have a part in the nation's future. Cashin argues that what we know as affirmative action—the race-based strategies that the right and left are fighting so fiercely over—will not solve the problem because it doesn't include discussion of the truly disadvantaged Americans, who are disproportionately black and brown schoolchildren isolated in communities with high poverty rates and poor schools. She writes:

> This differential experience of place greatly affects opportunity. Only about 30 percent of black and Latino families reside in neighborhoods where less than half of the people are poor. Put differently, less than one-third of the black and Latino children get to live in middle-class neighborhoods where middle-class norms predominate. Meanwhile, more than 60 percent of white and Asian families live in environs where most of their neighbors are not poor.

Her solution is for policymakers to substitute "place" for "race" when devising strategies to equalize educational opportunities. Such an effort would reshape the structural disadvantages crippling many children of color and potentially ease the racial resentment that affirmative action spawns among so many white Americans.

Her argument isn't new. Others like political scientist Robert Putnam, best known for his analysis of how inner-city communities declined as a result of white flight at the end of the twentieth century in his book *Bowling Alone: The Collapse and Revival of American Community* (Simon & Schuster, 2000), have posed versions of the same theory. In *Bowling Alone*, Putnam noted the decades-long decline in personal social interactions—he calls it "social capital"—among Americans. His analysis found that since 1950, the principles that Americans used to support, educate, and enrich the fabric of their social lives have withered as the nation became more politically egalitarian.

More recently, Putnam has argued that Americans, living in cultural cul de sacs, are reluctant to sympathize with fellow citizens, especially if they're from different economic strata. In an interview for "Convergence" and repeating comments he initially presented during a 2012 speech at the Aspen Ideas Festival, Putnam said race is waning and class is waxing as socially determinative factors in American mobility.

"You say poverty to most ordinary Americans, most ordinary voters, they think black ghettos," Putnam said. "But that's not the reality of the day. Class, not race is the dominant—and becoming more dominant—dimension of difficulty here."

"Relatively speaking, racial differences controlling for class are decreasing while class differences controlling for race are increasing in America," he said. "Nonwhite folks with a college education are looking more and more like white folks with a college education, and white folks who haven't gotten beyond high school are looking more and more like nonwhite folks who haven't finished high school."

Of course, such arguments strike some race-first observers as heresy. C.J. Lawrence, an attorney in Jackson, Mississippi, said all it takes is to monitor the news unfolding in places like Ferguson, Missouri, or Queens, New York, to prove that race remains the yawning gap in U.S. society.

"I just don't understand what planet these people are living on who say otherwise," Lawrence said in an interview. "Surely, they're not witnessing what's happening in the United States."

Lawrence's observations of the protests surrounding the police shooting last year of Mike Brown, an unarmed 18-year-old in Ferguson, a St. Louis suburb, inspired him to greater social activism, largely because so many Americans wanted to believe race no longer mattered or seem willing to believe the worst of black Americans.

The attorney, who uses the Twitter handle @CJ_musick_lawya, noticed the coverage of the Brown case and its violent aftermath repeatedly showed Brown in an unflattering light, unsmiling and standing on a porch while flashing a hand sign of his thumb and first two fingers extended.

So Lawrence offered up a cyberchallenge to his Twitter followers. He tweeted a pair of photographs of himself: one of him delivering a 2003 commencement address at Tougaloo College as President Bill Clinton laughed in the background and another of him clowning for a camera with a Hennessy bottle filled with cola. He posed a hashtag question for his followers: #IfTheyGunnedMeDown, which photo would flash across television screens and newspaper front pages?

The reaction went viral as friends and strangers posted their own two portraits, offering complex versions of their lives as scholars, workers, family members and caregivers juxtaposed with playful images of them scowling, flashing finger signs, holding weapons, or drinking alcoholic beverages.

In a series of email interviews with "Convergence," Lawrence explained that he was moved by media portrayals of Trayvon Martin, the 17-year-old high school student who was fatally shot in 2012 by George Zimmerman in Sanford, Florida.

"I was inspired by the fact that even during George Zimmerman's trial, the image the defense painted was one of Trayvon Martin being a menace, a narrative that seems palatable for that jury in Florida," he wrote. "It was believable to them that this poor kid that was simply walking home and being stalked by a stranger with the gun could somehow be in the wrong."

Lawrence said the media imagery is proof that Americans are continually impacted by racist ideas. Worse, he noted, their behavior reflects their beliefs. "If people don't want to pay taxes to support public schools or consciously decide to avoid living or interacting with people in certain communities or even refuse to support the president, I can only conclude that race is, in a large way, motivating their behavior," he said.

Cashin said she's sympathetic to this view, but, she remains unmoved in her belief that affirmative action isn't the sole answer to changing perceptions about people of color.

"I would trade the benefit of affirmative action for a country that does not fear and demonize people who look like you," she writes to her twin sons in the concluding chapter of her book. "We have to begin to heal this country, to set it on a new course of fairness. If we accept the system as it is—affirmative action for a few—we have given up, I think, on the idea of America. I'm not ready to do that."

Campus Police Departments Struggle with Issues of Race

By Peter Schmidt
The Chronicle of Higher Education, January 9, 2015

The head of the University of Pennsylvania's police union was not pleased to hear how Amy Gutmann had ended up lying on the floor last month at her own holiday party.

Ms. Gutmann, the university's president, had lowered herself onto her back to show solidarity with student demonstrators who staged a "die-in" at her party as part of national wave of protests over the killing of unarmed black men by police officers. The high-minded rationale for her action was exactly what inspired Eric J. Rohrback, president of the Penn Police Association, to regard it as a faux pas.

In a letter published by *The Daily Pennsylvanian*, the student newspaper, Mr. Rohrback said Ms. Gutmann had delivered "a slap in the face to every person that wears this uniform and serves this university." His letter accused the protesters of ignoring how the grand jury examining the shooting of Michael Brown of Ferguson, Missouri, had "fully exonerated the officer."

The tensions that have surfaced at Penn are similar to those found at many of the nation's colleges at a time of heightened attention to how the police treat members of minority groups. Several colleges' police forces have also been the subject of recent controversies stemming from allegations they had engaged in racial profiling.

Vassar College, in Poughkeepsie, New York, was accused last year of racial profiling after campus security officers confronted two black students for using their dormitory laundromat, and called the town police on a group of local black children and teenagers who had been noisy in the library. Catharine Hill, Vassar's president, announced in August that the college had taken several steps to deal with the problem, such as amending its anti-discrimination policies to explicitly prohibit racial profiling and hiring a consulting firm to assist in a review of campus security practices.

As reported in *The Chronicle* of Winston-Salem, North Carolina, students at Wake Forest University held a town hall in November to discuss black students' perceptions that the campus police ask them for their identification far more than they ask other students, and give disproportionate scrutiny to parties held by black fraternities and sororities. Regina Lawson, the university's police chief, told the audience that her department had established a new bias reporting system and plans to train its officers to avoid unconscious discrimination.

Police Backup

As proved by President Gutmann's participation in the Penn protest, however, college administrators who take a stand against alleged police misbehavior run the risk of alienating those they depend upon to maintain order on campus.

In his letter criticizing Ms. Gutmann's action, Mr. Rohrback said, "As a supervisor of law enforcement employees, she should at the very least remain neutral and not give in to mob mentality." Administrators scrambled to mend relations. Maureen Rush, vice president for public safety, said in a letter to the campus police department that Ms. Gutmann had responded "instinctively" to the protesters

> **Under a standard it adopted in 2012, the association requires that colleges have a written directive that prohibits officers from engaging "in bias-based enforcement activity" and profiling based on race, ethnicity, gender, sexual orientation, religion, or socioeconomic status.**

and "is 110 percent supportive of each and every member of our police department, and law enforcement in general."

At the University of Minnesota–Twin Cities, administrators have stood behind the university police department in a much more concrete and controversial sense, refusing demands from black faculty, staff, and student organizations that the campus police stop routinely publishing the race of suspects in campus crime alerts.

In a letter sent a year ago to Eric W. Kaler, the university's president, the campus's Black Faculty and Staff Association joined the department of African-American and African studies and other groups in protesting what they described as an upsurge in campus crime alerts that described suspects as black males. Arguing that the alerts had led to a rise in racial profiling, they called for the university to remove the suspects' race from crime alerts or provide a written justification for providing such information.

In an interview last month, Steve Henneberry, a spokesman for the University of Minnesota, said that there were discussions about such concerns but that the university's policy is to use racial descriptors in crime alerts. "A well-informed community is an asset to public safety," Mr. Henneberry said, "and that involves providing as much information as we can to our community."

Fighting Bias

The International Association of Campus Law Enforcement Administrators, which counts among its members the public-safety departments of about 1,200 American colleges, has sought to push colleges to end racial profiling through voluntary accreditation standards.

Under a standard it adopted in 2012, the association requires that colleges have a written directive that prohibits officers from engaging "in bias-based enforcement activity" and profiling based on race, ethnicity, gender, sexual orientation, religion, or socioeconomic status. It says such a directive should require that all officers receive entry-level and biennial training to prevent profiling, that all complaints of biased enforcement be investigated, and that complaints be reviewed annually.

It's unclear, however, how much weight those standards have. Just 18 college agencies have earned the group's accreditation, while 23 have earned accreditation jointly through the association and the Commission on Accreditation for Law Enforcement Agencies. Christopher G. Blake, chief staff officer of the law-enforcement administrators' association, said agencies without accreditation may well have developed their own policies against profiling.

The effectiveness of anti-bias training programs for police also remains in question.

Maria (Maki) Haberfeld, who studies racial profiling as a professor of police science at the John Jay College of Criminal Justice, says when police officers are caught engaging in biased enforcement, "the first and easiest thing to say is, 'We are going to retrain them.'" She says she is skeptical, however, that officers can be taught to operate without bias in a few training sessions, because bias against certain groups can be so entrenched in their thinking. Moreover, she says, "You can come up with the most wonderful training program, but if you are not offering it to the right people it is not going to improve anything."

David L. Perry, president of the law-enforcement administrators' association and chief of police at Florida State University, says one of the main factors keeping more campus agencies from being accused of racial bias or excessive use of force is "our foundation in community-oriented policing."

Gary J. Margolis, a former chief of police at the University of Vermont who now consults for campus police departments, says he believes such agencies "tend to be a little bit more sensitive to the dynamics of race just because of the nature of an academic learning environment," where race is often discussed.

If there is a major change that the recent police-shooting controversies is likely to bring about among campus police agencies, it may be in the popularization of the body-worn police cameras.

About 350 campus agencies have watched a webinar on such cameras that the law-enforcement administrators association offered in September, according to Tom Saccenti, who helped organize the presentation as chief of police at Furman University. He says the cameras, which his own agency began using in 2013, have helped in enforcing both laws and campus codes of conduct—not just by documenting what an officer is seeing, but by changing the behavior of those being filmed.

"It is accountability for both sides," Mr. Saccenti says. "The officer knows he is being recorded, but you can clearly see that there is a camera on the police officer. We have seen a change in behavior in a lot of people who we talk to because they know they are on a recording."

The Incidents That Led to the University of Missouri President's Resignation

By Elahe Izadi
The Washington Post, November 9, 2015

Tim Wolfe's resignation Monday as the University of Missouri System president came after months of escalating racial tension surrounding high-profile incidents on the flagship campus in Columbia, Mo., and student criticism about the administration's response.

Here's a rundown of what happened leading up to Wolfe's announcement that he was stepping down from his post leading the four-campus system.

Ferguson protests: 2014

Thousands of people took to the streets last year in Ferguson, Missouri, just hours away from Columbia, following the August 2014 police shooting of Michael Brown, an unarmed black 18-year-old.

Dozens of Missouri students joined demonstrators in August and again in November after a grand jury decided against indicting Darren Wilson, the white officer who fatally shot Brown. Following the initial protests, three Mizzou students started the activist group MU for Michael Brown, which later gave rise to a second group, Concerned Student 1950; that group's name was a nod to the year black students were first admitted to the university.

In light of the unrest in Ferguson, members of the student groups lamented the university's lack of official response to racial tensions on campus.

Swastika etched onto dorm stairwell wall: April

A swastika and the word "heil" were drawn in what appeared to be charcoal on the wall of a residence hall stairway in April. Authorities arrested freshman resident Bradley Becker days later and charged him with second-degree property damage motivated by discrimination. Becker pleaded guilty in October to a lesser charge and will serve two years probation.

Former civil rights lawyer named interim president at University of Missouri following student protests

Student body president called the n-word: September 12

Payton Head said he was walking with a friend when a pickup truck slowed down and a group of young people inside screamed a racial epithet at him. The Missouri Students Association president, who is black, shared the story in a social media post that went viral and prompted a response from Chancellor R. Bowen Loftin.

Head said at the time that he had been previously called a racial slur on campus, as well.

Black students' play rehearsal interrupted by racial slurs: October 5

Members of the Legion of Black Collegians were rehearsing on campus for a homecoming court performance when an "inebriated white man" walking by interrupted and called the students the n-word, the group publicly announced.

"There was a silence that fell over us all, almost in disbelief that this racial slur in particular was used in our vicinity," the group wrote.

Mandatory diversity training announced: October 8

The university said that all incoming freshman will have to receive online diversity training. The move was welcomed by some students. But activists were more skeptical, calling the move a "knee-jerk" reaction to improve the school's image.

Homecoming protesters block Wolfe's car: October 10

Police removed Concerned Student 1950 protesters who blocked the president's car during the campus homecoming parade. Wolfe did not leave his car to speak with the students.

"We disrupted the parade specifically in front of Tim Wolfe because we need him to get our message," graduate student Jonathan Butler, one of the protesters, told the [Colombian] Missourian. "We've sent emails, we've sent tweets, we've messaged, but we've gotten no response back from the upper officials at Mizzou to really make change on this campus. And so we directed it to him personally."

Student group demands Wolfe resign: October 20

Concerned Student 1950 released a list of demands, including [that] Wolfe apologize to the homecoming parade demonstrators and be removed from his post. The students also demanded increasing black faculty and staff; mandatory racial awareness and inclusion curriculum for all staff, faculty, and students; and additional funding and resources for mental health professionals, particularly those of color, to boost campus programming and outreach to students.

Feces used to draw swastika in residence hall: October 24

Months after the anti-Semitic symbol was found in the Mark Twain residence hall, officials found another swastika on Oct. 24. This one was drawn using feces smeared on the floor and wall of a bathroom.

"After this event, it has become clear to me that the inclusivity of our residence halls has been threatened," Resident Halls Association president Bill Donley said in a statement.

Wolfe meets with student group: October 26

Concerned Student 1950 announced it had met with Wolfe, but said that he wasn't meeting any of their demands.

"Wolfe verbally acknowledged that he cared for Black students at the University of Missouri, however he also reported he was 'not completely' aware of systemic racism, sexism, and patriarchy on campus," a statement from the group read.

Graduate student begins hunger strike: November 2

A 25-year-old graduate student announced a hunger strike that, he said, he would not break unless Wolfe resigned. Jonathan Butler, a member of Concerned Student 1950, said he was ready to die for his cause, and other students began camping out on campus in support.

"As much as the experiences on campus have not been that great for me—I had people call me the n-word, I had someone write the n-word on the door in my residence hall—for me it really is about a call for justice," Butler told the *Post*. "I'm fighting for the black community on campus, because justice is worth fighting for. And justice is worth starving for."

Wolfe apologizes, acknowledges racism: November 6

Wolfe released a statement Friday apologizing for how student protests at homecoming were handled and expressing concern for Butler's health.

"My behavior seemed like I did not care," Wolfe said of the parade incident. "That was not my intention. I was caught off guard in that moment. Nonetheless, had I gotten out of the car to acknowledge the students and talk with them perhaps we wouldn't be where we are today."

He added: "Racism does exist at our university, and it is unacceptable. It is a long-standing, systemic problem which daily affects our family of students, faculty and staff."

Football players threaten to boycott: November 7

A group of black football players announced that they were joining ongoing student protests and pledged to stop participating in football-related activities for the remainder of the season unless Wolfe resigned or was fired.

Head coach Gary Pinkel tweeted his support for his players and included a photo showing what appeared to include staff with both black and white players from the Mizzou football team.

This move, from one of the most popular, profitable and visible groups on campus, helped propel the situation into the national spotlight. It also raised the stakes for Wolfe; the university would have to pay $1 million to Bringham Young University if it canceled an upcoming game.

Wolfe pledges to stay: November 8

The president released a statement Sunday night, making no indications he had plans to step down and saying that his administration was "confident that we can come together to improve the student experience on our campuses."

"I am dedicated to ongoing dialogue to address these very complex, societal issues as they affect our campus community," Wolfe said.

Wolfe said the majority of Concerned Student 1950 demands were already in a draft strategic plan to improve system-wide diversity and inclusion.

Legislators call for Wolfe's resignation: November 8

Rep. Steven Cookson (R), chairman of the Missouri House Committee on Higher Education, said Wolfe "can no longer effectively lead" the university system and called Wolfe's reaction to protesters' concerns "callous." Another Republican lawmaker also urged Wolfe to resign.

Gov. Jay Nixon (D) said he supported the campus protesters. "These concerns must be addressed to ensure the University of Missouri is a place where all students can pursue their dreams in an environment of respect, tolerance and inclusion."

Some faculty members said they would stage a walk-out on Monday.

Wolfe resigns: November 9

At a special meeting called by the university's governing body, Wolfe announced his resignation.

From The Post:

"My motivation in making this decision comes from love," he said. "I love MU, Columbia, where I grew up, the state of Missouri.

"This is not the way change should come about," he said, calling on the community to stop yelling and start listening to one another. But he said, "I take full responsibility for this frustration. I take full responsibility for this inaction."

Wolfe said his resignation was effective immediately.

Yale Students and Staff Are in a Huge Debate over Offensive Halloween Costumes

By Megan Friedman
Cosmopolitan, November 10, 2015

Every Halloween, colleges across the country grapple with what to do when students wear offensive costumes on Halloween. This year, you could buy anything from a Caitlyn Jenner costume to a bloodied Walter Palmer costume, complete with Cecil the Lion's head. And every year, some genius thinks it's a good idea to wear blackface while dressing as a rapper. But when administrators at Yale tried to stop the issue before it started, it created a massive debate that is only getting louder.

According to the *New York Times*, Yale's Intercultural Affairs Committee sent a mass email to students before Halloween this year, advising them to avoid cultural appropriation when choosing a costume. "Halloween is also unfortunately a time when the normal thoughtfulness and sensitivity of most Yale students can sometimes be forgotten and some poor decisions can be made including wearing feathered headdresses, turbans, wearing 'war paint' or modifying skin tone or wearing blackface or redface," the email reads. The note included guidelines of how to avoid offending people with a costume, like asking yourself if the costume mocks another person's faith, race, or culture, and if anyone could take offense at what you're wearing.

One faculty member didn't agree with the sentiment. Erika Christakis, a lecturer at Yale, lives with her husband Nicholas in Silliman College, an undergraduate residential college where Nicholas, a faculty member, serves as "master" and she serves as associate master. She emailed all students and administrators at Silliman with her own response after some students complained, saying that colleges should let students make their own decisions. Erica Christakis, a child development specialist, said she worries these restrictions will prevent kids from dressing as characters outside their race, like a "blonde-haired child" who wants to dress like Mulan. "Is there no room anymore for a child or young person to be a little bit obnoxious . . . a little bit inappropriate or provocative or, yes, offensive?" she wrote. "American universities were once a safe space not only for maturation but also for a certain regressive, or even transgressive, experience." Her comments are similar to countless opinion columnists (and even President Obama) who believe college campuses have become too politically correct, stifling debate rather than creating a safe space for intellectual thought.

Hundreds of Yale students, alumni, faculty, and staff, signed an open letter in response to Erica Christakis, saying her email "infantilized" the people of color who requested cultural sensitivity on Halloween, and failed to distinguish between dressing as a specific character and dressing as a blanket stereotype of a race. "To be a student of color on Yale's campus is to exist in a space that was not created for you," the letter reads. "The purpose of blackface, yellowface, and practices like these were meant to alienate, denigrate, and to portray people of color as something inferior and unwelcome in society. To see that replicated on college campuses only reinforces the idea that this is a space in which we do not belong."

Students gathered on campus on November 5 and demanded Nicholas Christakis apologize for the comments, since he agreed with and added his own similar thoughts to his wife's email. In a moment caught on video, he refused, which led to a heated, passionate encounter with a student who insisted he step down. "You are a poor steward of this community!" a student shouted. "You should not sleep at night! You are disgusting." In the video, it seems like the students walk away before Nicholas Christakis can respond, but he later tweeted that "no one, especially students exercising right to speech, should be judged just on [the] basis of [a] short video clip."

This wasn't the only racial issue surrounding Halloween at Yale this year; a Yale fraternity was accused of having a "white girls only" party in New Haven, turning away any women of color. Yale president Peter Salovey and dean Jonathan Holloway met with a group of administrators and students, primarily of color, for an hours-long meeting. On Thursday, Salovey and Holloway emailed the student body in support of the original email, saying that the campus must be respectful of everyone.

"This conversation left me deeply troubled, and has caused me to realize that we must act to create at Yale greater inclusion, healing, mutual respect, and understanding," Salovey wrote in a message to students. "Remember that Yale belongs to all of you, and you all deserve the right to enjoy the good of this place, without worry, without threats, and without intimidation," Holloway added.

On Monday, more than 1,000 students and staff from multicultural groups on campus gathered in a March for Resilience in hopes of moving forward and turning the debate into a positive movement for cultural acceptance. According to the *Yale Daily News*, it turned into an impromptu dance party, with songs, speeches, and chants. "We out here, we've been here, we ain't leaving, we are loved," the marchers cheered.

> **The purpose of blackface, yellowface, and practices like these were meant to alienate, denigrate, and to portray people of color as something inferior and unwelcome in society.**

"Last week there was a lot of pain, and it was emotionally draining and traumatic for many people of color on campus, even though it was a necessary move," student Alejandra Padin-Dujon, a member of the cultural groups La Casa and the Af-Am House, told the student paper. "Right now, moving forward, we are looking to heal ourselves so that we can strengthen ourselves, regroup and push for specific demands and positive change for the future."

Woodrow Wilson's Legacy Gets Complicated

By Jennifer Schuessler
The New York Times, November 29, 2015

Was Woodrow Wilson a key founder of modern liberalism, a visionary whose belief in an activist presidency laid the groundwork for the New Deal and the civil rights legislation of the 1960s?

Or was he a virulent and unrepentant racist, a man who not only segregated the federal work force but nationalized the Southern view of politics, turning the federal government itself into an instrument of white supremacy for decades to come?

Wilson's record on race has long been debated among historians. But in the past two weeks, the topic has burst into broader view, thanks to student protesters at Princeton who have demanded, among other things, that the former president's name be removed from its prestigious Woodrow Wilson School of Public and International Affairs.

The protests have prompted a fierce round of op-eds and Facebook discussions, and not a few laments that few historical figures would be deemed pure enough to have their names inscribed on walls in today's heated atmosphere. (What's next, more than one Twitter wag asked, a demand to take the name of George Washington, a slave owner, off the nation's capitol?)

The debate comes amid a flurry of continuing renaming controversies on various campuses, including Georgetown, which recently announced that it was removing from campus buildings the names of two of its former presidents who had been involved in selling slaves, and Yale, which is hotly debating whether to rename a residential college named for John C. Calhoun, one of the nineteenth-century's foremost defenders of slavery.

But the controversy over Wilson strikes closer to home for many liberal-leaning historians and scholars, threatening a symbol whose broader vision many would wish to defend, while raising the uncomfortable question of whether Wilson's racism constitutes a blot on his record or an integral feature of the progressive tradition he helped to found.

"The irony here is that Wilson really is the architect of a lot of modern liberalism," said Julian E. Zelizer, a professor of history and public affairs at Princeton. "The tradition that runs through F.D.R. to L.B.J. and Obama really starts with his administration."

> **Wilson's attitudes and record on race, even his staunchest defenders agree, is hardly a pretty one. As president of Princeton, the Virginia-born scholar discouraged an African-American prospective student from applying, calling it "altogether inadvisable for a colored man to enter Princeton."**

Wilson has long been a favorite target of conservatives like Glenn Beck, who has blamed him for everything from overweening government to Nazi eugenics. Shortly after the Princeton protests, a writer for the Federalist, a conservative website, praised the students for targeting "an authoritarian hatemonger who also happened to be one of the most destructive presidents in the history of the United States."

Scholars, however, have generally taken a more sanguine view. Polls, like one earlier this year of several hundred members of the American Political Science Association, often rank him in the top 10 United States presidents. Defenders tick off a list of his accomplishments, including his leadership in World War I (he won the 1919 Nobel Peace Prize) and advocacy for national self-determination in international relations and, on the domestic front, the creation of the Federal Reserve, the Federal Trade Commission, the graduated income tax, and new antitrust and labor laws.

"Going to the mat for Wilson should not be hard," said David Greenberg, a historian at Rutgers University. "If your standards are liberal progressive values in general, Wilson deserves to be celebrated."

While the segregation of the federal government during his administration "deserves to be deplored," Mr. Greenberg added, evaluating Wilson solely by his record on race "stacks the deck."

But other scholars counter that Wilson's racism cannot be neatly cleaved off from his broader program, or from the broader political tradition he helped found.

"Historians usually say, 'Here was this amazing liberal progressive who was a racist, which is too bad, now let's go back to talking about the good things,'" said Eric S. Yellin, an associate professor at the University of Richmond and the author of "Racism in the Nation's Service," a study of the segregation of the federal work force under Wilson.

"But it's important to see that Wilson had a whites-only progressive view," Mr. Yellin said.

Wilson's attitudes and record on race, even his staunchest defenders agree, is hardly a pretty one. As president of Princeton, the Virginia-born scholar discouraged an African-American prospective student from applying, calling it "altogether inadvisable for a colored man to enter Princeton." His textbook *A History of the American People* referred to Reconstruction-era efforts to free the South from "the incubus of that ignorant and often hostile" black vote. As governor of New Jersey, his administration included no blacks.

After his election to the White House in 1912, Wilson, a Democrat, appointed a cabinet that was heavy on Southern racists, including William McAdoo as treasury secretary and Albert Burleson as postmaster general, both of whom quickly pushed to segregate their departments, demoting and firing many blacks.

Wilson, who also nominated an African-American for register of the Treasury (the nomination was withdrawn after Southern Democrats in the Senate raised a furor), did not spearhead those efforts, though he did go along with them, noted John Milton Cooper, a retired historian at the University of Wisconsin and the author of an admiring 2009 biography of Wilson.

"Trying to make Wilson into this gung-ho, committed white supremacist is just wrong," Mr. Cooper said.

But other historians say the matter ran much deeper than Wilson's personal feelings or intentions. Nathan Connolly, a visiting associate professor of history at New York University, said that while Wilson may not have spearheaded the segregation initiatives (which were not reversed by his Republican successors), when criticized for them by black leaders and others he "doubled down," rationalizing segregation as a strategy to keep the racial peace and a benefit to blacks themselves.

"It's important to remember that Jim Crow segregation was itself a Progressive Era reform," said Mr. Connolly, the author of *A World More Concrete: Real Estate and the Remaking of Jim Crow South Florida*.

And Wilson's racism, Mr. Connolly said, didn't stop at the nation's borders. The president's vision of national self-determination, he noted, did not extend to Haiti, the occupation of which Wilson authorized in 1915, partly to replace a national constitution that forbade foreigners to own land.

"Even the internationalism that people want to credit him with was deeply inflected by animus towards black people," Mr. Connolly said.

How to evaluate Wilson's historical legacy and whether to give him a place of honor on campus are different questions. And there, even some who support keeping Wilson's name on the policy school credit students with starting an important conversation.

Anne-Marie Slaughter, a former dean of the Wilson School, wrote on Facebook that when Christopher Eisgruber, Princeton's president, said that he would start a process to consider whether to rename the school, she thought it was "a crazy decision."

But Ms. Slaughter, now the president and chief executive of the nonpartisan think tank New America, said she had come to see the value of the debate itself, if not the removal of his name.

"It seems to me much more in keeping with values of liberal education that you keep the name and render the whole person, so you have to simultaneously confront that many great people have dark sides," she said.

Mr. Connolly said it might be more constructive to leave Wilson's name on the school but build, say, a monument to the occupation of Haiti in front.

The important thing, Mr. Connolly said, "is to write segregation and race into the story, not to write racists out of it."

5

A New Civil Rights
Movement and Current
Perspectives on Race

On August 8, 2015, protesters hold up a United We Stand banner during the march on Shaw Blvd, in St. Louis, Missouri. Several protest groups organized a march and block party on the weekend of the one year anniversary of Michael Brown's death.

A New Era of Civil Rights Challenges

The Civil War (1861–1865) ended the institution of slavery, but resulted in a population deeply divided over the issues of civil rights and racial integration. For more than a century after African Americans were given citizenship, throughout the South, in former slave states, residential areas and public services were segregated under a "separate but equal" legal doctrine that prohibited African Americans from using any public facilities or services reserved as "white only" by business owners and public utility companies. Public transportation, schools, restaurants, movie theaters, and even drinking fountains were divided into "whites only" and "blacks only." However, the facilities and services made available to African Americans were underfunded and in many cases distinctly inferior to those reserved for white Americans, and so a hierarchy of citizenship was established in which black Americans were legal citizens, but relegated to second-class status in their access to the benefits of citizenship. Although this policy was only legal throughout the South, in the North there was de facto segregation of neighborhoods and schools.

In the 1950s and 1960s, frustrated by decades of institutionalized segregation and discrimination, millions of African Americans and whites joined together in mass protests and demonstrations calling attention to the inequity of the "separate but equal" system. In the 1954 Supreme Court case *Brown v. Board of Education*, the Supreme Court ruled that the segregation of schools was unconstitutional. Over the next decade, the movement continued gaining traction in the federal government, eventually culminating in the 1964 Civil Rights Act, which officially made any form of state or local segregation or institutionalized discrimination illegal under United States law.[1]

It was clear to most Civil Rights leaders that simply making segregation illegal would not address the effects of decades of inadequate services and access to education and employment on the African American community. To address the deep and pervasive layers of discrimination, numerous federal and state measures were initiated under the banner of "affirmative action," a term established by President Kennedy in a 1961 executive order in which Kennedy stated that all federally-funded organizations would need to take "affirmative action" to ensure that all citizens were treated equally in employment.[2]

While affirmative action has taken a variety of forms, the process has essentially involved the distribution of federal funding to organizations, companies, and institutions that actively promote minority enrollment and employment. Federally-sponsored desegregation programs, for instance, brought African American students to traditionally white schools and brought white students to traditionally black schools in an effort to promote integration and allow students to benefit from being educated in racially diverse environments. Meanwhile, corporations, especially those receiving federal funding, were held responsible for meeting "diversity requirements" in hiring, toward the goal of encouraging minority involvement in American industry and professional environments. These measures have been the subject of intense debate since the 1960s. Some have claimed that affirmative action is necessary to counteract the lasting effects of racism and discrimination. Some critics claim that affirmative action has been ineffective at promoting true integration, and still others argue that the policy results in "reverse discrimination" wherein minority Americans are given an unfair advantage in education and employment.

The Rise and Fall of Affirmative Action

A 2013 survey by the Gallup Organization found that 59 percent of white and Hispanic Americans believed that colleges and universities should not take race into consideration in admission policies. Since the 1980s, affirmative action policies and laws have increasingly come under attack by white Americans who believe they have been subject to racial discrimination by being passed over for school enrollment or employment in favor of minority candidates.[3] Since the 1990s, several states have passed laws prohibiting "preferential treatment" in education and/or employment. Among the most recent developments in this debate was a state law passed in 2015 in Oklahoma making it illegal for employers or educational institutions to give preference to any individual because of race.[4]

The efforts of white Americans to fight the alleged racial discrimination of affirmative action are controversial because many believe that affirmative action and preferential treatment are still necessary to address continued racial disparities. Pew Research studies have found that while 70 percent of all Americans say they still support affirmative action, 76 percent of white Americans believe that affirmative action should not include giving preferential treatment to African Americans. By contrast, 58 percent of African Americans and 53 percent of Hispanics believed it was still necessary to actively promote minority involvement in industry and education.[5]

On the other side of the debate, Pew Research surveys indicate that 32 percent of all Americans believe that the United States has already made the changes necessary to promote racial equality. A majority of Americans, however, still believe that more changes are needed. But numerous polls have shown that a majority of Americans, both white and minorities, believe that further changes are needed to combat racial inequality. Pew Research studies published in 2015 indicate that 53 percent of white Americans believe that more "changes" were needed to address racial inequality, and that 44 percent of white Americans classify racism as one of America's leading social issues. However, as white Americans have turned against preferential treatment in affirmative action policies, there is little consensus about how to achieve integration without these controversial policies.

A New Civil Rights Movement?

In 2014–2015, the race debate returned to the front of America's social debate in the wake of protests and riots in numerous American cities protesting police and justice department treatment of African Americans. As the first widespread "race debate" of the twenty-first century proceeded throughout 2015, some in the media asked whether a new civil rights movement was emerging. The 2014–2015 protests and demonstrations were unique in the degree to which the modern movement depended on digital organization and activism. The BlackLivesMatter movement, for instance, began as a Twitter campaign that spread virally across the Internet, linking individuals across state lines and even internationally. Organization through digital social media demonstrated the potential for social issues to spread rapidly through a society increasingly linked together by these emerging forms of media.[6]

In a 2015 article in *Slate*, Rebecca Onion asked experts in civil rights history about how the modern movement resembled the Civil Rights era of the 1950s and 60s. Though historians were divided, they noted that the success of the 1950s and 1960s Civil Rights Movement depended on the mobilization of American youth. The ultimate impact of the modern movement will therefore depend on the ability of modern organizers and advocates to similarly motivate and organize young Americans in support of the emerging wave of Civil Rights activism.[7] According to this perspective, the success of the modern Civil Rights movement depends on the millennial generation: those Americans reaching adulthood in the 2000s. Though thousands of millennials took part in the 2014–2015 protests and marches, changing views of race among the millennial generation complicate efforts to engage the younger generation in substantive social activism and engagement.

Modern Perspectives on Race

In a 2014 survey of millennials conducted by MTV, researchers found 91 percent of millennials believed that everyone should be treated equally regardless of race and 58 percent believed that, as millennials moved into leadership positions, race would be a far less pressing issue in America. In addition, 73 percent of respondents believed Americans should strive to be "colorblind" in their treatment of others and 68 percent said that "focusing on race" prevents society from moving past racial inequality.[8] While the millennial view of race appeals to a generation removed from the struggles for equality that existed in the 1960s and 1970s, civil rights activists and historians argue that racism and the effort for racial equality are about far more than "differential treatment" and creating a society that is "colorblind." Racism is also a matter of addressing the effects of past inequities and a system of ingrained, sometimes unconscious racial bias and stereotypes that continue to support the existence of a racial hierarchy in America. According to this view, racial equality cannot be achieved by "ignoring" the racial divisions within but requires the willingness to actively root out and address the system of racial division that underpins all of the particular "expressions" of racial inequality that millennials would seek to avoid or call irrelevant.[9]

The modern race debate is also complicated by the rapid growth of the "mixed-race population," which is currently growing at three times the rate of the "single-race" population in America.[10] Multiracial Americans have long occupied a hazy middle ground between dominant and marginalized society and as this population grows, the future of race relations and civil rights struggles will increasingly depend on how multiracial individuals identify with race. Mixed-race individuals with lighter skin and ambiguous minority heritage more often identify as "white" or with "white culture," while other mixed-race individuals, particularly those of mixed African American descent, continue to identify as members of a racial minority. Pew Research studies indicate, for instance, that 61 percent of mixed-race individuals do not consider themselves "multiracial" but identify more strongly or entirely with one race.

The blending of racial groups dilutes the external signifiers that have long been used to identify individuals by race but does not reduce the significance of racial dynamics in American life, and the degree to which multiracial people are exempt from racial prejudice still depends on remaining signifiers of race. For instance, Pew studies found that only 6 percent of biracial white and Asian individuals report having been the victim of direct racial prejudice while more than 40 percent of mixed black and white individuals say they have experienced some form of discrimination or harassment in their lives.

Americans in the twenty-first century face a uniquely complex racial environment in which historical racial stereotypes and divisions are shifting. The ultimate goal of dismantling the deeply ingrained patterns of privilege and power that maintain class and race hierarchies requires sacrifice, determination, and engagement among generations further and further removed from the glaring racial divisions that motivated a nationwide movement at mid-century. For those interested in continuing the civil rights struggle, therefore, it is necessary to guide new generations in understanding the history and lasting effects of America's past struggles with racism, as well as how racism continues to shape American culture today.

Micah L. Issitt

Notes

1. Crosby, Emilye, "Civil Rights History from the Ground Up."
2. "Executive Order 10925," EEOC.
3. Jones, "In U.S., Most Reject Considering Race in College Admissions."
4. "Affirmative Action: State Action," *NCSL*.
5. "Public Backs Affirmative Action, but Not Minority Preferences," *Pew Research*.
6. Stephen, Bijan, "Get Up, Stand Up."
7. Onion, Jessica, "Are We in the Midst of a New Civil Rights Era?"
8. "MTV Survey on Millenials and Race," *MTV*.
9. Bouie, Jamelle, "Why Do Millennials Not Understand Racism?"
10. "Multiracial in America," *Pew Research*.

Growing Up "Post-racial," Teens Suddenly Find a World That Isn't

By Greg Toppo
USA Today, December 10, 2014

Chapter 1: Young and Postracial

The most racially diverse generation in American history works hard to see race as just another attribute, no more important than the cut of a friend's clothes or the music she likes.

But the real world keeps intruding, as it has the past few weeks with angry protests over the racially charged deaths of Michael Brown in Ferguson, Missouri, and Eric Garner in nearby Staten Island, New York.

"As a generation, we don't acknowledge color, but we know that the race problem is still there," says 16-year-old Nailah Richards, an African-American student at Medgar Evers College Preparatory School in Brooklyn. "We don't really pay attention to it, but we know it's there."

Nailah is one of the Millennials, the 87 million Americans born between 1982 and 2001. They are defined by opinion surveys as racially open-minded and struggling to be "postracial."

Pew Research says Millennials are the most racially tolerant of any recent generation—only 5%, for instance, say interracial marriages are "a bad thing for society" vs. 14% of Baby Boomers. And 93% of Millennials believe it's OK for African-American and white people to interracially date, 10 percentage points higher than Boomers, a 2010 survey shows.

"We don't really care if you're purple, brown, black—it doesn't even matter," Nailah says. "If you're a person, you are who you are."

But as they witness recent protests, and as their generation matures, Millennials are recognizing just how much race still matters to society, to their friends and family, and to themselves.

"I feel like if you don't acknowledge it, then it's like, 'Are you blind?' I feel like it has to be acknowledged," says Domonique Antoine, 16, one of Nailah's classmates. "It's something that has to be acknowledged because there's a certain level of privilege that African-American and Latino people—brown people—don't have."

"I don't think (racism) ever left," says Izabelle Denize, 22. "I think with every decade it transforms into something really different. For our generation you have these
criminal justice issues. Before, in the 1950s you had Jim Crow . . . . I think every
generation, it does look a little different."

Business consultant Howard Ross, author of the 2014 book *Everyday Bias*, says
Millennials are likely as surprised by the recent racially charged events as anyone.
"This is a generation of people who are now saying, 'Wait a second, we thought this
was *over*. We were *told* this was over. We thought we were moving forward and now
we see the same old stuff happening.'"

Millennials score 62 on the USA TODAY Diversity Index, a scale from 0 to 100
that measures the chance that two random people will be from a different race or
ethnicity. By comparison, Boomers score 45 and their parents, the so-called Silent
Generation, score just 36.

USA TODAY spoke with Nailah, Domonique and a handful of her classmates
and friends last week as they took a break from an after-school class at the Sadie
Nash Leadership Project, a non-profit education initiative near Manhattan's Grand
Central Station that attracts young women from all five city boroughs.

Most are non-white, and several are the first in their family born in the USA.

"I do wonder if the skin color that I am is going to determine my future and what
I'm going to do," says Esther Agyei, 16.

Born in Ghana, she still has close family there. Esther lives in the Bronx with her
mother. Teachers at Esther's school regularly tell her and her classmates that they
can "be anything you want to be," but she isn't so sure that all of the adults in her
life actually believe that. "I think they're lying—I mean, of course in school they're
pushing you to do your dream, whatever you want to do. But I think (in) reality,
that's not true. You go outside, I know that's not true."

Chapter 2: Where Skin Color Matters

Many young people still see the USA's intractable problems as rooted in race. In
a May 2012 report, Race Forward: the Center for Racial Justice Innovation found
that "a large majority" of young people in the Los Angeles area believed race and
racism still mattered significantly—particularly as they relate to education, criminal
justice and employment. In follow-up sessions in five cities in early 2012, the center
found that "racial justice" was the most significant interest among young people.

"Do I feel like I live in a post-racial society?" asks Izabelle. "Not at all. Not at all."

A recent Rutgers University graduate, Izabelle now serves on the Sadie Nash
board and mentors younger students. She grew up in and around Newark, but her
parents grew up in Haiti, where skin color matters perhaps even more than it does
in New Jersey. "Racism in Haiti looks a little different from racism in the United States," she says. "Having both of those perspectives tells me that being black
changes, but you still are 'The Other' in every context."

In his book, Ross notes that humans are "consistently, routinely, and profoundly
biased." The sooner we realize this and stop denying that bias plays out in our lives
every day, he writes, the better off we'll be. Actually, he notes, psychologists have

> **But as they witness recent protests, and as their generation matures, Millennials are recognizing just how much race still matters to society, to their friends and family, and to themselves.**

a term for our deep-seated preference to be around people who look and think and sound like us: homophily.

"We're drawn towards each other because our mirroring capacity, the part of our brain that wants to understand what we're dealing with, feels very comfortable with people like ourselves, because we kind of know what to expect," Ross says. "They're speaking our language, they're acting like we act, they're talking like we talk, they have the same concerns that we have. And so as a result, we're drawn to people like that. That's not necessarily a bad thing, but what's troubling is when that's the only connection we have."

Chapter 3: Following Friends Online

Researcher danah boyd, whose recent book, *It's Complicated,* examines how teens socialize online, notes that "the world in which teens live is segregated and shaped by race." Though teens do work to maintain cross-racial friendships, they're more likely to interact with people of the same race in class, in the lunchroom and online.

For five years, boyd, (who refers to herself in print in the lowercase) interviewed teens in 17 states and analyzed 10,000 social network profiles. She found that schools are rarely if ever explicitly segregated by race, but that the segregation happens in a kind of quiet, *de facto* way, both through class assignment and social pressures. boyd found that race was still a sensitive issue among teens and that they prefer not to talk about it, but that they still strongly identify each other racially.

Sixty years have passed since the U.S. Supreme Court ruled in the *Brown v. Board of Education* case that segregation of public schools was unconstitutional. But boyd found that most U.S. high schools "organized themselves around race and class through a variety of social, cultural, economic, and political forces." The borders of school districts often produce segregated schools as a byproduct of neighborhood segregation, and students are placed in classrooms and on academic tracks based on test scores that often correlate with socioeconomic status.

She also found that the early shift in social networking sites from MySpace to Facebook, primarily among white, upper-middle-class teens in 2006 and 2007, constituted a kind of "white flight" that mirrored suburban whites' move out of cities. MySpace was the subject of many "moral panic" stories in the media around that time, such as the "MySpace suicide" story in 2007 in Missouri. She found that kids were listening to their parents' fears: Facebook represented a clean, well-lit refuge from racial diversity. Social networking sites, she found, were basically the digital equivalent of the school cafeteria, reflecting kids' comfort—or discomfort—with kids of different racial and ethnic groups.

Social divisions, including racial divisions, "are not disappearing simply because people have access to technology," boyd says. "Tools that enable communication do

DIVERSITY, BY GENERATION

The USA TODAY Diversity Index is a scale from 0 to 100 that measures the chance that two random people will be from a different race or ethnicity.

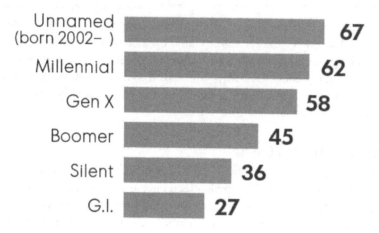

Generation	Index
Unnamed (born 2002–)	67
Millennial	62
Gen X	58
Boomer	45
Silent	36
G.I.	27

SOURCE: USA TODAY analysis of Census 2010 data

Paul Overberg and Janet Loehrke,
USA TODAY

 USA**TODAY**

not sweep away distrust, hatred and prejudice." The mere existence of new technology "neither creates nor magically solves cultural problems. In fact, their construction typically reinforces existing social divisions."

For instance, when she sat down to look at the Facebook profile of a white 17-year-old girl at a private East Coast high school, boyd found that though her school recruited students from diverse racial and ethnic backgrounds, most of those who had left comments on the student's profile were white. "Teens go online to hang out with their friends," she wrote, "and given the segregation of American society, their friends are quite likely to be of the same race, class, and cultural background."

When boyd visited one Los Angeles high school, she recalled, "I was initially delighted by how diverse and integrated the school appeared to be." But she found that during lunch and between classes, "the school's diversity dissolved as peers clustered along racial and ethnic lines."

That tracks closely with how their parents' generation experienced race, says Amy Stuart Wells, a professor of the sociology of education at Columbia University's Teachers College. Wells was the lead author of a large study of the USA's graduating high school class of 1980, who recounted their experiences in racially diverse schools. She found "a silent majority" of 40-somethings who said it made them more tolerant of other races.

Like boyd, Wells found that the students' closest friends tended to be of the same race, but she still says that consciously bringing together students of different races was useful. "If we think about desegregation as supposedly changing hearts and minds, I think it actually did that."

In many cases, her interview subjects were surprised, decades later, that institutions such as housing and employment didn't follow in the schools' footsteps. "They all said, 'We thought we were being educated for a different world. But the world didn't change—only our schools changed.' To me it's a big story about why the schools can't do it alone."

Wells, whose work has placed her across the interview table from thousands of parents, now says none of them has illusions about the importance of raising kids in a diverse society. "They know intuitively that putting your kid in a segregated school is not good preparation for the twenty-first century."

The century—and the changes it promises—are only beginning. Recent Census data show that 43% of newborns today are non-white, and that by 2043, the USA population will be majority non-white.

"It's our demographic destiny," Wells says. "At some point we have to realize that."

America's "Postracial" Fantasy

By Anna Holmes
The New York Time Magazine, June 30, 2015

On Father's Day, my dad and I had brunch with some close friends of mine. The conversation soon turned to their two sons: their likes, their dislikes, their habit of disrupting classmates during nap time at nursery school. At one point, as I ran my hand through one of the boys' silky brown hair, I asked whether they consider their kids biracial. (The father is white; the mother is South Asian.) Before they could respond, the children's paternal grandmother, in town for a visit, replied as if the answer were the most obvious thing in the world: "They're white."

I was taken aback, but I also realized she had a point: The two boys, who have big brown eyes and just a blush of olive in their skin, are already—and will probably continue to be—regarded as white first, South Asian a distant second. Nothing in their appearance would suggest otherwise, and who's to say whether, once they realize that people see them as white, they will feel the need to set the record straight? Most people prefer the straightforward to the complex—especially when it comes to conversations about race.

A Pew Research Center study released in June, "Multiracial in America," reports that "biracial adults who are white and Asian say they have more in common with whites than they do with Asians" and "are more likely to say they feel accepted by whites than by Asians." While 76 percent of all mixed-race Americans claim that their backgrounds have made "no difference" in their lives, the data and anecdotes included in the study nevertheless underscore how, for a fair number of us, words like "multiracial" and "biracial" are awkward and inadequate, denoting identities that are fluid for some and fixed for others.

This is especially true, I think, for the progeny of mixed-race black-white relationships: As the daughter of an African-American father and a white mother, born with olive skin, light eyes and thick, curly hair, I have been aware of a tension between the way the outside world sees me, the way the government sees me (I was already 27 when the census changed its options so Americans could check off two or more races) and the ways in which I see myself. Sometimes identifying as black feels like a choice; other times, it is a choice made for me.

Just a few years ago, the election of Barack Obama signaled to some that the country had arrived at a new reckoning with old categories, that many of America's racial wounds had healed, or that at least it was possible to move on from them.

The term *postracial* was everywhere: in thousands of newspaper articles and op-ed essays and on the lips of political pundits like Chris Matthews of MSNBC, who proudly

> **When people talked about being "postracial," they were often really talking about being "postblack"—or, more charitably, "post-racist-against-blacks."**

said that he forgot, for a moment, that Obama was black. Books were published on subjects like "postracial cinema," the "postracial church" and "postracial black leadership." Data from 2008–2009 showed that one in seven new marriages was between spouses of different racial or ethnic backgrounds. And an article from *The New York Times* in 2011 noted that some people felt that "the blending of the races is a step toward transcending race, to a place where America is free of bigotry, prejudice and programs like affirmative action."

The word *postracial* has been around since at least the early 1970s, when an article in this newspaper used it to describe a coalition of Southern government officials who believed that their region had "entered an era in which race relations are soon to be replaced as a major concern." That didn't happen. When a 21-year-old white supremacist was charged in the fatal shootings of nine African-Americans in Charleston, South Carolina, on June 17, it was a stark reminder that the past half decade has provided little evidence of reckoning or repair. According to a recent Gallup poll, more black Americans in 2015 than in 2014 regard race relations as one of the most pressing problems in the United States. As for the term *postracial*, well, it has mostly disappeared from the conversation, except as sarcastic shorthand.

This is probably how it should be. When people talked about being "postracial," they were often really talking about being "postblack"—or, more charitably, "post-racist-against-blacks." After all, blackness is seen as an opposite to the default—the ideal—of whiteness, and chattel slavery and the legacies it left behind continue to shape American society. Sometimes it seems as if the desire for a "postracial" America is an attempt by white people to liberate themselves from the burden of having to deal with that legacy.

As a child born a few years after *Loving v. Virginia*—the 1967 Supreme Court case that effectively ended miscegenation laws—to a mixed-race couple, I was keenly aware of the ways in which many people, especially liberal white people, saw me as an avatar for a colorblind civilization in which the best of white and black America banded together to move beyond this country's shameful history by birthing beautiful beige-colored babies. I was subject to a certain inquisitiveness, though well meaning, that I found irritating and doubted was directed at my darker-skinned brothers and sisters: questions about which parent was black and which was white; incredulity about my hazel eyes; inquiries about whether I consider myself African-American.

I was a curiosity, and a comfort: a black girl who was just white enough to seem familiar, not foreign, someone who could serve as an emissary or a bridge between blackness and whiteness. It's true that I can move about the world in ways that many other black people cannot; for one thing, I am rarely racially profiled. My choice, if you can call it that, to identify as black is much different from that of, say, my father or even my own sister, whose skin is at least three shades darker than mine. The eagerness with which people gravitate toward me is not shown to many of the other black people I know. These experiences led me to suspect that the breathless "postracial" commentary that attached itself to our current president had as much to do with the fact that he is biracial as with the fact that he is black. His blood relationship to whiteness and its attendant privileges serve as a chaser to the difficult-to-swallow prospect that a black man might achieve ownership of the Oval Office.

My interactions with the world also underscored that biracial children are not in any way created equal—others' interpretations of us are informed by assumptions based on appearance. Few black-white biracial Americans, compared with multiracial Asian-whites, have the privilege of easily "passing": Our blackness defines us and marks us in a way that mixed-race parentage in others does not. As the Pew survey explains, children of Native American–white parents make up over half of the country's multiracial population and, like Asian-white children, are usually thought of as white. The survey also reports that although the number of black-white biracial Americans more than doubled from 2000 to 2010, 69 percent of them say that most others see them solely as black; "for multiracial adults with a black background," Pew notes, "experiences with discrimination closely mirror those of single-race blacks."

On June 11, the same day that the Pew report was released, another provocative narrative about racial politics emerged: that of Rachel Dolezal, a 37-year-old white woman and N.A.A.C.P. leader in Spokane, Washington, who had been masquerading as black for over a decade. Some commentators dispassionately proposed that Dolezal's charade was yet another iteration of the white American tradition of co-opting the black American experience; others, like many of my biracial black-white friends, expressed outrage about her identity theft. Dolezal got to indulge in the myth of the self-made American, of choosing whom she wanted to be. But unlike actual black people, she could discard her putative blackness at any time, which made her performance all the more offensive and absurd. The spectacle of a naturally blond Montana native parading around broadcast and cable news studios insisting that she didn't identify as white reinforced the fact that for many Americans, blackness is impossible to divorce from ideas of what blackness looks like. (In Dolezal's case, that meant well-applied bronzer, braids and a weave.)

Being—or appearing—biracial is a real Rorschach test with regard to how our ideas about race have evolved. For every person who hardly bats an eye at the idea of a light-skinned biracial woman identifying as African-American, there's another person waiting to inform her that she doesn't "look very black" (the white husband of a Korean-American friend) or that she is not actually black at all (an African-American entrepreneur in a professional women's association to which I belong). Which is why, when people I meet ask me, "What are you?" my usual response is to look at them with amusement and shoot back, "What do you think I am?"

Will Today's Hispanics Be Tomorrow's Whites?

By Jamelle Bouie
Slate, April 15, 2014

The Trayvon Martin shooting was hardly in the national consciousness before fault lines emerged around the case. Was Martin as innocent as he seemed? Did Zimmerman fear for his life? Did Martin provoke the incident? Was Zimmerman a racist?

Perhaps most controversial among all of these was the question of identity. Yes, Trayvon Martin was black, but is Zimmerman white? For Martin's sympathizers, the answer was yes. For Zimmerman's, the answers ranged from "it doesn't matter" to he "is actually a Hispanic nonracist person who acted in self-defense."

In their early reports on the case, both CNN and the *New York Times* labeled him "white Hispanic," sparking thunderous condemnation from right-wing critics. At Fox News, contributor Bernard Goldberg *accused* the *Times* of race-baiting. "I guarantee you that if George Zimmerman did something good—if he finished first in his high school graduating class when he was younger—they wouldn't refer to him as a white Hispanic, he'd just be a Hispanic," he wrote. Likewise, *National Review*'s Jonah Goldberg *blasted* several news outlets for "playing the race card" with the term. And in typical paranoid style, *Breitbart*'s Ben Shapiro *accused* CNN of "labeling Zimmerman a 'white Hispanic' in order to maintain the false narrative that the killing was race-based."

For good reason, this debate—whether the half-Peruvian Zimmerman was "Hispanic" or "white"—was quickly overshadowed by the activism and acrimony around Martin's killing. But it's not unimportant, as it reflects the tension and confusion over race in a changing America and offers a twenty-first-century spin on one of the oldest questions in American life: Who is white? This debate is useful to keep in mind as we sift through the information in the Pew Research Center's new—and massive—look at America's shifting demographics.

According to Pew—and echoing the results in the last census—the United States is just a few decades away from its demographic inflection point. Come 2050, only 47 percent of Americans will call themselves white, while the majority will belong to a minority group. Blacks will remain steady at 13 percent of the population, while Asians will grow to 8 percent. Hispanics, on the other hand, will explode to 28 percent of all U.S. population, up from 19 percent in 2010. Immigration is driving this "demographic makeover," specifically the "40 million immigrants who have arrived since 1965, about half of them Hispanics and nearly three-in-ten Asians."

Will white Hispanics see themselves as part of a different race, or will they see themselves as just another kind of white?

But the thing to remember about the Hispanic category, for instance, is that it contains a wide range of colors and ethnicities. In the United States, Hispanics (or more broadly Latinos) include Afro-Brazilians, dark-skinned Puerto Ricans, indigenous Mexicans, Venezuelan mestizos, and European Argentinians, among others.

To say that America will become a majority-minority country is to erase these distinctions and assume that, for now and forever, Latinos will remain a third race, situated next to "non-Hispanic blacks" and "non-Hispanic whites." But, as the Zimmerman controversy illustrates, it's not that simple.

American racial categories are far from fixed, and who counts as white is extremely fluid. "A hundred years ago," writes Ian Haney López in *Dog Whistle Politics*, "firm racial lines elevated Anglo-Saxons over the supposedly degenerate races from southern and eastern Europe." For a large chunk of the nineteenth century—and a good deal of the twentieth—America's intellectual energy was devoted to policing the boundaries of "whiteness." Race "scientists" like William Z. Ripley measured human skulls and examined living standards to delineate the "races" of Europe, linking head shape to supposedly racial qualities like beauty and intelligence. Others used these supposedly objective factors to exclude a variety of different groups—Irish, Italians, Eastern Europeans—from the American racial category, envisioned as a white person of British or German stock. "White race taxonomy," writes Nell Irvin Painter in *The History of White People*, "was evolving into notions of immigration restriction and eugenics."

Over time, however, as new immigrants entered the country and old ones gained access to levers of power and influence, the boundaries grew to include them. As Painter explains, "In their penury and apparent strangeness, the new [Southern and Eastern European] immigrants after 1880 made Irish and Germans immigrants and. . . their more prosperous, better-educated descendants seem acceptably American."

It's hard to say history is repeating itself—the circumstances of the early twenty-first century are vastly different from those of the late nineteenth—but the current period does seem to rhyme with the past. Over the last 50 years of large-scale Latino and Asian immigration, we've seen waves of anti-immigrant hysteria (Proposition 187 in California and the minutemen along the Mexican border), attempts to keep high-achieving immigrants and their children out of elite institutions, and intermarriage leading to assimilation—one of the most famous comedians in the world, Louis C.K., is halfMexican, but to most Americans, he's just a white guy.

Which is to say that, before we begin to say anything about our majority-minority future, we have to consider the ways in which our existing social dynamics and racial boundaries will change in response to the demographic shift.

Going forward, will white Hispanics see themselves as part of a different race—light-skinned but distinct from whites—or will they see themselves as another kind of white? Will the government treat them as white in its forms and surveys, and will so-called traditional white Americans understand them as such? What about the children of mixed marriages? As Pew points out, we live in an age of intermarriage. More than 15 percent of new marriages are between partners of different races, and the large majority of them are Hispanic and Asian "out marriage" to whites. Will these children retain a racial identity, or will they join the vast tapestry of American whiteness?

These are critical questions, since—in a country where white Hispanics are just white, and Asians intermarry at high rates—the white population of the United States could stay steady or actually grow.

Of course, not all Hispanics and Asians will enter the white mainstream. We don't see them in popular culture, but there are sharp racial and class divisions in both groups. Low-income, dark-skinned Latinos and Pacific Islanders, for instance, face prejudice, racism, and a huge array of socioeconomic challenges. And going forward, that might stay the same, as their fair-skinned, more affluent counterparts "become" white. Or, put another way, now might be the last time we have a public debate over the whiteness of a figure like George Zimmerman. To Americans of 2050, the answer would be obvious: "Of course he is."

Pew ends its description of our changing demographics with a small rhetorical flourish: "We were once a black and white country. Now, we're a rainbow."

Or are we? After all, while *we* see the nineteenth century as a world of blacks and whites, that wasn't true for Americans at the time. They saw their United States as diverse as we see ours—a hodgepodge of races and ethnicities, with blacks as the insoluble element. The difference was their construction of race, which placed various Europeans on a convoluted hierarchy of racial difference.

Our hierarchies are a little flatter, and—in public life, at least—we aren't as obsessed with racial boundaries. But both still exist, and they take a familiar form: whites at the top, blacks at the bottom. The future could make a collection of minorities the majority in America, or it could broaden our definition of white, leaving us with a remix of the black-and-white binary. A country where some white people are Asian, some are Hispanic, and the dark-skinned citizens of America—and blacks especially—[are] still a world apart.

The Witnesses

By Jay Caspian Kang
New York Times Magazine, May 4, 2015

In the evening of April 25 at the corner of Pratt and Light Streets, in Baltimore's revitalized downtown district, more than 100 police officers in riot gear stood shoulder to shoulder, shields up. Six officers on horseback fidgeted behind them, staring down at a crowd of about 40, an odd mixture of protesters, journalists and protester-journalists. Earlier in the afternoon, well over a thousand people marched from the Western District police station to City Hall to protest the death of Freddie Gray, a 25-year-old black man whose spinal cord was severely injured while he was in the custody of the Baltimore Police Department. Only a handful of live-streamers, an older man in a kente-cloth *kufi*, five or six teenagers with bandannas drawn across their faces and two young women in cocktail attire who had just been kicked out of a wedding were left. Each person was filming the police.

In the coming days, riots would convulse the city, with young people running through the streets, looting stores and setting fires, and the National Guard descending on their neighborhoods. But this protest looked much like the ones that have characterized the growing movement against police violence. Bodies moved in the dark, but the faces—protesters and police officers alike—were lit up by the thin, lunar glow of cellphone screens.

One protester was DeRay Mckesson, a 29-year-old former school administrator who has spent much of the past nine months attending and catalyzing such protests, from Ferguson, Missouri, last summer and fall, to New York City and Milwaukee in December, to North Charleston, South Carolina, in April. Mckesson, who is from Baltimore, had returned to his hometown not long after Gray's death to join the protests. Now he stood in his usual pose—his slender back straight as a ramrod, phone held in front of angular face, camera lens pointed directly ahead.

The phalanx of police officers began tapping their riot shields with their batons and shouting, "Move back!" Then, in a sloppy, seemingly unrehearsed lock step, they advanced on the protesters.

Tap—

Moooove back.

Tap—

Moooove back.

Mckesson crouched down and angled his phone. On its screen, I could see the dramatic shot he had composed: the faces of police officers, flat and impassive. As the police marched their way up the street, Mckesson posted a Vine, a photo and a 30-second video to his 85,000 Twitter followers. "What in the world is going on?" he asked. "There's, like, how many hundred cops for 40 of us? This is wild." He walked backward at a slow pace, eyes on his screen.

"It's strange to come home after all that time in St. Louis," he said, calmly. "I know it's a cliché, but it's really driven home the saying: 'There's a Mike Brown in every town.'"

Since August 9, 2014, when Officer Darren Wilson of the Ferguson Police Department shot and killed Michael Brown, Mckesson and a core group of other activists have built the most formidable American protest movement of the twenty-first century to date. Their innovation has been to marry the strengths of social media—the swift, morally blunt consensus that can be created by hashtags; the personal connection that a charismatic online persona can make with followers; the broad networks that allow for the easy distribution of documentary photos and videos—with an effort to quickly mobilize protests in each new city where a police shooting occurs.

We often think of online activism as a shallow bid for fleeting attention, but the movement that Mckesson is helping to lead has been able to sustain the country's focus and reach millions of people. Among many black Americans, long accustomed to mistreatment or worse at the hands of the police, the past year has brought on an incalculable sense of anger and despair. For the nation as a whole, we have come to learn the names of the victims—Eric Garner, Tamir Rice, Tony Robinson, Walter Scott, Freddie Gray—because the activists have linked their fates together in our minds, despite their separation by many weeks and thousands of miles.

In the process, the movement has managed to activate a sense of red alert around a chronic problem that, until now, has remained mostly invisible outside the communities that suffer from it. Statistics on the subject are notoriously poor, but evidence does not suggest that shootings of black men by police officers have been significantly on the rise. Nevertheless, police killings have become front-page news and a political flash point, entirely because of the sense of emergency that the movement has sustained.

The movement began with a single image: Michael Brown, lying facedown on the asphalt, a stream of blood running from his head. That picture, combined with the testimony of witnesses who claimed to see the teenager surrender before being shot several times, brought hundreds of people from St. Louis out to the scene of his death the same evening. The following day, August 10, protests began on West Florissant Avenue nearby, as well as outside the Ferguson Police Department; the crowds demanded justice for Brown and that the name of the officer who shot him be released, prompting the police to come out in force. That night, the QuikTrip gas station on West Florissant burned, which in turn brought out the mainstream media and an even more militarized police response. By August 13, images from the Ferguson protests—plumes of tear gas, armored vehicles in the streets, packs

For him, the social network seemed to have become not just the site of revolution but the conduit for his ideas.

of heavily armed police officers wearing military fatigues—were leading the news.

Mckesson watched all this from Minneapolis, where he was working in the public-school system. He was struck by the distance between the sensational accounts of rioting he saw on television and the reports he was reading on Twitter from people in Ferguson, who claimed that the cops had been firing tear gas and rubber bullets into crowds of peaceful protesters. Mckesson decided to go see the protests for himself.

On the morning of August 16, Mckesson drove to St. Louis. Inspired, in part, by the Twitter accounts he had been following—at the time, Mckesson had fewer than 900 followers and tweeted inconsistently—he decided to live-tweet the trip. Setting out, he tweeted: "En route." A couple hours later, he tweeted: "So, this stretch through Iowa has trucks that aren't very good drivers." And when he finally arrived in St. Louis, Mckesson noted: "I should've gotten gas in Iowa. Much more expensive in St. Louis."

Mckesson arrived in Ferguson, and the next day he headed over to West Florissant, where he was tear-gassed. His terse, matter-of-fact updates, which had seemed almost comical when describing the banalities of everyday life, took on a forceful lucidity in the context of the protests, especially when they were accompanied by raw photographs from the scene.

"Y'all, tons of police," he tweeted that night. "Tear gas. It has begun #Ferguson." He added: "Also, the noise sirens are out. Tear gas feels like extreme peppermint tingling. F.Y.I. #Ferguson." Then, about an hour and 30 tweets later: "Phone is dying. I am nowhere near my car. I am lost in #Ferguson. Really bad car accident. Looting across from it. Pray for me. #Ferguson."

Mckesson was radicalized that night. "I just couldn't believe that the police would fire tear gas into what had been a peaceful protest," he told me. "I was running around, face burning, and nothing I saw looked like America to me." He also noticed that his account of that night's tear-gassings, along with a photo he took of the rapper J. Cole, had brought him quite a bit of attention on Twitter. Previously, Mckesson used the social-media platform to post random news articles that interested him, but now he was realizing its documentary power. He quickly grasped that a protester's effectiveness came mostly from his ability to be present in as many places as possible: He had to be on West Florissant when the police rolled up in armored vehicles; inside the St. Louis coffee shop MoKaBe's, a safe haven for the protesters in the city's Shaw neighborhood, when tear gas started to seep in through the front door; in front of the Ferguson Police Department when shots rang out. He had to keep up a steady stream of tweets and carry around a charger so his phone wouldn't die.

Mckesson eventually returned to Minneapolis, but by then he had committed himself to the protests. He started traveling down to St. Louis every weekend. On one of those trips, Mckesson met Johnetta Elzie, a fellow protester who goes by Netta. They became fast friends.

Elzie is "Day 1," the term given to Ferguson protesters who showed up on August 9. She grew up all around St. Louis, spending much of her childhood in the beauty salons where her mother worked. The day Michael Brown was killed, Elzie, who had been mourning the death of her mother, went down to Canfield Green, a housing complex near where Brown was shot, to pay her respects.

The first thing Elzie did was tweet: "It's still blood on the ground where Mike Brown Jr was murdered. A cone in place where his body laid for hours today. #STL #Ferguson." She experimented with other networks to see if they could do a better job of spreading what she was seeing. "I took an Instagram photo—there was one teddy bear; maybe three, four candles on the ground," she told me. "I even tried Tumblr, a social-media platform that I never use. Those videos got hundreds of thousands of reposts."

Over the next few weeks, Elzie, who studied journalism in college, emerged as one of the most reliable real-time observers of the confrontations between the protesters and the police. She took photos of the protest organizers, of the sandwiches she and her friends made to feed other protesters, of the Buddhist monks who showed up at the burned QuikTrip. Mckesson, too, was live-tweeting when he was back in Ferguson, integrating video and referring to protesters and police officers alike by name. Mckesson's tweets were usually sober and detailed, whereas Elzie's were cheerfully sarcastic, mock-heroic and forthright: a running account of events that felt intimate.

Other voices came to the fore as well. There was Bassem Masri, perhaps Ferguson's most famous live-streamer, who attracted tens of thousands of viewers to nightly feeds that showed what the protests looked like beyond the media barricades. Another local activist, Ashley Yates, created T-shirts and hoodies that read "ASSATA TAUGHT ME"—a reference to the former Black Panther Party member Assata Shakur—and that became part of the protest iconography. Clifton Kinnie, a senior in high school, organized other students throughout St. Louis. By the fall, these activists and a handful of others had gone from lone Internet figures to recognized faces of the movement.

Mckesson and Elzie focused much of their attention on criticizing the mainstream media, who devoted too much airtime, they felt, to violence and discord among the protest community. As a corrective, in mid-September, they teamed up with Brittany Packnett, the executive director of St. Louis's Teach for America program, and Justin Hansford, a law professor at St. Louis University, to publish the *This Is the Movement* newsletter, which scrutinized and curated the daily news out of Ferguson. A wide range of readers, from reporters to protesters to officials within the Department of Justice, subscribed. Pretty soon, Mckesson and Elzie were appearing regularly on TV and radio. The two cultivated appealing personas, becoming easily recognizable to their many followers. Mckesson had begun wearing red shoes and a red shirt to protests. Later, he replaced this outfit with a bright blue Patagonia vest, which he now wears everywhere he goes. (Someone created a DeRay's vest

Twitter account.) Elzie often wore dark lipstick, a pair of oversize sunglasses and a leather jacket: the beautician's daughter channeling a Black Panther.

Mckesson and Elzie have always insisted that the movement is leaderless, that it is a communal expression of pent-up anguish spilling onto the streets, but over the fall, they were frequently called upon to serve as its spokespeople. Elzie was invited to conferences and panels, and talked with established social-justice activists around the country about the actions in Ferguson. Mckesson, who was dutifully putting out the newsletter during this time while still working at his job in Minneapolis, began using Twitter to announce actions throughout St. Louis. He and Elzie would tweet a time and location and then wait for the people to show up. By October, they were also being followed by the police, who would sometimes arrive at the scene of the action before the protesters themselves.

Together, Mckesson and Elzie were developing a model of the modern protester: part organizer, part citizen journalist who marches through American cities while texting, as charging cords and battery packs fall out of his pockets. By November 24, when Robert McCulloch, the St. Louis County prosecutor, announced that Darren Wilson would not be indicted on murder charges, a network of hundreds of organizers was already in place, ready to bring thousands of people into the streets with a tweet.

I first met Mckesson on December 7, the 121st day of continuous protests in Ferguson. Three days before, a grand jury in Staten Island decided not to indict Officer Daniel Pantaleo, of the New York Police Department, on charges of killing Eric Garner, an unarmed black man, by choking him. Demonstrations broke out across the city, with major bridges and tunnels shut down every night by protesters, and Mckesson traveled to New York to join them. In Grand Central Terminal, I ran into a group of 30 protesters who had just performed a "die-in," lying quietly on the ground for four and a half minutes—the duration symbolizing the four and a half hours Michael Brown's body was left in the street. A handful of police officers stood by, looking bored and stern.

The crowd headed outside into a cold rain and started up the chants: "Black lives matter!" "I can't breathe!" "We need freedom from these racist-ass cops!" Three young white protesters in front of me—all dressed alike in thick, fur-fringed coats covered with see-through, formless rain ponchos—marched in a straight line with their phones set to video mode, holding them solemnly in the air like processional candles. At 42nd Street and Fifth Avenue, near the New York Public Library's main branch, I saw Mckesson, recognizing him by his blue Patagonia vest. He was walking at the edge of the crowd, head buried in his phone.

We walked with the group until it came to a halt in Times Square. Mckesson stood under a bank awning, shivering. When I asked why he didn't wear something warmer than a vest, he smiled and said, "I feel bulletproof in this."

An elderly man in an orange rain parka walked up to us and said he had been inspired by Mckesson's Twitter account and wanted to thank him for the work he did in Ferguson. "You just keep it up and stay safe," the man said. Mckesson, who speaks in a high-pitched, singsong voice, thanked the man for his kindness before turning his attention back to his phone.

After the protest, Mckesson and I retired to a nearby cafe in a Japanese bookstore. Mckesson took out a large charging device, roughly the size of a deck of cards, and plugged in his white iPhone 6 Plus. Then, reaching into a vest pocket, he pulled out another white iPhone and plugged that in as well. Dozens of Twitter notifications piled up on his screen, and Mckesson shared them with me. Earlier that day, he asked if any of his followers knew the address of William Bratton, New York's police commissioner, thinking that he might organize a protest.

In response, one person called Mckesson a "Mongoloid," while others asked if he was threatening Bratton's life. Some tweets were obliquely menacing: "I look forward to seeing your ass rightfully beaten" or "I hope one of his Rottweilers takes a bite out of your ass." The tone of these replies went beyond standard trolling—an odd familiarity ran through them. The Twitter users, especially the more vicious ones, seemed to actually know Mckesson and some of his fellow protesters.

"This is, like, every day," Mckesson told me. "The trolls are wild. They know where I am at all times."

Mckesson had come to New York to attend workshops and to spread the word about actions in the city. He wanted to see if the wave of dissent that had gathered in the streets of Ferguson and radiated out across the Internet could become something substantial and organized. Two weeks later, after a series of actions involving tens of thousands of people, the murder of two New York police officers had a chilling effect on the street protests. For now, though, Mckesson was in his element, using his phone to create a connection between the outrage on social media and the actions in the streets.

In the cafe, surrounded by shrink-wrapped pastries and a gathering of lucky cat figurines, he answered WhatsApp messages from fellow organizers and text messages from friends, and tried to fact-check a future tweet. When he wasn't sending out data, he was swiping down on Twitter to refresh his timeline with such frequency that it looked as if he were petting his phone.

"When I tweet, I'm mostly preaching to the choir," he said. "But the heart of the movement is in the actions. It's in shutting down streets, shutting down Walmarts, shutting down any place where people feel comfortable. We want to make people feel as uncomfortable as we feel when we hear about Mike, about Eric Garner, about Tamir Rice. We want them to experience what we go through on a daily basis."

Mckesson is a restless man. In the time we spent together, the only occasion I can recall him sitting in one spot for more than 15 minutes was in an Applebee's in St. Louis, where, after a long day of protests and TV interviews, he laid his head down next to a plate of salmon—he almost always orders salmon—and fell asleep. But his habit of seeing every minute of relaxation as a minute lost serves his activism well. In the rare quiet moments between police shootings and actions, Mckesson tweets and retweets stats, trivia, inspirational messages and the names of the dead.

NYC TV stations report crimes committed by blacks more frequently than they even occur.

Love is the Why.

Justice is not an abstract concept. Justice is a living Mike Brown. Justice is Tamir playing outside again. Justice is Darren Wilson in jail.

I once watched Mckesson spend a good five minutes trying to edit down a tweet that ran long before calling one of his closest friends. They talked through the tweet together. Ultimately they landed on this: "Blackness in America is never a question of afraid or unafraid; it's a matter of varying degrees of fear, as we are victims of state terror." This obsessive focus is evident in every part of Mckesson's life. He makes a point to never curse in public. He is too busy to watch movies or television. He does not have a boyfriend (some in the movement have objected to having a gay man in a prominent position). And although fellow protesters sometimes call him "the storyteller," his tweets gain their force from their concision and relentlessness rather than from narrative flair.

Mckesson grew up in Baltimore, the son of drug addicts; his mother left the family when he was 3, so his father and great-grandmother raised him and his sister. Starting in sixth grade, Mckesson was elected to the student government every year all the way through college. He went to Bowdoin, the small, elite liberal-arts college in Maine, paying part of his own way through a work-study job in the mailroom. During lulls, he would study the rows of mailboxes in the student union, trying to learn the name of every student on campus, hoping it would give him an edge in the coming campaigns. He also worked as a campus tour guide and diligently honed his patter. When he found that he was stumbling through the list of languages Bowdoin offered, he practiced reciting them. When he saw that prospective students weren't reacting to his presentation as enthusiastically as he hoped, he tweaked his delivery until he got it right. There is a touching earnestness to Mckesson that makes you want to believe everything he says.

"There was a whole generation of Bowdoin students who came to the college because of the campus tours DeRay would do," said Barry Mills, the president of Bowdoin, who considers Mckesson a close friend. "He's always known how to inspire a group of people, so it doesn't surprise me that he's become a thought leader for what's going on out in Ferguson."

After graduating in 2007, Mckesson joined Teach for America and taught middle school for two years in East New York, Brooklyn, before moving back home to Baltimore to work in H.R. for the city's schools. He developed a reputation as a ruthless administrator—every hiring and firing was justified, in his own mind, by what was best for the kids in the district.

His career, both academic and professional, was built on an unusual faith in effecting change from within a bureaucratic organization, whether a student government or the city public-school system. But when he saw Michael Brown lying dead in the street, he felt as if he had come up against the edge of that belief. "I kept thinking, Kids can't learn if they're dead," he told me.

There is an indelible picture of Mckesson taken on his first full day in Ferguson. He is standing by the side of the road, right fist raised defiantly in the air; in his left hand, he holds a cardboard sign that reads: "My Blackness Is Not a Weapon. #handsup #dontshoot." Behind him are the dull greenery of St. Louis in August and hints of the one-story, uniform brick houses off West Florissant. After a night of photographing and documenting everyone else at the protest, Mckesson, the education executive with a six-figure salary, finally turned the camera around on himself, revealing the awkward resolve of a student-body president who had lost confidence in all those systems and was trying something new.

In March, Mckesson and Elzie traveled to Selma, Alabama, for the fiftieth-anniversary commemoration of Bloody Sunday, the pivotal moment in the civil rights era when protesters marching on the Edmund Pettus Bridge were brutally attacked on national television by Alabama state troopers. I stood with Mckesson on the bridge. "We're really up high," he said, staring down at the brown waters of the Alabama River. "Can you imagine having all those troopers on horseback riding toward you, trying to beat you down? Where do you run? You definitely can't jump over the side here." All day, hundreds of tourists had been walking over the bridge, solemnly touching its supports and snapping selfies in front of its historical markers. If Mckesson was feeling the sway of the fiftieth anniversary, he betrayed no emotion. Instead, he asked me how far I thought the drop was down to the river, and started searching Google for answers.

Mckesson and Elzie have each expressed ambivalence over whether the youth movement should try to draw from the popular image of the civil rights movement. They worry that the constant comparisons with something that happened 50 years ago will dilute the immediacy of today's protests. Much as they admire the Rev. Dr. Martin Luther King Jr.—each is well versed in his writings—they feel his legacy has been distorted. He is held up as an avatar of genteel protest, invoked by conservative politicians and leaders in the black community as a way to discredit their movement. Mckesson and Elzie frequently point out that King was in fact a revolutionary who believed in the power of confrontation, and that it's a crime against American history to confuse the real King with an appealingly passive one. To make their point, they participated in an action called #ReclaimMLK, which sought to counter "efforts to reduce a long history marred with the blood of countless women and men into iconic images of men in suits behind pulpits."

"Also," Elzie often says whenever someone brings up King as a way of questioning their work, "they killed him too."

If you ask Mckesson and Elzie why there is no central figure in today's movement, they will again insist on the advantages of leaderlessness. If you bring up legislative reform, they will point out that the Voting Rights Act of 1965 has been all but rolled back and that their aims go well beyond small changes to the criminal-justice system. If you bring up nonviolence as the only civilized way to effect change, they will recite King's words: "A riot is the language of the unheard," or they will say they don't condone rioting, but they understand it. Their resistance to confining the civil rights movement to a museum made Mckesson and Elzie an awkward fit for Selma, which was filled with people doing just that.

At dinner that night in Montgomery, Mckesson and Elzie received the news that a 19-year-old unarmed black man, Tony Robinson, had been shot and killed in Madison, Wisconsin. They spent the meal with their heads bent over their phones, compiling and tweeting out all the information they could confirm through their sources in the Madison protest community. Piece by piece, a digital portrait of Robinson emerged: a photo of him in a graduation gown, his arm around a female friend; a few tweets he sent out in the days before his death. Then, around midnight, dinner long gone by, Mckesson sighed and held up his phone to show Elzie a photo of the front steps of Robinson's home, which were streaked with blood. "That's where they dragged him out of his house," Mckesson said.

The next morning, in the lobby of the education center at Selma's George C. Wallace State Community College, Mckesson and Elzie took selfies with Diane Nash and her son Douglass Bevel. In the early 1960s, Nash, along with Bernard Lafayette Jr., John Lewis and others, founded the Student Nonviolent Coordinating Committee (S.N.C.C.). She also helped organize the Freedom Riders, helped lead the march from Selma to Montgomery and played a key role in the push to integrate lunch counters throughout the South. Between photos, Nash talked to another admirer about a call she had received from one of Bobby Kennedy's aides, who pleaded with her to cancel an action because Kennedy thought there was a good chance people would be killed.

Mckesson and Elzie seemed almost star-struck, peppering Nash with questions about the civil rights movement and then posting her answers on Twitter. Mckesson told Nash she needed to get on Twitter to share her wisdom.

"Twitter?" Nash asked. "I just figured out how to have a Facebook."

"Twitter is the revolution, Ms. Nash," Mckesson said.

For him, the social network seemed to have become not just the site of revolution but the conduit for his ideas. Two days later, on the anniversary of Bloody Sunday, Mckesson was scheduled to speak at a rally before a ceremonial crossing of the bridge. As we drove from Montgomery to Selma, Mckesson wrote drafts of tweets on his phone.

"I do this to make sure what I say can be tweetable," he explained. "And it helps me be precise in what I say."

He muttered lines to himself. "We must always confront," he said, but something about the phrase displeased him. He deleted the words and started from the top.

Mckesson and Elzie arrived in Selma and walked to the Brown Chapel A.M.E. Church, the starting point for the original march across the bridge. Inside, Attorney General Eric Holder Jr. was addressing the congregation. The crowd outside was made up largely of union members carrying placards for their local chapters. Mckesson, Elzie and Packnett, who arrived the night before, tried to find a contact who would take them to the foot of the bridge, where Mckesson would speak. After 20 minutes of confusion, they walked back through the crowd to a small auditorium off Broad Street, where Bernard Lafayette Jr. was holding a book signing. When they walked in, an elderly woman said, loudly enough for all to hear, "Social media just showed up."

In the end, Mckesson did not get to deliver his speech. The Reverend Al Sharpton, who followed Holder, went long, and there was no time left.

In an interview with *People* magazine to promote the release of the film *Selma*, Oprah Winfrey voiced some of the questions skeptics have had about the modern protest movement. "I think it's wonderful to march and to protest, and it's wonderful to see, all across the country, people doing it," she said. "But what I'm looking for is some kind of leadership to come out of this to say: 'This is what we want. This is what has to change, and these are the steps that we need to take to make these changes, and this is what we're willing to do to get it.'"

Certain factions of the movement have made explicit demands. During the Eric Garner protests in New York, a group called the Justice League NYC, which is affiliated with Harry Belafonte, came out with a list that included the immediate firing of Officer Pantaleo and the appointment of a special prosecutor. In the wake of the Department of Justice's report on Ferguson, some people within the St. Louis protest community demanded the recall of Mayor James Knowles III. But on the whole, the movement does shy away from specific policy prescriptions. Instead, the work seems to be aimed at an abrupt, wide-scale change in consciousness, channeling the grief and anger that these police killings engender around the country. The pipelines for that energy are still under construction, but asking the leaders of the youth movement what they plan on doing with it is akin to barging into a funeral and asking the mourners why they haven't donated their inheritance to charity yet.

Soon after I met them, Mckesson and Elzie took me on a tour of some of the sites around St. Louis where black men have been killed by the police. Many of the buildings that burned during the protests were standing in ruin. "They want to leave them all up," Elzie said, referring to the St. Louis city government. "They want this to be a museum of black rage." As we drove from the Six Stars Market, where Kajieme Powell, 25, was shot in August, to the gas station where Antonio Martin, 18, was killed in December, Elzie talked about the emotion behind the movement and how, for many people in St. Louis, the Ferguson protests represented the first time they were able to collectively voice their frustrations with the police. "Our demand is simple," Elzie said. "Stop killing us."

The starkness of that demand has been enough to create some measure of change, purely by creating an atmosphere of awareness and constant urgency around an issue that was previously ignored. Although Ferguson's mayor was not recalled, the Department of Justice report did lead to the resignation of the police chief, the city manager and a handful of city employees who sent racist emails. The swiftness with which the movement now acts, and the volume of people it can bring out to every protest, have turned every police killing into a national referendum on the value of black lives in America.

In April, after cellphone video footage showed a North Charleston police officer firing eight times at the back of a 50-year-old black man named Walter Scott as he was running away, the officer was arrested and booked on murder charges the same day, and nearly every prospective candidate in the coming presidential election sub-sequently released a statement, expressing horror at Scott's death and promising to address criminal-justice-system reform. Later that month, after riots broke out in Baltimore, Hillary Clinton gave a speech at Columbia University in which she explicitly allied herself with the goals of the Black Lives Matter movement, and im-plicitly rejected some policies that her husband put in place during his presidency. Her proposals were hardly specific or new: widespread adoption of body cameras by police officers, "a renewed focus on working with communities to prevent crime" and a call for a "true national debate" on how to end the "era of mass incarceration," but the fact that Clinton chose to address these issues at such length suggests that police reform will be an unavoidable subject during the campaign season. "What we've seen in Baltimore should, indeed does, tear at our soul," Clinton said. "And from Ferguson to Staten Island to Baltimore, the patterns have become unmistak-able and undeniable." She listed the names of Walter Scott, Tamir Rice, Eric Gar-ner and Freddie Gray, and called for "real reforms that can be felt on our streets, in our courthouses and our jails and prisons, in communities too long neglected."

Perhaps the most telling evidence of change was the charges filed on May 1 against six Baltimore police officers related to the death of Freddie Gray, which ranged from misconduct in office to second-degree depraved heart murder. While making the announcement, Marilyn Mosby, the Baltimore state's attorney, said: "To the people of Baltimore and the demonstrators across America, I heard your call for 'no justice, no peace.' Your peace is sincerely needed as I work to deliver justice on behalf of this young man."

The attention that political figures are paying to the movement points to real anxiety that African-American voters who supported President Obama won't turn out again. "This issue is at the forefront of people in the black community," Quentin James, co-founder of the public-affairs firm Vestige Strategies, which specializes in engaging communities of color, told me. "Not voting is a choice, and many may choose to stay home. If you look at a pivotal state like Ohio, African-Americans ended up overvoting in 2012. If they undervote in 2016, the election becomes a little bit shakier."

In talking about the problem of police violence at all, these national political figures are reversing a three-decade presumption within the Democratic Party, one established by Bill Clinton himself in 1994, that there is zero incentive to advocate for the rights of criminal suspects. "The narrative used to be: 'We support the police and whatever police unions say,'" James said. "That has changed. Technology, hav-ing a video camera anywhere, has changed the game."

Most of the activists are deeply skeptical that the candidates will follow through on their promises. Rachel Gilmer, the associate director for the African American Policy Forum, pointed to the long history of Democratic candidates who have "em-braced rhetoric that implies their willingness and readiness to produce systemic change. However, once they've solidified our support and are elected into office, we've seen that they aren't willing to confront or align themselves with the powers, systems and interests that continue to exploit black lives." Gilmer went on to say that, absent a candidate who would be willing to address white supremacy directly, many within the movement would be content to opt out of voting for "the lesser of two evils."

But perhaps the question of political follow-through is misplaced. "Black lives matter" is a vital statement, especially when people are confronted with all the footage that shows police officers who may not agree. But it is more a provocation than a platform, a phrase that might be more appropriate for a rally than a sustained political movement. Jim Crow was an evil that could be addressed by Congress and argued against before the Supreme Court. But how do you legislate the worth of black lives? Could a law force a police officer to cut out the possible prejudice and fear he feels when he sees a young black man, however seemingly unarmed, reach for his waistband?

For now, the victories of the movement are difficult to quantify—the paradox, perhaps, of a movement that exists to raise awareness of death. Shortly after Tony Robinson was shot and killed in Madison, Mike Koval, the city's police chief, released the name of the officer involved and visited Robinson's mother. In an interview with CNN, Koval said: "We have a person of color cut down in his prime—he was unarmed—by a police officer. So whether I like it or not, I am inextricably tied to the Ferguson phenomenon."

"Do I think that was influenced by the protests in Ferguson?" Mckesson said. "Yes. But Tony's still dead, so how do you call that a win?"

On April 26, a bright, warm Sunday in Baltimore, Mckesson attended Freddie Gray's wake. Across the street from the funeral home, a group of demonstrators held up signs that read: "We are ONE Baltimore," "Our hearts are with you" and "We grieve with you." Television crews had set up nearby. A cable-news anchor grabbed Mckesson and said, "It's the esteemed DeRay." The two had met back in St. Louis. Mckesson agreed to come back later that afternoon to record a short interview.

> **The swiftness with which the movement now acts . . . [has] turned every police killing into a national referendum on the value of black lives.**

Inside, Gray's body was laid out behind a gauzy shroud. His head, swollen and shiny, was covered by a white baseball cap. A pair of spotless white sneakers had been placed on his feet.

Looking at the body, I couldn't help thinking that in the coming months, more incidents would arise in more American cities. Nobody can predict where and when these killings may happen, only that they will happen, and that the movement will continue to draw attention to them, and that the sense of grief within black America and of constant siege at the hands of the police will not abate.

"They never look like they do in life," Mckesson said. "Being back here, it reminds me of how many funerals we attend."

We walked back to Mckesson's rental car. A big man in a tank top stood in the center of the road, holding up a sign that asked passing drivers to honk for Freddie Gray. "We come in peace!" he screamed. "We come in peace!"

I asked Mckesson what his thoughts were after seeing Gray's body.

"I just tweeted my thoughts," Mckesson said. Over the five months I had been following him and Elzie around, from Ferguson to New York to Selma and now to Baltimore, I found that Mckesson often tweeted the answers to my questions before I could think to ask them. I took out my phone to check Twitter, but this time Mckesson saved me the effort.

"I'm not desensitized to death," he said. "I just expect trauma now and am trying to steel myself for what's coming next." For the first time since I met him, Mckesson seemed overcome by emotion. He turned his head away and covered the bridge of his nose with his hand.

"It's going to be a long summer," he said.

Head of Hispanic Advocacy Group: Trump's Remarks Racist

By Gabriel Debenedetti
Politico, July 14, 2015

Donald Trump is no Republican sideshow, the country's largest Latino advocacy organization is warning. He's a real, potentially long-term hindrance to the party's chances of capturing any significant portion of the Hispanic vote in 2016's presidential election.

That's the message Janet Murguía, the leader of the National Council of La Raza, sent in an interview ahead of her Tuesday afternoon speech that will close the group's annual convention—and that will label the presidential candidate's remarks about Mexican immigrants, "by definition, racism."

In a speech to an audience of Hispanic activists that heard Democratic presidential candidates Hillary Clinton, Bernie Sanders and Martin O'Malley pitch themselves while they criticized Trump on Monday, Murguía plans to call on Republican leaders and candidates to aggressively repudiate Trump's statement—and reiterations—that Mexican immigrants are "bringing drugs, they're bringing crime, they're rapists," according to an advance copy of the speech provided exclusively to *Politico*.

"To the leadership of the Republican Party and its candidates for president, I have this to say: What's your excuse?" she will ask. "The clock is ticking. Trump keeps doubling down."

The stark warning sent by the former Clinton administration official whose group has previously hosted Republican presidents—including George H.W. Bush and George W. Bush— came as Trump climbs in national and early-state polls. His shadow looms over the annual convention of the generally left-leaning grass-roots group that supports immigration reform, a convention that saw no Republican candidates in attendance this year.

While Democrats have universally decried Trump's comments—and used them to portray the Republican Party as a backward and bigoted institution—some Republicans have been far more cautious, eyeing the candidate's rising poll numbers as evidence of actual support on the ground for his message.

The message sent by the influential Latino group Tuesday is unlikely to immediately sway large swaths of GOP leadership, but it puts further pressure on a party that has struggled to relate to the crucial voting bloc in recent years.

"Head of Hispanic Advocacy Group: Trump's Remarks Racist" by Gabriel Debenedetti. Originally published in *Politico*, July 14, 2015.

Murguía said she has not heard from any Republican leader since Trump entered the race with a strict anti–illegal immigration message, and other candidates—including Jeb Bush—declined invitations to Kansas City. (Trump was not invited.)

GOP leaders' refusal to repudiate Trump weighs more heavily on the party every day as it strays further from its post-2012 report outlining a path to reconciling with Latino voters, Murguía said, though she does plan to acknowledge Bush and Sen. Lindsey Graham as two candidates who have distanced themselves from Trump in her address.

> While Democrats have universally decried Trump's comments—and used them to portray the Republican Party as a backward and bigoted institution—some Republicans have been far more cautious, eyeing the candidate's rising poll numbers as evidence of actual support on the ground for his message.

Pointing to businesses that have severed ties with the billionaire and name-checking Republican leaders who made controversial but principled choices for minority groups—from Abraham Lincoln, to Ronald Reagan, to Nikki Haley—the Hispanic leader will make the case that there is an easy way for GOP members to show Latino voters that they care.

"Are they so afraid of the 'Trump wing' of the party that they're willing to pass up a chance to make their case to the nation's largest ethnic minority and its fastest-growing group of voters?" she will ask.

"They're perilously close to really damaging their brand with Latino voters, and time is not their friend," she said in a back room of the sprawling convention center hosting the conference on Monday evening. "The longer this goes, the more difficult and damaging it is with the Latino vote."

After Barack Obama was reelected in 2012 the Republican National Committee commissioned a so-called autopsy report that eventually outlined ways for the party to climb back into the White House. A top priority was appealing to Hispanic voters, but many of its recommended steps for doing so—like embracing comprehensive immigration reform—have fallen by the wayside.

"What's so remarkable here is they wrote their own playbook about what went wrong and what they needed to do to fix it with the Latino electorate after the poor showing by candidate Romney last time," Murguía said. "And yet, it feels like at every turn they have ignored it, walked away from it, refused to follow it, and it's hard to know why. Because they actually did have a good plan when they had that autopsy."

The recent dustup over Trump's comments has seen Democratic candidates push immigration reform particularly strongly on the campaign trail, further drawing contrasts by portraying Trump as a de facto spokesman for his party.

"The real problem isn't that the Republicans have such a hate-spewing character running for president—the problem is that it's so hard to tell him apart from other candidates," said O'Malley, the former Maryland governor, on Monday afternoon.

"I don't have to wait to become president to take a stand right here, right now, against the divisive rhetoric that demonizes immigrants and their families," Clinton said soon after.

Still, Murguía said, even if the controversy helps elect a pro–immigration reform Democrat, if there is no clean resolution within the Republican Party, longer-term fixes to the immigration debate are unlikely to come anytime soon.

"When one party is AWOL in a presidential election as it relates to a significant voting bloc, it's not good for us at the end of the day, to get those permanent solutions that we need," she explained. "It's a bad sign for the future of the country if the parties are not showing up to engage voters directly."

The Rebirth of Black Rage

By Mychal Denzel Smith
The Nation, August 13, 2015

There are two quotes from September 2, 2005, that have become fixtures in our cultural and political language, and each sums up the ways in which Americans with differing perspectives came to view the disaster of Hurricane Katrina. The first is from George W. Bush: Five days after Katrina tore through the Gulf Coast region, the president landed in Louisiana facing heavy criticism for his administration's slow response to the devastation. Touring the state with FEMA director Michael Brown—the only person who'd been more heavily criticized for the government's inadequate response—Bush turned to the man he'd placed in charge of disaster relief and said, "Brownie, you're doing a heckuva job." Part of Bush's appeal had always been his folksiness, but it offered no solace here. His comment only served to further exemplify his ineptitude.

The other quote—what Bush would later call the worst moment of his presidency—came at an unexpected time from a rather unexpected source.

Later that same evening, after Bush's "heckuva job" comment, NBC did what television networks do during times of disaster and hosted a celebrity telethon. Faith Hill, Harry Connick Jr., Claire Danes, Hilary Swank, Lindsay Lohan, Leonardo DiCaprio, and others stood before an audience of millions, accompanied by the pictures of despair that were still streaming from the gulf—New Orleans in particular.

Also invited was Kanye West, one of the more popular entertainers in the country at the time. He was paired with Mike Myers, famous for his performances as Austin Powers and as the voice of *Shrek*. Myers read from a teleprompter about the suffering in New Orleans, attempting to build up sympathy before the big ask. When it was West's turn, he deviated from the script and started speaking from his heart.

"I hate the way they portray us in the media," Kanye said. "You see a black family, it says, 'They're looting.' You see a white family, it says, 'They're looking for food.' And, you know, it's been five days because most of the people are black. . . . America is set up to help the poor, the black people, the less well-off, as slow as possible."

Myers attempted to rebound, returning to the teleprompter script. The folks in the control room at NBC must have been hoping that West would do the same. Perhaps they weren't familiar with his brash reputation, or perhaps they thought he would rein himself in, in service of charity. But Kanye wasn't done: He still needed to deliver what would become one of my generation's greatest moments of live television. Speaking as if he were reading from the teleprompter, his cadence straddling the line between stiff and natural, he looked straight into the camera and said, "George Bush doesn't care about black people."

Had this happened even five years earlier, it would have been newsy fodder for comedians and might even have made its way into some year-end retrospectives. But it would also have receded more easily into a cultural footnote, a had-to-see-it-to-believe-it moment in television. In September 2005, however, millennials were already taking more direct control of our media diets; we were deciding for ourselves which moments were fleeting and which were definitive. YouTube had launched earlier that year and was already starting to catch on; the idea of the Internet providing video on demand was becoming more of the norm. I was back on campus for my second year of college when this telethon aired, and for weeks afterward, if someone mentioned that they had missed Kanye's declaration, another person would open a laptop, conduct a quick Google search, and pull up the video for a crowd of onlookers. Facebook, founded the previous year, didn't yet support video links, but we could all post on one another's walls some variation of jokes involving West, Bush, or not caring about black people. With these new technological possibilities, and the most succinct political statement of the year, West was able to further ingratiate himself with a generation of young people who already loved his music, but who now had, in him, our first relatable expression of black rage on a national stage.

* * *

Black rage, as a political message, had all but disappeared from the cultural and political landscape by the time my generation came of age. The aspirations of the black political class had shifted from the anger that animated the civil-rights and Black Power era to seeking influence through electoral politics, where black rage does not translate into votes. Jesse Jackson had gone from agitator and organizer to presidential candidate, while Oakland, New Orleans, Chicago, Baltimore, New York, and many other cities had voted their first black mayors into office, and Douglas Wilder, in my home state of Virginia, had become the nation's first elected black governor. The Rev. Al Sharpton could still command media attention, but his expressions of rage were diluted by his celebrity-activist status and the larger-than-life persona that made him a prime target for caricature.

The world of hip-hop that West came out of had also long since excised political anger in favor of narratives of material wish fulfillment. Of course, there were always artists like Dead Prez and the Coup, groups with a radical, socialist Black Power message, but the days of Public Enemy and NWA selling millions of records of uncut black rage and becoming part of mainstream American culture were no more. Whereas Ice Cube had once crashed the *Billboard* charts with an album featuring the song "I Wanna Kill [Uncle] Sam," by the time Kanye West reached prominence, most rappers were searching for an "In da Club" clone.

That's what was important about West's "George Bush doesn't care about black people" comment. This kind of rhetorical expression of black rage was marginalized throughout most of the relatively prosperous 1990s, when there was no longer a Reagan or a Bush to serve as an identifiable enemy, and the nation's children were being taught that racism was essentially over because we were committed to celebrating multiculturalism.

The second Bush proved an easier foil than his Democratic predecessor, but his historic appointments of Colin Powell and Condoleezza Rice gave him the sort of symbolic cover we've come to accept as evidence that racism is a nonfactor. In 2001, when Bush took office, a Gallup poll showed that 32 percent of black people believed that "relations between blacks and whites" would eventually be worked out, and by 2004 that number had risen to 43 percent.

Black rage, at its most potent, cuts through that kind of bullshit. Black rage announces itself at the Women's Convention in Akron, Ohio, and says, "Ain't I a woman?" Black rage stands before hundreds of thousands at the Lincoln Memorial and says, "America has given the Negro people a bad check, a check which has come back marked 'insufficient funds.'" Black rage says to the Democratic National Convention, "I'm sick and tired of being sick and tired." Black rage says "Fuck tha Police" and "Fight the Power."

At its best, black rage speaks to the core concerns of black people in America, providing a radical critique of the system of racism that has upheld all of our institutions and made living black in America a special form of hell. But that anger has not only drawn attention to injustice; it has driven people to action, sparking movements and spurring them forward. At the very least, the public expression of black rage has allowed communities and people who have felt isolated in their own anger to know that they are not alone.

This is what West's telethon moment did. It was replayed over and over, adopted as slang, fit to whatever situation one was in, because it gave language to the pain we felt watching the nightmare in New Orleans play out after Hurricane Katrina made landfall. When the levees broke and the water rose, a city full of black people attempted to wade through it alone. The sick, the young, the elderly were being left for dead in one of the most wealthy countries in the world. The media spoke of people attempting to survive as if they were savages (a study by linguist Geoffrey Nunberg showed that in articles that used either "refugee" or "evacuee" to describe the survivors, "refugee" was far more likely—68 versus 32 percent—to appear in stories that also mentioned "poor" and/or "black" people). And you couldn't help but think, because you knew it was true, that had this been a city with a larger white population, there wouldn't have been so much death and destruction, or at least there would have been greater relief.

When West said, "George Bush doesn't care about black people," he wasn't just speaking about George W. Bush. It was an indictment of an America that doesn't care about black people and that elected a president to carry on the tradition.

* * *

There was a sign, a few years later, that the black rage to which Kanye gave voice might turn into a movement. In 2007, young people of color led the charge seeking justice for the Jena Six, a group of teenage boys in Jena, Louisiana, who had been charged with attempted murder for what amounted to a schoolyard fight. Thousands of young black people used social media to raise awareness of their case, with new Facebook groups dedicated to justice for the Jena Six appearing nearly every day during the summer of 2007. Hundreds traveled to Louisiana, and thousands marched on the day that Mychal Bell was to be sentenced; he had been convicted of lesser but still serious felony charges that could have sent him to prison for up to 22 years. Thousands of students organized protests on their college campuses in solidarity. Al Sharpton called it the "beginning of the twenty-first-century civil-rights movement." At the time, it truly felt that way.

But then Barack Obama happened.

In 2008, young black people turned out to vote for Obama at historic levels, helping to ensure that he would become the first black president of the United States. But this meant the activist energy that had been building since Hurricane Katrina, and had caught a bit more momentum with the Jena Six, was being redirected to electoral politics and the messaging of Obama's candidacy. Black rage was being channeled into black hope. On its face, that isn't entirely bad, but the particular brand of black hope that Obama represented was one that muted black rage, and its possibilities, altogether.

This was first evident in Obama's famous speech on race. During the 2008 campaign, the then-senator had to address the controversy that had arisen around his attendance at the Trinity United Church of Christ in Chicago, presided over by the Rev. Jeremiah Wright. The pastor was in the spotlight after tapes were uncovered by ABC News in which he was heard saying things like "God damn America for treating our citizens as less than human. God damn America for as long as she acts like she is God and she is supreme." Obama's association with Wright was used by his opponents to paint him as some kind of secret black radical, obviously unfit for the presidency. Obama needed to distance himself from the pastor who had officiated at his wedding and baptized his children.

> **Black rage is about holding America accountable. It does not distract "attention from solving real problems"; it illuminates those problems and asks America to confront their roots.**

He accomplished this in what has become known as the "Philadelphia race speech." In it, Obama denounced Wright's inflammatory rhetoric, saying that his words had the "potential . . . to widen the racial divide" and that he obviously didn't agree with everything his former pastor had to say. But he also said that Wright was like family and that the Obamas couldn't disown him.

The speech was regarded as an instant classic, a treatise on race in America that we all needed to hear, from the first viable black presidential candidate in our history. But it was also the first major speech by the first viable black presidential candidate to throw water on the flames of black rage.

"That anger may not get expressed in public, in front of white coworkers or white friends," Obama said. "But it does find voice in the barbershop or the beauty shop or around the kitchen table. At times, that anger is exploited by politicians, to gin up votes along racial lines, or to make up for a politician's own failings. . . .

"That anger is not always productive; indeed, all too often it distracts attention from solving real problems; it keeps us from squarely facing our own complicity within the African-American community in our own condition; it prevents the African-American community from forging the alliances it needs to bring about real change."

But black rage is about holding America accountable. It does not distract "attention from solving real problems"; it illuminates those problems and asks America to confront their roots. If black rage has prevented alliances from forging, those are likely not alliances that would have yielded much in the way of progress anyway.

As president, Obama continued to blunt the edge of black rage, at a time when the reasons for that anger were stacking up in plain sight. In fairness, his job as president is not to represent black America—and if he were ever to register any type of anger in office, the already racist coverage that follows him would only worsen. That doesn't, however, mean that he needed to make black anger seem unjustified or undignified. As president, he speaks with a different moral authority for many people. Because he is the first black president, that moral authority is all the more highly regarded when he is speaking about race.

When Henry Louis Gates Jr. was arrested in front of his own home, Obama's response was to call him to the White House garden for a beer summit with the arresting officer, thereby sending the message that racial profiling is, meh, not that big a deal. It didn't even matter that this happened to a celebrated Harvard professor and PBS documentarian who serves as an avatar for black mainstream assimilation and acceptance—or that Gates himself had been enraged. Obama's solution was to calm the black anger down, come together over a pint, and talk it out.

This invalidation of black rage felt even more insidious when Obama used the tragedy of Trayvon Martin's death and the subsequent acquittal of George Zimmerman to reinforce ideas about black male criminality. In his remarks following the verdict, Obama at first did what no other president has had the capacity to do: He spoke about Martin's death in very personal terms, including the experience of being racially profiled and living with the burden of the stereotypes attached to young black men. It represented the best of what having a black president has meant. But then he pivoted and said, "I think the African-American community is also not naive in understanding that, statistically, somebody like Trayvon Martin was probably statistically more likely to be shot by a peer than he was by somebody else."

False moral equivalencies of this kind are a pattern for the president when discussing race. Whereas Obama was uniquely positioned to relate Martin's story to his own, as the first black president, he has also been uniquely positioned to speak with authority on the ways that racism has built America. But even when he's risen to the task, Obama has done so by making the perceived moral failings of black

Americans as much a part of that story as racism itself. His rhetoric provides further ammunition for those who believe that black people's anger at racism is unjustified.

* * *

But Martin's death and Zimmerman's acquittal also represented a turning point. The generation that heard Kanye West say "George Bush doesn't care about black people," then pushed the vote for the first black president, then watched America continue to not care about black people, simply has had enough. As the deaths of young, unarmed black people continue to become headlines, and social media holds more hashtag funerals, the hope has turned to despair, and the despair into rage. That rage consumed the streets of Ferguson when Michael Brown was killed; it set fire to the streets of Baltimore when Freddie Gray was killed; and it sent Bree Newsome up the flagpole at the South Carolina state Capitol to bring down the Confederate flag in the wake of nine people being killed in the Emanuel African Methodist Episcopal Church. Black rage is back, cutting to the core of white supremacy and demanding that America change.

This movement, known across the country and the world as "Black Lives Matter," has pushed an agenda to address police violence, racial profiling, and racial inequality onto the national political stage. When black rage is felt, organized, and radically expressed, this is what it does best—shift consciousness and make the needs and concerns of black America part of the body politic. It has made presumptive Democratic presidential nominee Hillary Clinton take notice, and it has even moved Obama. At the 2015 NAACP convention, the president delivered his strongest speech yet on criminal-justice reform, calling for the end of mass incarceration, the reduction or elimination of mandatory-minimum sentencing, the restoration of voting rights for the formerly incarcerated, the end of rape in prisons, and more—without the added moralizing about sagging pants, missing fathers, and "acting white" that he'd grown so fond of.

An opportunity may have been missed in those post-Katrina days, when the words "George Bush doesn't care about black people" still buzzed. But a decade later, the resurgence of black rage in the political sphere is finally ready to make America face its racist past and present. Or burn it down trying.

A Different Take on Race

By Joseph P. Williams
U.S. News & World Report, October 2, 2015

Asked about racial strife in America, this prominent, groundbreaking black politician, long on ideas but not governing experience, called for unity, not conflict.

"Our strength as a nation comes in our unity," he said in a national radio interview. "We are the United States of America, not the divided states. And those who want to divide us are trying to divide us, and we shouldn't let them do it."

Pop quiz: Was it Barack Obama, a bright young Senate candidate and future president, in his famous "No red or blue states" speech at the 2004 Democratic convention? Or was it Ben Carson, retired pediatric neurosurgeon, African-American up-from-poverty hero and current 2016 Republican front-runner?

While one can imagine Obama, then a liberal rising star, uttering the quote, the real answer is Carson. But that's pretty much where any confusion between the nation's first black president and the man who wants to succeed him begins and ends on the issue of race.

At a time when the nation's first black president is speaking openly on the black-white divide, passionately describing how African-Americans are hamstrung by slavery's legacy, Carson's taking what could be called a tough-love approach: Rather than pointing out what racism has done to black America—and how whites can help fix it—the doctor would rather talk about what the black community can do for itself.

"Both of my older cousins died on the streets where I lived," Carson wrote about his hardscrabble Detroit childhood in a *USA Today* editorial in July. "I thought that was my destiny. But my mother didn't. She changed all of that. She saved my brother and me from being killed on those streets with nothing but a library card."

For whites irritated by the Black Lives Matter movement, criticism of police and the Confederate flag—and Obama's two terms—it's just what the doctor ordered. It's also a significant factor in Carson's meteoric rise from obscure presidential also-ran to serious contender with better polling numbers than heavyweights Jeb Bush and Ohio Governor John Kasich.

For black voters who've kept the GOP at arm's length for generations, however, the use-your-bootstraps prescription is a tough sell. Though Carson's a genuine African-American hero, his self-empowerment message echoes the same conservative orthodoxy that walks past structural racism and lets white people off the hook.

"He really embraces the individualism that the Republican Party espouses," says Andra Gillespie, an Emory University political scientist who specializes in race, referring to Carson's path from fatherless black child living in poverty to groundbreaking neurosurgeon to high-profile presidential candidate. "It would not be unusual for him to [avoid being] at the forefront of racial issues."

> **"He's a Republican. He speaks at conservative forums, which are mainly forums for white people," Lublin says. "Certainly black Twitter isn't rushing to gush about Ben Carson."**

Or, as *Chicago Tribune* columnist Dawn Turner wrote in a September 15 editorial, "Carson's feel-good story allows Republicans to feel good about themselves. They can vote for a black guy (whose name isn't Obama) and maintain the myth that race is no longer a hindrance in this country and the only thing black folks have to do is work hard (as if many blacks don't already) and they too can achieve the American Dream."

Unlike Obama, who convened a White House summit to examine tensions between police and black communities, Carson says the Black Lives Matter movement, which put the issue on the national agenda, is a divisive group that unfairly demonizes police. While Obama, speaking about the Baltimore riots, said unresolved racism contributes to poverty and anger that spurs riots, Carson insists that African-Americans can rise above racism, which he calls "a sickness," with focus and hard work, just like he did.

While his fans say Carson's success in the GOP presidential campaign is evidence of the long-promised "postracial America" Obama's 2009 inauguration was to have ushered in, analysts say his campaign is evidence that the fault line of race is as deep as ever, and Carson's using his position on it to win over whites.

That's because "black voters don't make up the base of the Republican Party," says Andra Gillespie. In 2007, she says, "Obama had to worry about it—if he did not get black votes, he was not going to win."

Obama in 2007 also faced intense scrutiny on whether a black man could win over white Democratic liberals to become president. Carson's most ardent supporters are white evangelical Christians, a key component of the Republican base.

When Obama became a serious White House contender, African-American voters ironically were skeptical that a biracial politician who grew up with his white mom in Hawaii could understand their interests. Carson, who came of age in a majority black city surrounded by urban blight, has no such racial authenticity issues, but African-Americans who embrace his own remarkable up-from-poverty story say his conservative principles miss the big picture.

While he acknowledges racism exists—he scolded his GOP competitors who refused to use the term to condemn the June slaughter of nine black churchgoers by a white supremacist in Charleston, South Carolina—Carson told the National

Urban League in July that individuals can escape structural racism if they work hard and rise above "ignorant Americans."

When he argues that the black community needs to reject government handouts and the Democratic Party's "welfare state," Carson offers "validation for positions held by [white] Republicans" that structural racism doesn't exist, or are uncomfortable with a black president insisting it does, says David Lublin, an American University professor.

"We haven't arrived in a more postracial political world," Lublin says. "Racial polarization in our politics have been steadily growing."

He points out that whites who support Carson back many of his hard-line policies, like his stance on immigration or his belief that a Muslim president would be more loyal to the Quran than the Constitution he or she would be sworn to uphold. Both positions will likely drive Latinos and Muslim-Americans—two growing voting blocs largely comprised of people of color—into the waiting arms of the Democratic Party.

At the same time, Lublin says, Obama's white constituency has faded; in his 2012 reelection, the president drew far fewer white votes than he did in his groundbreaking 2008 campaign, when he drew in white voters "at the same or higher rates as [former President Bill] Clinton."

Ultimately, Carson is largely playing to his strengths as a conservative Republican, Lublin says. Like Obama in 2008, the retired surgeon doesn't want to come off as "the last angry black man," a turnoff to white voters who choose the party's nominee.

"He's a Republican. He speaks at conservative forums, which are mainly forums for white people," Lublin says. "Certainly black Twitter isn't rushing to gush about Ben Carson."

Gillespie concurs Carson isn't, and probably will never be, a racial firebrand demanding white accountability.

"That's not his lane," she says. "He is not someone who built his career advocating for civil rights."

And while Obama may talk about race more now than at the beginning of his presidency, don't expect Carson, a statistical longshot for the presidency, to follow suit.

As black people, "We're right to be angry," Carson wrote in *USA Today*, "but we have to stay smart."

For Black Millennials, a Determined Hope Tempered by Frustration

By Henry Gass
Christian Science Monitor, November 6, 2015

By some very prominent measures, black America is more politically powerful than ever before. The president is black, as is the current front-runner for the Republican nomination for president, Ben Carson. There are more black members of Congress than ever before, and black mayors govern major cities from Philadelphia to Denver.

And yet, in personal lives, African Americans still say they feel overly targeted for petty crimes such as traffic stops and major ones such as drug use. Young blacks feel more accepted than ever—embraced by Americans popular culture and no longer subject to the overt racism of Jim Crow—yet still separate.

In short, black Millennials are conflicted, and research out this week shows how that mingled sense of new opportunity and old frustration has found powerful expression since protests broke out over the police shooting of a black youth in Ferguson, Missouri, last year.

Black Millennials are more confident than any other young group that they can make a difference through political participation—71 percent, compared with 52 percent of white Millennials and 56 percent of Latino Millennials, according to the study by the Black Youth Project at the Center for the Study of Race, Politics, and Culture at the University of Chicago. Yet more than half of black Millennials also said they had been the victim of police violence or harassment or knew someone who had.

The result has been the rise of a new black civil rights movement—headlined by Black Lives Matter—that is heady with its own success, yet in some senses also angry that it needs to exist.

"Yes, we have organizing happening, we have a black president, we have a black man leading the Republican primary," says Robert Ruffins, a twenty-something former teacher who is now a community organizer in New Orleans. "But at the other end of it, the reason we have so much of this organizing is a recognition of what hasn't happened."

"It's a weird moment," he says.

The confusion is representative of a larger paradox within black political activism that has been growing since the election of President Obama in 2008, but which has intensified since Ferguson. Young blacks have faith in their ability to agitate and disrupt, but they have little faith in the politicians who must ultimately turn that activism into law.

"Black millennials report the highest level of confidence that they have the skills and knowledge to exercise their political voices and participate in politics," writes Jon Rogowski, a political scientist at the University of Washington in St. Louis and a co-author of the "Black Millennials in America" report, in an e-mail to the *Monitor*. "But [they] also express the greatest frustration with current political leaders."

The generation that proved decisive in sending Mr. Obama to the White House twice may now be losing its faith in institutional politics, Professor Rogowski adds.

"For many young people, the Obama presidency has been disappointing in the sense that his presidency, many argue, has not brought about the systemic change he seemed to promise in 2008," he says. "In addition [to voting], we also see that young Black adults report being politically engaged in a number of ways beyond voting compared to young whites, and #BlackLivesMatter represents one example."

Jason Kennedy and Devon Simon, both black 19-year-olds, shake their heads when asked if they feel politically empowered.

"I feel like what I have to say doesn't really matter and will never be taken into consideration or [taken] that seriously," says Mr. Kennedy as the pair grab lunch in a Wendy's in Boston.

The perception could be generational, says Rogowski. Older generations might feel that their mission was accomplished with the election of Obama, but Millennials have been conditioned to expect more.

"Like all Millennials, [we] grew up in world of unparalleled choice. We expect our voices to be heard," says Mr. Ruffins, the community organizer in New Orleans. "We have grown up with an expectation of being powerful."

But "when that power is taken away from us, when we're stopped on the street and no amount of education or respectability politics, no amounts of rights you have, can protect you from literally having your life taken away, that creates a weird tension," he adds. "We believe we're powerful because we've been told we're powerful, but we're confronting the limits" of that.

Daunashia Yancey, also a Millennial, is on the front lines of that confrontation. A member of Black Lives Matter Boston who was involved in a tense conversation with Hillary Clinton in August, Ms. Yancey says that the group's success stems in part from the fact that it is a "multitactic movement" that includes traditional efforts like voter registration drives and direct actions like blockades and occupations.

"There's a lot of things you can do in the political system, but there's also a lot of things that you can't," she adds. "By working outside of the traditional or the set way that folks are supposed to work within politics, by stepping outside of that we actually get a little bit further."

Ruffins echoes her frustrations with the traditional ways of politics: "I think our generation trusts the system, but I think that trust might be wearing out."

The Truth about the White Working Class: Why It's Really Allergic to Voting for Democrats

By Sean McElwee
Salon.com, November 29, 2015

What's up with working-class whites? It's a question that's been asked for decades, and has been raised again recently in the discussion surrounding an Alec MacGillis piece examining Matt Bevin's recent election gubernatorial win in Kentucky, which could leave many in Kentucky without Medicaid. Though there are many explanations for why working class whites vote Republican and many are certainly true, the overwhelming reason is rather simple: racism.

To see why working-class whites—defined as non-Hispanic whites without a college degree, although there are extensive debates as to the best way to define "working-class"—aren't voting Democratic, I use the American National Election Studies 2012 survey. To begin, I examined raw vote shares among working-class whites, and then vote shares among working-class whites in the South (the former

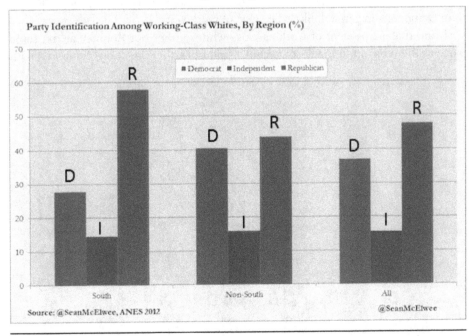

Party Identification Among Working-Class Whites, By Region (%)

Source: @SeanMcElwee, ANES 2012

@SeanMcElwee

"The Truth about the White Working Class: Why It's Really Allergic to Voting for Democrats" by Sean McElwee. Originally published by Salon.com, November 29, 2015.

11 states of the Confederacy) and non-South. Immediately, it is obvious that a key divide is the South/non-South distinction: only 28 percent of Southern working-class whites identify as Democratic, compared with 40 percent of non-South working-class whites.

Next, I examined whether racial stereotyping had any effect. The stereotype question asks respondents to rate Blacks on a scale of 1 (hard-working) to 7 (lazy). I examined the party identification of working-class whites in each category and the results are rather suggestive: among working-class whites who ranked Blacks as hard-working, 40 percent were Democrats and 38 percent Republicans, among those who said Blacks are lazy, 20 percent were Democrats and 60 percent were Republicans.

But how does this affect the votes of working-class whites? My next analysis teases out whether social issues play a role in white votes, as Thomas Frank has suggested; whether it's concerns about the role of government, as John Judis (and others) have argued; or whether it's racism, as Ian Haney-Lopez has argued.

Specifically, I examine three questions that allow respondents to place themselves on a scale and also place the major parties (or candidates) on the same scale. I examine three questions: a four-point scale regarding abortion, a seven-point scale regarding government services and spending, and a seven-point scale regarding aid to Blacks. The first two ask respondents to put themselves on a scale and also place the Republican and Democratic party on the scale, the last asks the respondents to place themselves as well as Mitt Romney and Obama on the scale (this may skew results because people may perceive Obama as more supportive of aid to Blacks than Democrats in general, likely because of racism).

I find that 62 percent of working-class whites either put Romney at the same place as them on aid to Blacks or within 1 point in either direction, compared with

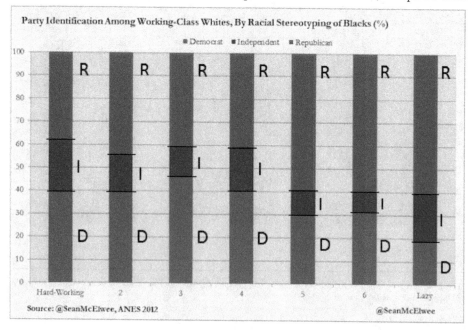

Party Identification Among Working-Class Whites, By Racial Stereotyping of Blacks (%)

Source: @SeanMcElwee, ANES 2012   @SeanMcElwee

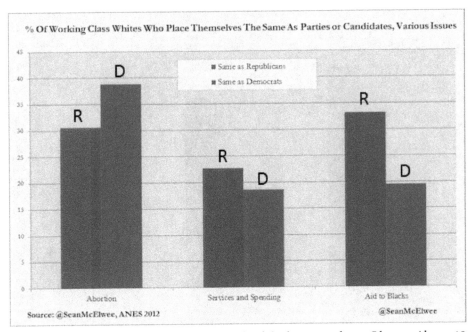

% Of Working Class Whites Who Place Themselves The Same As Parties or Candidates, Various Issues

Source: @SeanMcElwee, ANES 2012   @SeanMcElwee

only 35 percent of working-class whites who felt that way about Obama. About 40 percent of working-class whites placed themselves at the same place or within one point in either [direction] as Democrats on government services or spending, compared with 53 percent who perceived closeness with the Republican party. On the abortion scale 31 percent of respondents placed themselves as the same as Republicans, compared with 39 percent who felt the same way about Democrats. Because abortion was only a four-point scale, I didn't compare what percentage of people placed themselves within one point of either party (the chart shows the percentage placing themselves the same as the parties).

Working-class whites say they are overwhelmingly more liberal than the Republican party on abortion and modestly more liberal on government services and spending. However, they are more conservative than Romney on aid to Blacks. When compared to the Democratic party, working-class whites say they are more conservative on abortion (only slightly) and dramatically more conservative on services and spending. More than 70 percent of working-class whites say they are more conservative than Obama on aid to Blacks. This suggests that working-class whites see themselves as far closer to the Democratic party on abortion and further away from the party on services and spending. They see themselves furthest away from Obama on the issue of aid to Blacks.

These results are suggestive, and they fit into a broader academic literature. In a recent National Bureau of Economic Research working paper, Ilyana Kuziemko and Ebonya Washington find that racism can explain almost all of the decline of Southern white support for Democrats between 1958 and 2000. Larry Bartels performed a similar (although far more detailed) analysis in a 2006 paper criticizing Frank and found similarly, that working-class voters were closer to Republicans on economic and racial issues, but agreed with Democrats on abortion and women's role in the

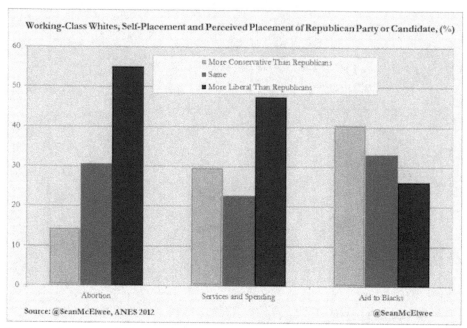

family. In his masterful work, *Why Americans Hate Welfare*, Martin Gilens finds that opposition to welfare is driven by racial stereotypes about blacks. In a seminal book, *Race and the Decline of Class in American Politics*, Robert Huckfeldt and Carol Weitzel Kohfeld show that the more a state-level Democratic party relies on Black votes, the less likely low-income whites in the states were to vote Democratic. Ian Haney-Lopez argues that Republican politicians have consciously played up racial tensions and animosity to peel white votes away from the Democratic party.

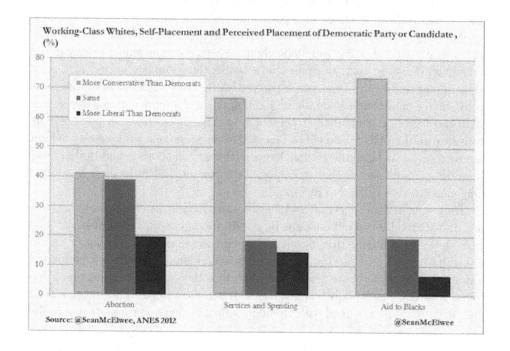

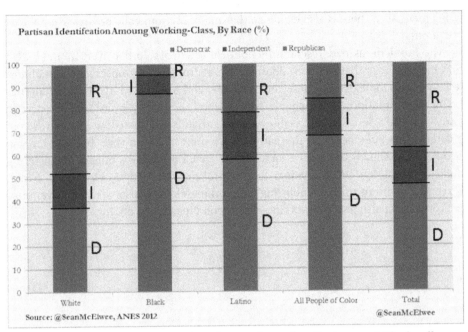

Partisan Identifcation Amoung Working-Class, By Race (%)

Source: @SeanMcElwee, ANES 2012   @SeanMcElwee

Another clue comes from the fact that working-class Latinos and Blacks all over-whelmingly prefer Democrats, and the non-white working class as a whole prefers Democrats to Republicans 68 percent to 16 percent. The only defectors are the white working class.

So if the working class generally likes Democrats (with the exception of working-class whites), why do Democrats lose elections? The key is turnout, a point MacGillis makes, citing some of my research.

The core question then, for Democrats, is how to mobilize the low-income voters who are disproportionately harmed by Republican policies. Here, the Affordable Care Act includes a self-inflicted wound by Democrats. For decades, many states have failed to meet the NVRA requirement, which states that Medicaid offices and other public assistance agencies ask recipients whether they want to register to vote. Further, NVRA covers the federally mandated health care exchanges, but the Obama administration has failed to require the exchanges to offer participants an opportunity to register to vote. Both offer a huge missed chance to register millions of new voters, disproportionately low-income and non-white.

Understanding why Democrats have lost working-class whites is a key to understanding the future. On the positive side, the decline of the white working-class and the increasing racial diversity of the nation could help Democrats, if they could mobilize non-white members of the working-class to vote at the same rate as working-class whites. As I've noted, the rise in diversity of the general population has only slowly been reflected in the diversity of the electorate. On the other hand, the idea that Democrats are losing votes because of their socially progressive stances on abortion and gay rights are clearly incorrect. Further, while it's clear that economic progressivism might struggle because Americans fail to link public policy to rising inequality, there is also evidence that many economically progressive policies are popular.

The problem, as new research by political scientists Torben Iversen and David Soskice shows, is that the U.S. doesn't have a strong union movement to mobilize low-income people. As they note, and as Fowler and Michele Margolis show, another factor is information: When people are informed they shift toward the Democratic party. Political scientists Jan Leighley and Jonathan Nagler note that people who see greater differences between the parties were more likely to vote, but low-income people are less likely to perceive large differences. Progressives must see registering and mobilizing low-income voters as a central priority. Supporting unions, which serve an important role in mobilizing the working-class, is also vital. However, progressives must also give the working-class a good reason to vote for them.

Bibliography

"Across Racial Lines, More Say Nation Needs to Make Changes to Achieve Racial Equality." *Pew Research*. Pew Research Center. Aug 5 2015. Web. Dec 12 2015.

"Affirmative Action: State Action." *NCSL*. National Conference of State Legislatures. Apr 2014. Web. Dec 6 2015.

American Civil Liberties Association. "Campaign for Smart Justice." *ACLU*. 2015. Web. Dec 6 2015.

Anderson, Melinda D. "The Other Student Activists." *Atlantic*. Atlantic Monthly Group. Nov 23 2015. Web. Dec 13 2015.

Bidwell, Allie. "Report: Higher Education Creates 'White Racial Privilege.'" *US-NEWS*. U.S. News & World Report. Jul 31 2013. Web. Dec 10 2015.

Bidwell, Allie, "STEM Workforce No More Diverse Than 14 Years Ago." *US News*. U.S. News and World Report. Feb 24 2015. Web. Dec 15 2015.

Bouie, Jamelle. "Easy AA." *Slate*. The Slate Group. Jun 29 2015. Web. Dec 12 2015.

Bouie, Jamelle, "Why Do Millennials Not Understand Racism?" *Slate*. The Slate Group. May 16 2014. Web. Dec 10 2015.

Brown, Alyssa, "Views of Race Relations as Top Problem Still Differ by Race." *Gallup*. Gallup, Inc. Jun 11 2015. Web. Dec 10 2015.

Brown, Dorothy, "How Home Ownership Keeps Blacks Poorer Than Whites." *Forbes*. Forbes, Inc. Dec 10 2012. Web. Dec 10 2015.

Child, Ben, "Hollywood Fails to Represent US Ethnic Diversity, Study Says." *The Guardian*. Guardian News and Media. Aug 5 2014. Web. Dec 16 2015.

Clark, Jonas, "In Search of the American Dream." *The Atlantic*. Atlantic Monthly Group. June 2007. Web. Dec 2 2015.

Clement, Scott, "On Racial Issues, America Is Divided Both Black and White and Red and Blue." *Washington Post*. Nash Holdings. Dec 27 2014. Web. Dec 15 2015.

Coates, Ta-Nehisi, "There Is No Post-Racial America." *Atlantic*. Atlantic Monthly Group. July 2015. Web. Dec 10 2015.

Cohen, Patricia. "Racial Wealth Gap Persists Despite Degree, Study Says." *New York Times*. New York Times Company. Aug 16 2015. Web. Dec 2 2015.

Cottom, Tressie McMillan, "The Discomfort Zone." *Slate*. Slate Group.

Crosby, Emilye, *Civil Rights History from the Ground Up*. Athens, GA: University of Georgia Press, 2011. Print.

Curwen, Thomas, Jason Song and Larry Gordon, "What's Different about the Latest Wave of College Activism." *Atlantic*. Atlantic Monthly Group. Nov 18 2015. Web. Dec 10 2015.

Demby, Gene, "Is the Millennial Generation's Racial Tolerance Overstated?" *NPR*. National Public Radio. Jun 24 2015. Web. Dec 12 2015.

DeParle, Jason, "Harder for Americans to Rise from Lower Rungs." *New York Times*. New York Times Company. Jan 4 2012. Web. Dec 10 2015.

Dixon, Travis. "Good Guys Are Still Always in White? Positive Change and Continued Misrepresentation of Race and Crime on Local Television News." *Communication Research*. Apr 2 2015. Web. Dec 1 2015.

"Executive Order 10925," *EEOC*. U.S. Equal Employment Opportunity Commission. 2015. Web. Dec 6 2015.

Falola, Toyin, "The African Diaspora." Rochester, NY: University of Rochester Press, 2013. Print.

Fulwood, Sam III, "Race and Beyond: The Media's Stereotypical Portrayals of Race." *American Progress*. Center for American Progress. Mar 5 2013. Web. Dec 2 2015.

Gibbons, Ann, "How Europeans Evolved White Skin," *Science Mag*. American Association for the Advancements of Science. Apr 2 2015. Web. Nov 30 2015.

Gioia, Ted, *The History of Jazz*. New York: Oxford University Press, 2011. Print.

Goyette, Braden, Wing, Nick, and Danielle Cadet. "21 Numbers That Will Help You Understand Why Ferguson Is about More Than Michael Brown." *Huffington Post*. Aug 25 2014. Web. Dec 12 2015.

Gugliotta, Guy, "The Great Human Migration." *Smithsonian*. Smithsonian Institution. Jul 2008. Web. Dec 10 2015.

Guskin, "5 Facts about Ethnic and Gender Diversity in U.S. Newsrooms." *Pew Research*. Pew Research Center. Fact Tank. Jul 18 2013. Web. Dec 10 2015.

Hadjiargyrou, Michael. "Race Is a Social Concept, Not a Scientific One." *Live Science*. Purch Media. Aug 29 2014. Web. Nov 30 2015.

Hamblin, James, "Medicine's Unrelenting Race Gap." *Atlantic*. Atlantic Monthly Group. Dec 10 2014. Web. Dec 10 2015.

Heath, Brad, "Racial Gap in U.S. Arrest Rates; 'Staggering Disparity.'" *USA Today*. Gannet Pulishing. Nov 19 2014. Web. Dec 8 2015.

Hook, Janet, "U.S. Split Along Racial Lines on Backlash against Police, Poll Finds." *Wall Street Journal*. Dow Jones & Co. May 3, 2015. Web. Dec 12 2015.

Ingraham, Christopher, "White People Are More Likely to Deal Drugs, but Black People Are More Likely to Get Arrested for It." *Washington Post*. Nash Holdings. Sep 30 2014. Web. Dec 7 2015.

Jones, Jeffrey M. "In U.S., Most Reject Considering Race in College Admissions," *Gallup*. Gallup Inc. Jul 24 2013. Web. Dec 6 2015.

Khan, Razib. "Tutsis and Hutus Are Genetically Different. Does That Matter?" *Discover*. Discover Magazine. Oct 16 2011. Web. Nov 30 2015.

Levine, Sam. "Eric Holder: Ferguson Police Created a Toxic Environment." *Huffington Post*. Mar 4 2015. Web. Dec 12 2015.

Levitin, Michael. "The Triumph of Occupy Wall Street." *The Atlantic*. Atlantic Monthly Group. Jun 10 2015. Web. Dec 10 2015.

"MTV Survey on Millenials and Race." *MTV*. Viacom Media Networks. May 15 2014. Web. Dec 12 2015.

"Multiracial in America," *Pew Research*. Pew Research Center. Jun 11 2015. Web. Dec 12 2015.

Newport, Frank and Joy Wilke, "American Rate Economy as Top Priority for Government." *Gallup*. Gallup, Inc. Jan 16 2-14. Web Dec 10 2015.

Nilsen, Sarah and Sarah E. Turner, eds, *The Colorblind Screen*. New York: New York University Press, 2014. Print.

"Nine Charts about Wealth Inequality in America," *Urban*. Urban Institute. Feb 2015. Web. Dec 10 2015.

Onion, Jessica, "Are We in the Middle of a New Civil Rights Era?" *Slate*. Slate Magazine. Aug 6 2015. Web. Dec 12 2015.

"Othello." *PBS*. WHYY Station. Masterpiece Theatre. 2013. Web. Dec 10 2015.

"Policing for Profit in St. Louis County." *New York Times*. New York Times Company. Nov 14 2015. Web. Oct 12 2015.

"Public Backs Affirmative Action, but Not Minority Preferences." *Pew Research*. Pew Research Center. Jun 2 2009. Web. Dec 5 2015.

"Report of The Sentencing Project to the United Nations Human Rights Committee," *The Sentencing Project*. Aug 2013 Pdf. Dec 12 2015.

Riese, Matt, "The Biological Meaning of 'Race.'" *UCSC*. University of California Santa Cruz. UCSC Center for Biomolecular Science & Engineering. 2005. Pdf. Nov 30 2015.

Shin, Laura, "The Racial Wealth Gap: Why a Typical White Household Has 16 Times the Wealth of a Black One." *Forbes*. Forbes, Inc. Mar 26 2015. Web. Dec 2 2015.

Stephen, Bijan, "Get Up, Stand Up." *Wired*. Conde Nast. Nov 2015. Web. Dec 13 2015.

Sussman, Wobert Wald, "The Myth of Race." Cambridge: Harvard University Press, 2014. Print.

"2015 Hollywood Diversity Report: Flipping the Script." *Bunchcenter*. Ralph J. Bunche Center for African American Studies at UCLA. Feb 2015. Pdf. Dec 12 2015.

Wazwaz, Noor. "It's Official: The U.S. Is Becoming a Minority-Majority Nation." *US News*. U.S. News & World Report. Jul 6 2015. Web. Dec 12 2015.

Wong, Alia, "The Renaissance of Student Activism," *Atlantic*. The Atlantic Monthly Group. May 21 2015. Web. Dec 10 2015.

Ye Hee Lee, Michelle, "Does the United States Really Have 5 Percent of the World's Population and One Quarter of the World's Prisoners?" *Washington Post*. Nash Holdings. Apr 30 2015. Web. Dec 6 2015.

Websites

African American Policy Forum (AAPF)
http://www.aapf.org/

The African American Policy Forum (AAPF) is a think tank that connects academics, activists, and policy-makers to promote efforts to dismantle structural inequality, using new ideas and innovative perspectives to transform public discourse and policy. AAPF promotes frameworks and strategies that address a vision of racial justice that embraces the intersections of race, gender, class, and the array of barriers that disempower those who are marginalized in society. AAPF is dedicated to advancing and expanding racial justice, gender equality, and the indivisibility of all human rights, both in the United States and internationally.

American-Arab Anti-Discrimination Committee (ADC)
http://www.adc.org/

Founded by former U.S. Senator James Abourezk in 1980, ADC is a civil rights organization committed to defending the rights of people of Arab descent and promoting their rich cultural heritage. Today the largest Arab American grassroots organization in the United States, ADC supports the human and civil rights of all people and opposes racism and bigotry in any form.

American Civil Liberties Union (ACLU)
https://www.aclu.org/issues/racial-justice

The ACLU champions segments of the population who have traditionally been denied their rights, with much of its work today focused on equality for people of color, women, gay and transgender people, prisoners, immigrants, and people with disabilities. Its work on racial equality falls into categories such as criminal justice, economic justice, inequality in education, affirmative action, and American Indian Rights.

Black Lives Matter
http://blacklivesmatter.com/

Black Lives Matter is a chapter-based national organization working for the validity of Black life and working to (re)build the Black liberation movement. #BlackLivesMatter is a call to action and a response to the virulent anti-Black racism that permeates our society. Black Lives Matter is a unique contribution that goes beyond extrajudicial killings of Black people by police and vigilantes, using social media to organize events and raise awareness around the country.

Congressional Black Caucus (CBC)

https://cbc-butterfield.house.gov/

Since its establishment in 1971, Members of the Congressional Black Caucus (CBC) have joined together to empower America's neglected citizens and address their legislative concerns. For more than 40 years, the CBC has consistently served as the voice for people of color and vulnerable communities in Congress and has been committed to utilizing the full constitutional power, statutory authority, and financial resources of the government of the United States of America to ensure that everyone in the United States has an opportunity to achieve the American Dream.

National Association for the Advancement of Colored People (NAACP)

http://www.naacp.org/

The mission of the National Association for the Advancement of Colored People is to ensure the political, educational, social, and economic equality of rights of all persons and to eliminate race-based discrimination, including the following objectives: to achieve equality of rights and eliminate race prejudice among the citizens of the United States; to remove all barriers of racial discrimination through democratic processes; to seek enactment and enforcement of federal, state, and local laws securing civil rights; and to inform the public of the adverse effects of racial discrimination and to seek its elimination.

National Council of La Raza (NCLR)

http://www.nclr.org/

Since 1968, the National Council of La Raza has remained a trusted, nonpartisan voice for Latinos. The organization serves this community through research, policy analysis, and state and national advocacy efforts, as well as through programs work in communities nationwide. NCLR partners with affiliates across the country to serve millions of Latinos in the areas of civic engagement, civil rights and immigration, education, workforce and the economy, health, and housing.

Southern Christian Leadership Conference (SCLC)

http://sclcnational.org/

Since the SCLC's beginnings with the Montgomery Bus Boycott in 1955, when Rosa Parks was arrested for refusing to give up her seat to a white man on the bus, the SCLC has worked in the spirit of Martin Luther King, Jr., with a commitment toward the following objectives: to promote spiritual principles within its membership and local communities; to educate youth and adults in the areas of personal responsibility, leadership potential, and community service; to ensure economic justice and civil rights in the areas of discrimination and affirmative action; and to eradicate environmental classism and racism wherever it exists.

Southern Poverty Law Center (SPLC)

https://www.splcenter.org/

The Southern Poverty Law Center is dedicated to fighting hate and bigotry and to seeking justice for the most vulnerable members of our society. Using litigation, education, and other forms of advocacy, the Center works toward the day when the ideals of equal justice and equal opportunity will be a reality.

Index